Transitions and Social Change

The Early Lives of American Men

This is a volume in

STUDIES IN POPULATION

A complete list of titles in this series appears at the end of this volume.

Transitions and Social Change

The Early Lives of American Men

Dennis P. Hogan

Population Research Center
and Department of Sociology
University of Chicago
Chicago, Illinois

ACADEMIC PRESS
A Subsidiary of Harcourt Brace Jovanovich, Publishers
New York London Toronto Sydney San Francisco

ACADEMIC PRESS, INC.
111 Fifth Avenue, New York, New York 10003

United Kingdom Edition published by
ACADEMIC PRESS, INC. (LONDON) LTD.
24/28 Oval Road, London NW1 7DX

Library of Congress Cataloging in Publication Data

Hogan, Dennis P.
Transitions and social change.

(Studies in population)
Bibliography: p.
Includes index.
1. Men--United States--History--20th century.
2. Life cycle, Human. I. Title. II. Series.
HQ1090.3.H63 305.3'0973 81-7889
ISBN 0-12-352080-0 AACR2

PRINTED IN THE UNITED STATES OF AMERICA

81 82 83 84 9 8 7 6 5 4 3 2 1

To Mary

Contents

IV. The Consequences of Early Life-Course Transition Behavior

Preface

This book is about the timing and synchronization of transition events that mark the passage of American males from adolescence to adulthood. The transition events examined include the completion of formal schooling, the establishment of relative financial independence through entry into the first full-time civilian job, and the formation of a new family of procreation through first marriage. The timing and synchronization of these transition events are examined for single-year birth cohorts of men born from 1907 to 1952. Intercohort variations in the transition to adulthood are explained with reference to a variety of demographic, social, and economic conditions that define the unique history of each birth cohort. In addition to varying across cohorts, the transition to adulthood varies among individuals according to social class, size of community during adolescence, and paternal ethnic ancestry. The timing and ordering patterns of the transition events are shown to have implications for occupational and earnings attainments both early and in midcareer and to influence the stability of the first marriage.

This study is based on data collected in the 1973 Occupational Changes in a Generation II Survey, which was carried out in conjunction with the March demographic supplement to the Current Population Survey. The survey respondents included more than 33,500 men, aged 20 to 65, in the civilian noninstitutional population. The large number of respondents permits the description of the transition experiences of detailed subgroups in the population, as well as of 46 single-year birth cohorts. The survey is unique in its inclusion of a broad array of family background data and career socioeconomic attainment information, along with the data about the timing of transition events that are essential to this study.

This is a theoretical study that poses a number of research questions about the transition to adulthood and attempts to answer these questions through empirical demographic research. It is hoped that my research methods will provide technically correct answers to the research questions yet be as understandable as possible to the average social science reader. A variety of more complex statistical techniques for the analysis of longitudinal data were not used (despite their appropriateness for the research issues addressed here) because those methods are difficult for the average reader to comprehend. The methods of analysis employed represent the best compromise between the twin goals of presenting a comprehensive, correct analysis and presenting an intelligible analysis. This study, then, is aimed at the wide audience of demographers, sociologists, historians, and psychologists who are interested in life-course research. It is intended to appeal to persons at all levels of methodological sophistication—both professionals and graduate students.

The book is organized into four parts. Part I describes the theoretical background and the major objectives of the study (Chapter 1), and discusses the data, the measurement of critical variables, and the research methods (Chapter 2). Part II documents intercohort changes in the transition behavior of twentieth-century American males (Chapter 3), and identifies the social structural conditions and historical events instrumental in these changes (Chapter 4). Subgroup differentials in the timing and sequencing of early life transitions and intercohort changes in the effects of subgroup membership on transition behavior are analyzed in Part III. The subgroups of interest include social classes (Chapter 5), communities of various sizes (Chapter 6), and paternal ethnic ancestry (Chapter 7). In Chapter 8, the simultaneous effects of the three types of subgroup membership are described, and the subgroup differentials in transition behavior are related to the intercohort changes documented in Chapter 3. In Part IV, the focus of the study shifts to the analysis of the later life-course consequences of the timing and sequencing of early life transitions. The career consequences of transition behavior are traced for occupational attainment (Chapter 9) and earnings attainment (Chapter 10). The effects of early-life transition behavior on the stability of the first marriage are examined in Chapter 11. The major conclusions of the study and their implications for the transition behavior of cohorts born after 1952 are discussed in Chapter 12.

Acknowledgments

This research was supported by a Spencer Research Grant from the Division of the Social Sciences of the University of Chicago and by the University of Chicago Population Research Center. After the initial draft of the book was completed, I attended the 1980 Summer Institute on Life-Span Human Development sponsored by the Center for Advanced Study in the Behavioral Sciences and the Social Science Research Council Committee on Life Course Perspectives on Middle Age. The Summer Institute provided a splendid intellectual and physical environment in which to discuss my research, reflect on the analysis I had written, and begin to revise the book.

I gratefully acknowledge, with special thanks, the intellectual inspiration and personal encouragement provided by Glen H. Elder, Jr. My decisions about the research questions to be posed by this work and the research methodology to be adopted were greatly influenced by his recent work on the life-course perspective and his identification of unanswered research questions. I also benefited from Elder's forthright and constructive criticisms of the research plan and of the initial draft of the manuscript.

Michele Pazul and Paul Frenzen, graduate students at the University of Chicago, assisted in the project. Pazul prepared and maintained the OCG-II data file, and produced most of the survival-table and log-linear models required in the study. Frenzen assembled the cohort data file utilized in Chapter 4 and did both the computer tabulations for that chapter and estimated the occupational mobility models of Chapter 9.

Besides handling data processing, both Pazul and Frenzen were always ready to discuss the analysis with me and to comment on chapter drafts.

I greatly appreciate the secretarial assistance provided by Wilhelmina Crawford, whose persistence and craft transformed my handwritten constructions into the finished tables reproduced in this volume. Crawford, along with Debra Milton and Faye Gilbert, typed the various drafts of this book. That these three people tolerated my frequently illegible script is surprising; that they did so without complaint is amazing. Adele Pardee of the Population Research Center and Hana Okamoto of the Department of Sociology provided the assistance that freed me from administrative detail and allowed me to pursue the intellectual concerns of this project.

Over the course of this project, many persons have provided encouragement and advice. These include Evelyn Kitagawa, Philip Hauser, and Teresa Sullivan (my colleagues at the Population Research Center), and William Julius Wilson, James Coleman, Morris Janowitz, Amy Ong Tsui, Michael White, François Nielsen, Thomas DiPrete, and Mariah Evans of the Department of Sociology. Rachel Rosenfeld, Kenneth Spenner, Clifford Clogg, Beverly Duncan, and Christopher Winship were willing sources of helpful advice. I am especially grateful to Bernice Neugarten, who discussed the research issues of this study with me. I have incorporated many of Neugarten's ideas into this analysis. Finally, I wish to acknowledge the helpful comments of J. J. Card and William McKinley Runyan of the 1980 Summer Institute on Life-Span Human Development, and those of Phyllis Moen of Cornell University. I acknowledge, with great thanks, the contributions of these people.

I

Introduction to the Study

OBJECTIVES

This book describes a study of the early life transitions of twentieth-century American men. The completion of schooling marks the conclusion of a youth's formal training for adulthood. Entry into the first, full-time civilian job indicates the age at which a young man becomes a productive, economically self-sufficient member of the society. With his first marriage, a man begins a family of procreation and becomes socially accepted as a potentially reproductive member of the society. Considered jointly, these three transitions transform a young man who is dependent on his family and the larger society into a productive and reproductive adult.

These transitions are age-graded, but their timing and sequencing has varied among twentieth-century birth cohorts. These intercohort differences result partly from the historical changes in social structural conditions experienced by the cohorts at the time of their transition from youth to adulthood (for example, industrialization, urbanization and suburbanization, the expansion of the public school system). Intercohort differences in transition behavior are produced also by historical events—such as the Great Depression, the two World Wars, and the Korean and Vietnam Wars—which affected cohorts differently, depending on their ages at the time the events occur. The first objective of this study is to describe these intercohort changes in transition behavior and to identify the social structural conditions and historical events that produced these changes.

Within cohorts, the timing and sequencing of early life transitions may vary among men occupying differing positions in the social structure. Social class and ethnic ancestry differences in transition behavior are expected insofar as the educational and occupational aspirations and attainments of the social classes and ethnic groups vary. The timing and sequencing of early life transitions may also vary among men from communities with differing opportunity structures. The ways in which family and community characteristics affect transition behavior may differ among the cohorts as men respond to the unique combination of social structural conditions and historical events experienced by their cohort. The second objective of this study is to describe social class, ethnic ancestry, and community-size differences in transition behavior, and to identify any intercohort variations therein.

The life-course perspective on individual behavior suggests that the timing and sequencing of early life transitions will influence the later life course. A career beginning with an early or late timing, or with an unusual sequencing in relation to other transitions, may hinder career achievements. An early or late marriage, or a marriage occurring prior to the other transitions, may be associated with increased tension and discord early in the marriage and, ultimately, with a higher probability that the marriage will end in divorce. The third objective of this study is to measure the effects of the timing and sequencing of early life transitions on men's occupational and earnings attainments and marital stability over the later life course.

In a review of the literature on adolescence, Glen Elder (1980:33) remarked:

> The impact of major historical transformations that occurred between late-nineteenth-century America and the 1970s—especially the Great Depression and the two World Wars—as well as class and ethnic differences in life-course change have yet to be explored in detail.

This study is intended to provide such a comprehensive description and explanation of the ways in which social structural conditions, historical events, and position within the social structure have affected the early life-course transitions of twentieth-century American men. This study also attempts to accomplish an important goal of any truly comprehensive study of the early life transitions of twentieth-century American males: to direct attention to consequences of these transitions in the later life course.

In *The Sociological Imagination* (1959:175), C. Wright Mills remarked:

> The biographies of men and women, the kinds of individuals they have become, cannot be understood without reference to the historical structures in which the

> milieux of their every-day life are organized. Historical transformations carry meanings not only for individual ways of life, but for the very character—the limits and possibilities of the human being.

The study described in this book attempts to link historical circumstances, position within the social structure, and individual biography in the description, explanation, and understanding of the causes and consequences of the early life transitions that mark the passage from youth to adulthood. This is a very ambitious undertaking, and it succeeds only occasionally. Ultimately, however, I believe that this study, through its application of sociological and demographic techniques of analysis within a life-course framework, has succeeded in expanding our knowledge about the early life transitions of American men. A selective review of the existing literature on the early life-course behaviors of American men and a discussion of data and methodology sets the stage for this analysis.

1

The Passage to Adulthood

Every human society is composed of members who enter the society through birth, age over the course of time, and ultimately exit from the society through death. A society maintains its continuity by a dynamic process through which young persons who have been inculcated with the knowledge, skills, beliefs, and norms of the culture replace persons who have died. It is through this process of cohort replacement that human societies achieve a degree of permanence despite the transitory lives of their members (Ryder, 1965).

Although cohort succession guarantees cultural continuity, it also provides an important mechanism for social change. Members of a birth cohort are born during the same time interval (for example, during a single calendar year) and age together. The persons in a birth cohort experience historical events at the same chronological age. The members of a cohort therefore share the "historical structures in which the milieux of their everyday life are organized [Mills, 1959:175]." They thus develop a common set of experiences that define a unique cohort identity.

Different birth cohorts experience the same historical events at different ages. Since the effects of historical events usually vary among age strata, the meaning and significance of every historical event differs among birth cohorts. For example, the outbreak of World War II in 1941 had different meanings for the cohorts of 1901, 1921, and 1931. Because of age, few men in the 1901 cohort served in the military during World War II; they remained at home and reaped the benefits of the high employment rates and prosperous economic conditions associated with the wartime economy. Persons born in 1921 were of prime military-service age during the early 1940s; the educations, early careers, and family lives of many members of this cohort were interrupted by the war. The cohort of 1931 was too young to serve in World War II, but many of these young people grew up in homes where the father or older brothers were absent due to wartime service. Because the impact of most historical events varies among age strata in this fashion, the histories of birth cohorts become increasingly differentiated over the lifetimes of their members. Thus, every member of a birth cohort shares a set of experiences common to the members of that cohort—experiences that differ from those of persons in earlier or later cohorts.

The members of every birth cohort are born with a variety of ascribed characteristics deemed important by their society, including such attributes as sex and race. Most babies are born into families that care for them during the period of childhood dependency and train them in the ways of the society. Families differ in regard to a variety of socially significant characteristics, many of which are imparted to the child during the process of socialization. In this way, the members of a single birth cohort become differentiated in regard to such characteristics as ethnicity, religion, and primary language.

The family background composition of a birth cohort depends on the personal attributes of adults of childbearing age, and on differentials in the rate and tempo of childbearing. Both of these factors have varied among cohorts over time, producing variation in the compositions of successive birth cohorts. The survival chances of members of a birth cohort depend on their demographic characteristics and socioeconomic circumstances (Kitagawa and Hauser, 1973; Riley, 1976). Mortality differentials therefore produce changes in the composition of a cohort as it ages.

The social position of individuals structures the way in which they experience historical events. For example, Elder (1974b) has demonstrated that the effects of the Great Depression on the life experiences of adolescents varied according to the social-class position of the family and the extent of family income loss. Thus, the historical milieu experienced by an individual is determined by birth cohort, but the nature of the experience is filtered by the individual's position in the social structure. The study of the early life transitions of twentieth-century American men, therefore, demands attention to differentials among social groups as well as change among cohorts.

EDUCATION, WORK, AND ADOLESCENCE

Over the past two centuries the United States has undergone a transformation from a rural–agrarian society to an urban–industrial society. New beliefs, attitudes, skills, and behavior were needed in an urban–industrial society. The skills of older generations, though appropriate for a rural–agrarian society, became obsolete with this societal transformation. Instead of upgrading the skills of the older cohorts, new personnel were trained to fill the positions of the urban–industrial society. This training could not be carried out within families, since many parents were ignorant of the desirable skills and lacking in the appropriate beliefs and attitudes. The modern system of mass public education was created in order to carry out this training and socialization function (Bowles, 1972; Bowles and Gintis, 1976; Kett, 1977). The schools trained the children born in the more recent birth cohorts. The shift from a rural–agrarian to an urban–industrial society occurred as the better educated cohorts succeeded the older, less educated cohorts.

These intercohort changes were characterized by intracohort variation. Initially, schooling was not publicly supported, so that there were costs associated with sending a child to school. Also, children enrolled in school represented opportunity costs for their families because of the potential income from child labor that was lost. The upper class and middle class families thus were more able than the working class, lower class, and farm families to enroll their children in school (Kett, 1977; Kaestle and Vinovskis, 1978). The lower class families adopted various strategies to obtain the education necessary for the success of their children. For example, a study of the expenditure patterns of Irish families in the United States showed that the older children in these families often left school early, entered the labor force, and contributed to the family income, whereas the younger children were kept in school to learn the new skills and to earn the diploma necessary for career success in the urban–industrial society (Modell, 1978).

Over the course of the last century, intercohort improvements in the socioeconomic characteristics of family of origin have produced increases in the average educational attainments of the cohorts. But an even more important source of the intercohort improvements in educational attainment have been the widespread introduction, and subsequent expansion, of the modern system of mass public education (Featherman and Hauser, 1978; Mare, 1979). As publicly supported education at the elementary school and secondary school levels became available, the children of lower classes, working classes, and farm families enrolled in school at rates approaching those at which children from wealthier backgrounds enrolled. These trends were accelerated by the adoption of child-labor prohibitions and requirements for mandatory school attendance.

In recent years, enrollments in the secondary school system have become nearly universal across social classes, and the locus of intercohort educational upgrading has shifted to the college level (Mare, 1979). As was earlier the case for graded schooling, a college education has become the route to career success. Despite some recent suggestions that Americans have become "overeducated," few members of recent cohorts could have anticipated career success in the absence of education beyond high school (Blau and Duncan, 1967; Freeman, 1976; Featherman and Hauser, 1978).

However, social class differentials in educational attainment, which have been greatly reduced at the graded school level, are still found at the college and graduate levels of education. In part, these result from social class differences in parental and teacher encouragement to students and in students' educational aspirations. But controlling for these factors, the better economic resources of middle class and upper class families have enabled their children to attend and complete college more frequently than children from poorer socioeconomic backgrounds (Sewell, 1971).

In a similar fashion, the educational attainments of men from rural communities, and of men of Southern European and Eastern European Catholic origins have lagged (Blau and Duncan, 1967; Sewell, 1971; Featherman, 1971). Parents with more favorable socioeconomic origins thus have used their resources to better their children's educational attainments, assuring a degree of intergenerational socioeconomic transmission.

Of course, among the recent cohorts many persons of relatively poor socioeconomic backgrounds have attended and completed college. They have done this in part by attending the less expensive public institutions of higher education. Family economic strategies also have included student loans, part-time employment of students, and support from students' working spouses. Government financial assistance programs (Educational Opportunity Grants, National Defense Student Loans, and G.I. Bill benefits) have been important sources of support for college students of all socioeconomic backgrounds. Such government aid programs, however, are insufficient to vitiate the economic disadvantages associated with birth to low socioeconomic status families (Sewell, 1971).

The prolongation of school enrollment has been associated with delays in labor-force entry. Although the relationships between the two are complex, most persons are not simultaneously enrolled in school and employed full-time in the labor force. Ordinarily, full-time labor-force entry is postponed until an interruption in schooling or the completion of schooling (Modell *et al.*, 1978; Sweet, 1979). The prolongation of school enrollment and attendant delays in labor-force entry have created a lengthy period of economic dependency among youth. This period encompasses the early stages of physical maturation but extends well past the achievement of physical maturity. Whereas members of birth cohorts in prior centuries passed directly from the status of children to the status of adults, the cohorts of this century have been socially defined as passing through an intermediate stage of adolescence (Kett, 1977). The sharp age-grading within the school system and the increased societal usage of chronological age as a legal demarcation of social status have accentuated the distinctiveness of adolescence. Initially, adolescence was viewed as ending with the completion of school (at age 18 or 19), but the extension of school enrollment for many cohort members into the early twenties has lengthened the period of youthful dependence. This new age-status group has developed its own subculture (Coleman, 1961; Friedenberg, 1963; Panel on Youth, 1974).

In premodern cultures, the passage of children into adult roles commonly is marked by rites of passage. In urban–industrial societies, the development of a protracted period of adolescence has been accompanied by disappearance of most formal rites of passage. However, the completion of key transitions generally indicates the achievement of adult status. Such transitions include the completion of formal schooling, the achievement of relative economic independence through the beginning of a first full-time job, and the establishment of a family of procreation through first marriage. The timing and sequencing of these transitions have depended upon the characteristics of men's birth cohorts and their family backgrounds.

A MODEL OF THE LIFE COURSE

A schematic model of the life course of twentieth-century American males is displayed in Figure 1.1. The transition experiences of all men are determined by the character and history of their birth cohort, and by their family background. Although the transition to adulthood is a relatively diffuse process among these men, the model hypothesizes that it is not an unregulated process. It is hypothesized that the members of every cohort, and social groups within each cohort, are characterized by values systems that specify the preferred levels of educational and occupational attainments. It further is supposed that each group faces

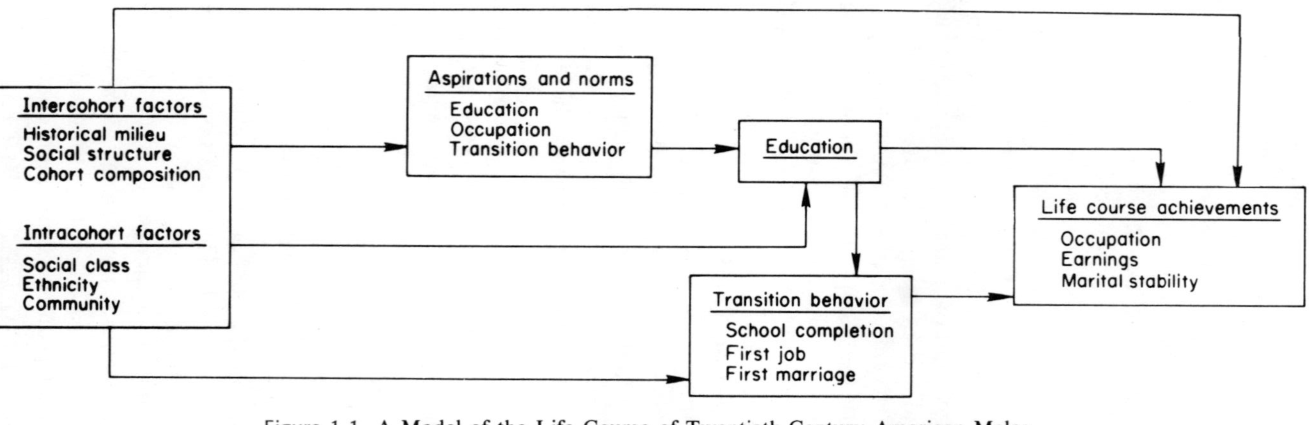

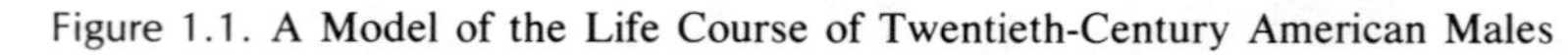
Figure 1.1. A Model of the Life Course of Twentieth-Century American Males

normative regulations regarding the "social time" in the life course of individuals at which it is appropriate to complete school, begin work, and first marry (Elder, 1978a). The available empirical evidence tends to support the hypothesis that these normative concepts not only specify the ideal age for each event but extend to suitable age ranges, outside of which the transition would be too "early" or too "late." But this evidence is based on only a small sample of middle class, middle-aged persons (Neugarten *et al.*, 1965).

It is hypothesized that these normative schedules not only specify the appropriate age for each event, but also prescribe an appropriate sequence of events. Modell (1980) has used public opinion poll data to document that people believe marriage should occur only after the achievement of economic sufficiency targets. Chapter 2 of this book documents that men tend to delay marriage until after the completion of their schooling.

Individuals try to coordinate the timing of the various transitions in conformity with norms about transition behavior, while also attempting to achieve their educational and occupational aspirations. The occupations to which men aspire depend partly on the educations they expect to complete. The timing of school completion depends on educational attainment. The timing of labor-force entry and first marriage, in turn, are influenced by age at school completion. Educational aspirations thus are an important determinant of occupational aspirations and transition norms. The level of education completed is a major determinant of transition behavior and achievements in the later life course. Consequently, education is viewed as the central event in the early life course; educational achievements mediate the effects of transition norms on transition behavior. Birth cohort and family background thus influence transition norms, but the effect of these norms on actual transition behavior are mediated through educational attainments. Empirical support for this assertion is provided by Bayer (1969) who demonstrated that socioeconomic status of family background had no direct effect on marriage plans of adolescents but indirectly affected their marriage plans through plans about their educational attainments.

Educational and occupational attainments, as well as the timing and sequencing of early life transitions, involve "problems of coordination, resource management, and adaptation [Elder 1974a:176]." Therefore, the resources and opportunities available to a cohort directly affect the educational and occupational attainments of its members, and the timing and sequencing of their transitions. Similarly, the social and economic resources available to men from a single cohort who have differing family backgrounds determine their ability to adhere to normative regulations about transitions and to achieve the education and occupations to which they aspire. The model of the life course adopted in this study therefore posits that characteristics of birth cohort and family background influence educational attainment directly because of differing levels of facilitating resources, as well as indirectly through their effects on educational aspirations. These background factors also are hypothesized to influence transition behavior directly because of the availability of facilitating resources, as well as indirectly via educational achievements. The test of this hypothesis is a principal goal of this study.

The life-course perspective suggests that the timing and sequencing of early life transitions constitute contingencies in the personal biography that have persisting effects on achievements in the later life course. These effects are hypothesized to exist quite apart from the influences of educational attainment. The available empirical evidence provides limited support for this hypothesis. Featherman and Carter (1976) report that among a cohort of men born in 1939 and 1940, those men who delayed the completion of schooling through an interruption in their education earned about $2400 less annually (when interviewed in 1972) than did men with similar background characteristics who did not experience such a delay. Men who begin working or marry relatively early (compared with other men at the same level of education) have slightly lower levels of occupational attainments than other men (Duncan *et al.*, 1972). Early marriage also is associated with a higher rate of marital instability (Hogan, 1977). The hypothesis that the timing and sequencing of transition events influence later life course achievements is subjected to empirical test in this study.

The effects of family background on educational and occupational aspirations have been thoroughly studied (Sewell and Hauser, 1975). The effects of birth cohort and family background on educational and occupational attainments also have been carefully studied (Blau and Duncan, 1967; Featherman and Hauser, 1978). Birth cohort and family background differentials in transition norms are a neglected, but important area of investigation. Unfortunately, transition norms cannot be examined in this study because of the lack of requisite data. This is an important area for future research.[1] This study focuses on the remaining

[1]Elder (1974a:176) has remarked:

> No large sample study has provided evidence on normative expectations and sanctions regarding the timing and synchronization of social roles and transitions over the life span. . . . The process by which age norms or timetables are constructed, transmitted, and learned remains largely unexplored territory.

I am now researching some of these questions, using data collected in James Coleman's "High School and Beyond Study."

neglected connections in this model of the life course. The total effects of birth cohort and family background factors on transition behavior are examined, as are the direct effects of these factors, controlling for differences in educational attainment. The total effects of transition behavior on career achievements and marital stability are identified, as are the effects net of cohort, family background, and educational attainment. In this way, the study attempts to link historical circumstances, position within the social structure, and individual biography in the description, explanation, and understanding of the causes and consequences of the early life transitions marking the passage from youth to adulthood.

2

Data and Methods

This study describes the transition behavior of American males in their passage from youth to adulthood. The study's three principal objectives were:

1. To compare transition behaviors of cohorts born during the twentieth century
2. To compare transition behaviors within cohorts of subgroups based on social class, ethnic ancestry, and size of community of origin
3. To identify effects of early life transitions on life course career and family achievements.

Requisite data included date of birth, age at the occurrence of key transition events, social class origins, size of community during adolescence, and ethnic ancestry. We needed information on the family and career attainments of men in their later life course, and the data had to reflect a broad cross-section of birth cohorts over the twentieth century. Finally, the sample had to be large enough to permit the accurate representation of the transition behaviors of fairly detailed subgroups in the population.

DATA

The Survey

The data for this study were drawn from the Occupational Changes in a Generation II (OCG-II) survey, which was carried out in conjunction with the March 1973 demographic supplement to the Current Population Survey (CPS). The eight-page OCG-II questionnaire was mailed out 6 months after the March CPS and was followed by mail, telephone, and personal callbacks. The respondents, comprising 88% of the target sample, included more than 33,500 men, aged 20 to 65, in the civilian, noninstitutional population. Blacks and Hispanics were sampled at about twice the rate of other men, and almost half of the black men were interviewed personally. Data collected in the OCG-II survey were matched to the CPS data collected from each respondent.[1]

Life-Course Transition Variables

The CPS/OCG-II data met all the requirements for use in this study. Although the survey did not collect complete life histories regarding school enrollment, employment, residence, marriage, or paternity, it did ascertain the month and year of occurrence for completion of the highest grade in school, first full-time civilian job after completion of school, and first marriage. It also gathered data about military service, including dates of first entry and final discharge. Respondents were also asked whether they ever discontinued schooling for 6 months or longer; if they had, they were asked for the date the first interruption began and the highest grade completed prior to the first interruption.

In the OCG-II interview schedule, following a question on the highest grade of school completed, the respondent was asked: "In what month and year did you COMPLETE your highest grade of school?" Thus, the date of school completion for OCG respondents refers to the completion date of the highest school grade the respondent finished, not the date at which the respondent last attended school.

Following the questions on the highest grade of school completed and the date of completion, each respondent was asked to "describe the FIRST, FULL-TIME CIVILIAN JOB you had AFTER you completed your highest grade in school." No respondents currently enrolled in school answered these first-job questions. Under this definition, a man who worked full-time at a civilian job and then discontinued that job in order to finish an additional year of schooling correctly reported as his first job the job he held after completely finishing school.

The OCG-II survey was designed to provide data for a study of the socioeconomic attainment process of American males; the questions were not developed with the idea of using the data to study the transition to

[1]A complete description of the OCG-II survey is provided in Featherman and Hauser (1978).

adulthood. The basic model of the socioeconomic attainment process developed by Blau and Duncan (1967) viewed men as first completing their educations and then entering the work force in their first, full-time civilian job. This post-schooling career entry position provided a basis for later career mobility.

Nonetheless, detailed cross-tabulations of age at first job by educational attainment suggested that as many as 12.5% of the respondents to the Occupational Changes in a Generation I question, "Please think about the first full-time job you had after you left school (Do not count part-time jobs or jobs during school vacation. Do not count military service.)," answered by naming a job they held prior to completing their highest grade in school (Blau and Duncan, 1967:167). The OCG-II question developed by Featherman and Hauser was intended to provide a closer fit between the first job named by the respondents and the assumption of the status-attainment model that first job begins after the completion of schooling. Featherman and Hauser (1975:238) describe their modified first-job question as follows:

> While retaining the concept of first job in the replicate study, we expanded the series of questions on education and the timing (dates) of schooling so as to eliminate respondents who would not appropriately be asked the first-job question (e.g., those currently enrolled in school) and to assist in the reconstruction of events surrounding the transition from school to work. Additionally, we rephrased the defective first-job item in consonance with greater clarity.

Despite these changes, more than 12% of the 1973 respondents reported a first job that began prior to the completion of education. Apparently the respondents have a definite concept in mind when they reply to a question concerning their first job, a concept that seems fairly constant regardless of the question's format. Thus, while most men have periods of part-time employment while enrolled in school and other men have brief periods of full-time employment during an interruption in schooling, most men can identify one job they have held as their "first job."[2]

[2]For purposes of this analysis it would perhaps have been preferable to have a first-job variable defined without reference to school enrollment. For example, a definition of first job as the first full-time job held for twelve months or longer would elicit information about the point of significant labor-force entry—significant in the sense that it was full-time and lasted long enough to represent the beginning of a meaningful job history. Such first-job information would make it easier to classify persons according to the true ordering of first job and school completion. However, a definition of this type might introduce a bias against men who begin working relatively young, who are unskilled, or who are members of a minority since such men less commonly remain continuously employed in the same job for twelve months.

The persons whose experiences were most distorted by the OCG-II definition of first job are those who worked during an interruption in schooling. Therefore, in describing intergroup differentials in age at school completion and age at first job, data on prevalence of interruptions in schooling (which suggests the extent to which temporary labor-force entry prior to completion occurred) were examined. The description of age at first job used the first, second, and third quartiles rather than the mean and standard deviation to describe the central tendency and variation in each group's first-job transition. This reduced the effect of the skewed age at first-job reports of those men who interrupted schooling to work and then reported a "first job" beginning after the completion of schooling at a relatively late age.

As discussed below, men were classified according to temporal sequencing of education, first job, and marriage. Men who married before completing schooling were correctly classified into an *extreme nonnormative* category regardless of the timing of their first job. The men who began their first, full-time job prior to completing school but who married after completing school were correctly classified into the *intermediate nonnormative* category, if they reported the beginning date of their first job as earlier than the date of school completion. Only men who had a full-time first job prior to completing school that did not continue after school, who did not marry until after completing school, and who followed OCG-II instructions to report the date they began the first job held after the completion of schooling were incorrectly classified into the *normative* ordering category. The normative ordering category includes a majority of respondents. The inclusion in the normative ordering group of a few men who, under other first-job definitions, began their first job prior to completing school, has no substantial impact on the overall characteristics of the normative group.

The OCG-II survey defined age at first marriage in a straightforward manner. Respondents who answered "yes" to the question "Have you EVER been married?" were asked "When did you FIRST get married?" Respondents were given one blank each on the self-administered questionnaire for the month and year of the marriage date. (A similar procedure was used to ascertain the date of school completion and beginning of first job.)

Unfortunately, the CPS/OCG-II survey provided only the age for each respondent, not date of birth. Thus respondents' birthdates were estimated from their age in March 1973.[3] Age (in months) at the com-

[3]Birth cohorts in this study were defined according to age in March 1973. Members of a birth cohort refer to men born from March to December in that calendar year or in January or February of the following calendar year. For example, the birth cohort of 1907 refers to men born March 1, 1907 to February 29, 1908.

pletion of each transition event then could be calculated from the estimated birthdate and the reported date of the event. In cases where the year but not the month of an event was reported, age at the event was calculated assuming a July month of occurrence.

These procedures permitted the classification of 91.1% of the respondents for age at school completion, 89.2% for age at first job, and 97.4% for age at first marriage. (These percentages include respondents who had not experienced a transition by the date of interview.)

Social Background Variables

The OCG-II survey ascertained social class origin, size of original community, and ethnic ancestry, as well as other information on respondents' family backgrounds. These three background factors—social class, size of community, and ethnicity—were selected as independent variables in this study because they are the factors most consistently mentioned as important influences on early life transitions (Elder, 1974a, 1978a, 1978b; Haraven, 1978; Katz and Davey, 1978; Modell *et al.*, 1976; Neugarten and Moore, 1968). These factors are important in part because of their relationship to normative ideals about the appropriate ages for specific life transitions. But these factors also differentiate people according to the social and economic resources available to them in effecting transition behavior (see Modell and Haraven, 1978).

In the OCG-II survey, respondents reported the occupations their fathers (or other family heads) held when the respondents were about sixteen years of age. Respondents' reports of fathers' occupation, industry, and class of worker were used to array persons into five social class strata: upper white-collar (salaried and self-employed professionals, managers, officials, and proprietors); lower white-collar (sales and clerical workers); skilled blue-collar (craftsmen); unskilled blue-collar (service workers, operatives, and laborers); and farm (farmers, farm managers, and farm laborers). These social classes are ranked according to status levels, with the men from upper white-collar origins enjoying the highest social status and the men from farm origins experiencing the lowest status background.[4] The data permitted the classification of 93.5% of the respondents according to their social class origins; nonrespondents to the father's-occupation question were excluded from the analysis of social class differentials in transition behavior.

Respondents answered an OCG-II question about size of community

[4]These social class groupings are based on the standard definitions used in social mobility work (see, for example, Blau and Duncan, 1967; Hauser and Featherman, 1977; Featherman and Hauser, 1978).

while growing up, and the CPS reported the size of community of residence in 1973. In the OCG-II survey respondents were asked: "Where were you living when you were 16 years old?" Respondents living in the same community at the time of the survey as they had lived in at age 16 marked an answer to that effect. Respondents who had lived in a community at age 16 that was different from their 1973 community indicated whether the community they had lived in at age 16 was: (*a*) a large city of 500,000 population or more; (*b*) a large city of 100,000 to 500,000 population; (*c*) a suburb near a large city; (*d*) a middle-sized city or small town (under 100,000 population) but not a suburb of a large city; (*e*) open country (but not on a farm); or (*f*) on a farm. It thus was necessary to refer to the CPS report on size of community of residence in 1973 in order to classify men who had not migrated into a community of origin category. Unfortunately, sizes of current place of residence were divided into somewhat different categories by the CPS and the OCG-II: (*a*) SMSA by size and whether in or outside of the central city; (*b*) not SMSA–urban; (*c*) not SMSA–rural nonfarm; or (*d*) not SMSA–rural farm.

Both the CPS and the OCG-II types of community-size information were used to classify all respondents by size of place of residence at age 16 as follows: (*a*) large city (large city for men who had moved since age 16; SMSA, in central city, for men who had not moved); (*b*) suburb of large city (suburb near a large city for men who had moved; SMSA, outside central city, for men who had not moved); (*c*) small city (nonsuburb under 100,000 population for men who had moved, and urban non-SMSA for men who had not moved); (*d*) rural nonfarm; or (*e*) rural farm. These procedures permitted the classification of 99.1% of the sample according to their size of community of origin; respondents who did not report their size of community of origin were excluded from the analysis of community-size differences in transition behavior.

By the definitional procedures used, respondents who grew up in the central city of an SMSA of 50,000 to 100,000 people were classified as having grown up in a small city if they had migrated since age 16 but as having grown up in a large city if they had not migrated. This discrepancy could not be avoided with the data provided by the CPS and OCG-II surveys. Also, some persons who had not moved were assigned to a larger community-size classification than truly represented their community of residence at age 16 because of city growth between 1973, the year of the survey, and the year the respondent was 16.

Ethnic ancestry was determined by responses to the question: "What is the original nationality of your family on your FATHER's side? That is, what was it before coming to the United States? (Example: Polish,

German, Spanish, Russian)," and to the CPS question on race. On the basis of the race data, respondents were classified as black or nonblack. Nonblack respondents were assigned an ethnic ancestry based on their first response to the question on paternal ethnic ancestry. Eight ethnic groups were examined: British (English, Scottish, and Welsh); Irish; German; other Northern and Western European; Eastern European and Russian; Southern European; Hispanic; and black. About 93.3% of the respondents could be assigned to one of these eight ethnic groups; the remaining survey respondents were excluded from the analysis of ethnic differentials in transition behavior.

The timing of early life transitions is closely related to the level of schooling completed. Therefore, in the analysis it was necessry to examine subgroup differentials in the transition behavior of men at each level of education. CPS data—on the highest grade of school attended and completed—were used to determine the highest grade of schooling each respondent had completed. Respondents were then classified into six educational levels, based on years of schooling completed: No education or elementary school (0 to 8 years); some high school (9 to 11 years); high school graduate (12 years); some college (13 to 15 years); college graduate (16 years); graduate or professional school (17 or more years). We were able to assign every respondent an educational level, because missing education responses to the CPS were allocated by the Bureau of the Census prior to the release of the data.

Population Coverage

This analysis describes the transition behavior of several relevant subgroups of men born from 1907 to 1952: (*a*) the 46 birth cohorts; (*b*) 46 cohorts who were in military service; (*c*) 46 cohorts who were never in military service; (*d*) 30 groups of men defined by combinations of the variables of social class background and level of education; (*e*) 30 groups of men defined by size of place of residence at age 16 and level of education; and (*f*) 48 groups of men defined by paternal ethnic origin and level of education. A precise description of the transition behavior of each of these groups required sufficient sample sizes. The large number of sample respondents to the 1973 CPS/OCG-II survey provided a satisfactory basis for this analysis. The number of respondents from each birth cohort ranged from 465 for the cohort of 1907 to 1049 for the cohort of 1952. Birth cohorts were represented by an average of about 730 respondents (standard deviation is 126). For the social class by level of education classification, the sample sizes ranged from 117 respondents of low, white-collar origins with 0 to 8 years of schooling to 3715 respondents who were high school graduates from an unskilled, blue-collar background. The mean sample size over the 30 social class by education subgroups was 1023 (with a standard deviation of 858). A similar range of sample cases was observed for the other subgroups examined. Only 5 of the 246 subgroups whose transition behaviors are described in this analysis were represented by fewer than 100 sample cases: veterans born in 1952 and blacks and Hispanics with four years of college or more. Each of these 5 subgroups was represented by at least 50 sample cases.

One source of potential bias in the use of the 1973 CPS/OCG-II data is the restriction of the sample coverage in the OCG-II to the civilian, noninstitutional population. Men who, in 1973, were on active duty in the armed forces, in hospitals for long-term care, or in prison, were excluded from the OCG-II survey population. The survey represented all other men aged 20 to 65 in March 1973, including men enrolled in college and living in dormitory or fraternity housing. Of the total population of men aged 20 to 24 (including armed forces personnel in the United States and overseas), 10.0% were excluded from survey coverage because of active duty in the Armed Forces, and an additional 1.3% were excluded as inmates of institutions. Of men 25 to 34 in 1973, 4.3% were excluded because of military service and 1.2% as inmates of institutions. Population coverage in the 1973 survey thus was 88.8% of the men ages 20 to 24, 94.5% of men ages 25 to 34, 96.2% of men ages 35 to 44, and more than 98.5% of men ages 45 and older. Regardless of the birth cohort, therefore, population coverage for the entire cohort was nearly complete. The poorest population coverage was found among men born from 1948 to 1952, but even for these men it was 88.8%.

The analysis also distinguished cohorts of men who were military service veterans and men who had never served in the military. The OCG-II exclusion of men currently in the military service did create problems of population coverage for birth cohorts of military service veterans. Among men born 1947 to 1952, 10.0% were on active duty in the Armed Forces, and another 19.2% were military service veterans. About one-third of the birth cohorts of veterans born 1947 to 1952 therefore were excluded from population coverage in the OCG-II survey. The problem was much less severe among men born 1938 to 1947. Fewer than 11% of the men from these birth cohorts who had military service experience were excluded from population coverage in the OCG-II survey. Thus, the parameters reported here of the transition behavior of military service veterans born 1947 to 1952 must be interpreted with extreme caution. The population coverage for all other birth cohorts of veterans, for all civilian cohorts, and for the total birth cohorts were based on relatively complete population coverage, and can be interpreted with confidence.

A second source of potential bias in the use of the 1973 CPS/OCG-II data is the differential mortality among older birth cohorts. In this study, the parameters of the transition process were estimated for birth cohorts from the retrospective reports of a sample of men surviving in 1973. Calculations based on retrospective reports are valid only to the extent that the transition experiences of men surviving in 1973 did not differ from the transition experiences of men born in the same year who lived through the transition to adulthood but died before 1973. Kitagawa and Hauser (1973) have provided evidence that the mortality risks of men vary by marital status and educational attainment; married men and men with higher educations enjoy the lowest mortality rates. I applied period life table survival rates for each decade to men from three different birth cohorts in order to estimate what proportion of men aged 16 (who had at least begun the transition to adulthood) survived until the 1973 OCG-II survey.[5] Approximate proportions of men surviving from age 16 to the date of the survey were 65% of the 1907 birth cohort, 84% of the 1917 cohort, and 94% of the 1927 cohort.

We have no historical data on the ages of birth cohorts of men at the time of school completion, first job, and first marriage. As a result, we cannot assess the extent to which differential mortality may bias the OCG-II estimates of the parameters of the transition behavior of cohorts born in the early part of the twentieth century. Some reassurance that the biases are not large is provided by a comparison of the age-at-marriage data from the 1962 and 1973 Occupational Changes in a Generation surveys. This comparison shows that there are no statistically significant differences in the probability of early marriage (before age 23) and late marriage (age 23 or older) among cohorts of men born from 1917 to 1931 and first married by March 1962. Nor does the association between age

[5]Abridged life table survivorship rates were available for census years during this century (U.S. Department of Health, Education and Welfare, 1964). Age-specific survivorship rates for each decade were calculated by averaging the survivorship rates for the census years marking the beginning and end of the decade. Men born in each cohort were then survived forward by 10-year intervals using a weighted combination of survivorship rates for each decade. For example, men born in 1907 were aged forward ten years assuming that the survivorship rates from birth to age 10 experienced by the cohort were those of the 1900–1909 decade for 2.5 years (from mid 1907 to the end of 1909) and the 1910–1919 decade for 7.5 years (from the beginning of 1910 until mid 1917). Men were survived forward in this fashion until 1973. The proportion surviving in 1973 divided by the proportion surviving at age 16 (determined by linear interpolation) yielded the final estimate of the percentage of each cohort reaching age 16 who lived until the date of the 1973 survey.

at marriage and birth cohort, education, and race vary between OCG-I and OCG-II (Hogan, 1976: Table A.1).

The high reliability of the OCG-based transition parameters for the single-year birth cohorts can be illustrated also by a comparison of the age-at-marriage estimates for single-year cohorts of men from the 1970 United States Census and the 1973 OCG-II survey. Winsborough (1978) provided Census-based estimates of the first, second, and third quartiles of the age-at-marriage transition for cohorts born from 1911 to 1944. Chapter 3 of this book provides estimates of the same age-at-marriage parameters for birth cohorts of men based on the OCG-II data. Table 2.1 compares the OCG-based and Census-based parameters of the age-at-marriage transition of the birth cohorts of 1911 to 1944.

The correlations between the OCG-based and Census-based estimates of the first, second, and third quartiles of the age-at-marriage transition of these 34 birth cohorts are each better than 0.96. The mean and standard deviation of the first and second quartiles of the birth cohorts age-at-marriage transition all agree to within 0.1 year. The OCG-II estimate of the third quartile of the age-at-marriage transition was based on the experiences of relatively few sample respondents. Therefore, the OCG-II and Census estimates of the mean and standard deviation of the third quartile differ, but by one-third year or less. Nonetheless, the correlations between the OCG-II and Census estimates is still very high (.97). Although the greater sampling variability of the

Table 2.1
Comparison of Census and Occupational Changes in a Generation-II Estimates of the Parameters of the Age at Marriage Transition, Single-Year Birth Cohorts of American Males Born 1911–1944

Measures	Transition Parameter			
	First Quartile	Second Quartile	Third Quartile	Interquartile Range
Mean				
Census	21.58	24.11	28.07	6.51
OCG-II	21.54	24.02	27.73	6.20
Standard Deviation				
Census	0.69	1.05	1.64	1.00
OCG-II	0.72	1.02	1.45	0.81
Correlation	.967	.969	.973	.921

OCG-based third quartile also affects the mean and standard deviation of the interquartile range of the age-at-marriage transition over the 34 birth cohorts, the correlation between the OCG-II and Census estimates of the interquartile range is quite high (.92).

METHODS

Our research objectives and the nature of the data available for this study were the primary factors considered in selecting the methods of analysis. In addition, we attempted to adopt an analysis strategy that would yield intelligible, as well as comprehensive and complete, results.

The Censoring Problem

Some men in the survey had completed the school-leaving, first-job, and first-marriage transitions by the date of the OCG-II survey. Other men had not yet completed one or more of the transitions by the survey date. The experiences of men who had not yet completed a transition but might complete that transition at a later date are censored by the date of the survey. This problem is especially severe among members of the more recent birth cohorts, whose experiences were censored by the survey at a relatively early age. If the transition behaviors of birth cohorts of men are described based only on the experiences of those men who have completed a given transition, the more recent birth cohorts are represented only by those men who have completed the transition at a relatively early age (since men who will complete the transition at a later age will do so after the date of the survey). In general, the transition experiences of any population subgroup with a relatively young age composition will be incorrectly described if men whose experiences are censored are not taken into account.

Survival Tables

The single-decrement survival table provides a method of overcoming this censoring bias. Modeled on the demographic life table, the single-decrement survival table includes the experiences of the censored population in the calculation of age-specific rates of occurrence up until the age at which the population is censored. The age-specific rates of occurrence of an event thus are estimated on the basis of the total population exposed to the risk of the event, without regard to whether each person ultimately does experience the event (Gross and Clark, 1975).

An illustrative survival table for the first-marriage transition of a group of men aged 20 to 65 at the time of observation is shown as Table 2.2. Column 1 indicates the exact ages of individuals at the beginning and end of each interval. For example, a man enters interval 20–21 on his twentieth birthday and exits from the interval on his twenty-first birthday.[6] Column 2 indicates the number of persons reaching the beginning of the age interval prior to the survey who had not yet married by that age. For example, 855 men were born into this social group, and 830 of the men reached their twentieth birthdays prior to the survey date without marrying. Column 3 shows the number of persons in this social group who were of a given age at the time of the survey. For example, 10 men in this group were age 20 (i.e., in the 20–21 interval) at the time of the survey. A man who enters a given age interval, and whose experience is censored during that interval is assumed, on average, to have been exposed to the risk of marriage during one-half of the age interval (in this example, for one-half year). Thus, of the 830 men entering the age interval 20–21, 10 men contribute an average of only one-half year exposure each to the risk of marriage. The remaining 820 men are assumed to contribute one year of exposure each to the risk of marriage. The total number of years of exposure to the risk of marriage during the 20–21 age interval thus is 825.0 (see column 4). The number of persons marrying during each age interval is shown in column 5. The number of persons marrying during an interval (column 5) divided by the person-years of exposure to the risk of marriage during that interval (column 4) indicates the age-specific proportions of men marrying (column 6). Column 7 shows the proportion of persons not marrying during the age interval (1.0 minus column 6). Column 8 displays the cumulative proportion still unmarried at the end of an age interval. For example, given the age specific rates of marriage estimated on the basis of the experiences of these men, 0.971 of a hypothetical cohort of men living throughout the period of observation would still be single at the end of the age interval 19–20 (that is, on their twentieth birthdays). This proportion multiplied by the proportion of persons not marrying during the 20–21 interval (0.954) yields an estimate of the proportion of the hypothetical cohort of men not yet married by age 21 (0.926).

[6]In this illustrative table, age intervals are shown in years. The experiences of persons up to age 12 are combined together, and the marital experiences after age 29 of persons who reach age 30 without marrying are not shown. In practice, all survival table estimates were based on one-month intervals; the results were printed for yearly intervals. The rates for all 780 months of experience (from age 0 through age 65) were calculated.

Table 2.2
Example of a Survival Table for Age at First Marriage, American Males Aged 20 to 65

Age Interval	Number Entering Interval	Number Censored During Interval	Number Exposed to Risk of Marriage	Number Marrying During Interval	Proportion Marrying During Interval	Proportion not Marrying During Interval	Cumulative Proportions Still Unmarried at End of Interval
(1)	(2)	(3)	(4)	(5)	(6)	(7)	(8)
0-12..........	855	0	855.0	0	.000	1.000	1.000
12-13..........	855	0	855.0	0	.000	1.000	1.000
13-14..........	855	0	855.0	1	.001	0.999	0.999
14-15..........	854	0	854.0	0	.000	1.000	0.999
15-16..........	854	0	854.0	0	.000	1.000	0.999
16-17..........	854	0	854.0	0	.000	1.000	0.999
17-18..........	854	0	854.0	2	.002	0.998	0.997
18-19..........	852	0	852.0	5	.006	0.994	0.991
19-20..........	847	0	847.0	17	.020	0.980	0.971
20-21..........	830	10	825.0	38	.046	0.954	0.926
21-22..........	782	16	774.0	81	.105	0.895	0.829
22-23..........	685	36	667.0	99	.148	0.852	0.706
23-24..........	550	28	536.0	103	.192	0.808	0.570
24-25..........	419	25	406.5	63	.155	0.845	0.482
25-26..........	331	14	324.0	73	.225	0.775	0.374
26-27..........	244	13	237.5	49	.206	0.794	0.297
27-28..........	182	13	175.5	34	.194	0.806	0.239
28-29..........	135	10	130.0	28	.215	0.785	0.188
29-30..........	97	5	94.5	21	.222	0.778	0.146
.	.	.	.	.	.	.	.
.	.	.	.	.	.	.	.
.	.	.	.	.	.	.	.

Transition Parameters

In this study, using exact age at the completion of each transition event (or exact age at the time of the interview for respondents with censored experience), single-decrement survival tables were calculated for each transition (school completion, first job beginning, and first marriage). These survival tables were weighted, and sample sizes were adjusted to reflect survey departures from simple random sampling procedures. Thus the tables provided unbiased estimates of the parameters of the transition process for any subgroup examined. Survival tables for each transition were calculated for several relevant subgroups of men, as described earlier.

Several commonly used and readily understood measures were chosen to summarize the results of these survival-table calculations. The approximate age at which a group began a transition was represented by the first quartile calculated in the survival table. For example, in Table 2.2, 25% of the group first married between ages 22 and 23 (from column 8, the cumulative proportion not married was .829 at age 22 and .706 at age 23; 25% of the group were first married at the age at which 75% have not yet married). By linear interpolation, the first quartile age at marriage for the population of Table 2.2 was 22.64. The median age at transition (50th percentile) was used to describe the typical age of a group at a transition. The approximate age at which a group completed a transition was specified by the age at which 75% of the group finished the transition. The interquartile range was used as an indicator of the length of time taken by a group to complete a given life-course transition. The length of time taken by a group of men to complete the overall transition to adulthood was operationally defined as the difference between the first quartile of the school-completion transition (when the transition to adulthood began for a group) and the third quartile of the marriage transition (when the transition to adulthood ended for a group).[7]

Previous research has shown that age at school completion and age at first marriage are related to each other among individuals in a way

[7]The use of quartiles and interquartile ranges to describe the transition behavior of specific groups has been suggested by Winsborough (1978). Modell *et al.* (1976) used the first and ninth deciles and the interdecile range to describe the transition behaviors of synthetic cohorts. My decision to use the interquartile range was based largely on practical considerations. First, the ninth decile would be based on the experiences of only a small number of sample men for each subgroup and therefore would be more subject to sampling error than would the third quartile. Second, for many of the more recent cohorts, the third quartile of each transition could be determined, but because of censoring, the ninth quartile was indeterminate.

that suggests an ordering norm (Hogan, 1978b). To demonstrate this, a contingency table of age at completion of school by age at marriage was divided into two subtables—one in which marriage occurs prior to leaving school (including the lower left triangular cells of the original matrix) and the other in which marriage occurs at the same age as, or after, the end of formal education (including the diagonal and upper-right triangular cells of the original matrix). These two subtables were treated as categories of an ordering dimension, producing the three-way matrix on which the models of Table 2.3, panel A were based.

The first line of this panel indicates that the null hypothesis of no association between age at leaving school and age at marriage was rejected (χ^2_{LR} = 1994.4, with 304 degrees of freedom). Of the total association between these two variables, about one-third was due to the tendency of men to finish school before marrying (Table 2.3, panel A, row 3). (This statement is equivalent to the observation that age-specific marriage rates are higher among men who have completed school than among those still in school; see Winsborough, 1979.) Another one-third of the association was due to the relationships between the ordering tendency and both age at completion of schooling and age at marriage (Table 2.3, panel A, row 5). This relationship reflects the greater tendency of men who finish school at a relatively early age to marry after school completion as compared with men who finish school at a relatively advanced age. The association between the timing of school completion and marriage was even stronger when the respective age-specific rates (i.e., the margins for marriage age and age at leaving school) were allowed to vary among 10-year birth cohorts (compare rows 4 and 6 of Table 2.3, panel B). Although two-thirds of the association between age at school completion and age at marriage was accounted for by the tendency to order the two events, the remaining one-third of the association was due to the variation of age-specific marriage rates among men with different ages at school completion (Table 2.3, panel C, row 2). In this study, the sequential ordering of transitions was examined; the small associations among the transition events due to factors other than ordering were ignored.

These models, therefore, verify that among individual men, age at marriage is associated with age at termination of schooling. As Elder (1974a) suggests, apart from their tendency to finish school and to marry during certain age ranges, men tend to time marriage to follow the completion of schooling. This observation provides empirical justification for the hypothesis that the ordering of transition events between adolescence and adulthood can be classified according to how well it conforms to a socially preferred sequence. The three transition events between ado-

Table 2.3
Log-Linear Tests of Temporal Ordering Relationship of Age at Completion of Schooling and Age at First Marriage, U.S. Males Born 1907–1952[a]

	Model[b]	χ^2_{LR}	df	P	Δ	χ^2_H/χ^2_T
A.	[E] AGEXED BY [M] AGEXIM BY [O] ORDERING Matrix					
	1. [E][M]	1,994.37	304	.000	11.52	100.00
	2. [E][M][O].	1,392.90	303	.000	9.26	69.84
	3. A2 vs. A1 (Net [O]). .	601.47	1	.000	2.26	30.16
	4. [EO][MO]	665.17	268	.000	6.34	33.35
	5. A4 vs. A2.	727.73	35	.000	2.92	36.49
B.	[E] AGEXED BY [M] AGEXIM BY [C] CHT10X Matrix					
	1. [E][M][C].	6,780.18	1419	.000	21.99	100.00
	2. [EC][MC]	2,977.13	1279	.000	13.82	43.91
	3. [EC][MC][EM]	957.18	975	>.5	7.21	14.12
	4. B3 vs. B2 (Net [EM]) .	2,019.95	304	.000	6.61	29.79
	5. [EM][C].	4,911.60	1115	.000	18.81	72.44
	6. B5 vs. B1 (Gross [EM])	1,868.58	304	.000	3.18	27.56
C.	[E] AGEXED BY [D] DIFFAMAE Matrix					
	1. [E][D]	13,990.05	381	.000	32.51	100.00
	[E] AGEXED BY [O] ORDERING Matrix					
	2. [E][O]	9,741.57	16	.000	21.87	69.63
	3. C1 - C2.	4,248.48	365	.000	--	30.37

[a]In this, as in all other tables, the sample cases have been weighted to reflect true population proportions. The estimated sample frequencies have been adjusted to reflect departures from a simple random sample. Certain cells in the above table are structural zeros; the chi-square statistic and its degrees of freedom are calculated accordingly.

[b]AGEXED = Age at completion of highest grade of schooling (0-10/11-12/13/14 . . . 25/26/27-28/29-31/32-35/36-65). For the matrices of Panels A and B this variable is categorized as (0-10/11-12/13/14/ . . . /25/26/27-28/29-30/31-39/40-65).

AGEXIM = Age at first marriage (13-17/18/19/ . . . /30/31-33/34-39/ 40-64).

ORDERING (Schooling completed before marriage/schooling after marriage).

DIFFAMAE = Age at marriage—Age at completion of schooling (LE -6/ -5/ . . ./0/1/2/ . . . /15/GE 16).

CHT10X = Ten-year cohorts (1907-16/1917-26/1927-36/1937-46/1947-52).

The notation indicates those marginal tables that are fit (i.e., used to predict cell frequencies) under that model. [E][M] indicates that the AGEXED margin and the AGEXIM margin are fit. [EM] indicates that the AGEXED by AGEXIM is fit.

lescence and adulthood can be classified according to how well it conforms to a socially preferred sequence. The three transition events examined in this study were characterized as occurring in a typical (presumed normative) order only when a man first, completed school; next, started to work; and last, married. A single inversion from this normative rank order occurred when a man either began a job before finishing school or married before beginning work but after completing school. An extreme, atypical ordering pattern occurred whenever a man married before completing his education; this produced at least two inversions in the normative order.

Men were classified on the temporal ordering variable using estimated age (in months) at the time of each transition. In cases where two events occurred in the same month, the ordering closest to the typical, presumed normative pattern was assigned. In this study, a person was assigned a temporal ordering classification only if he had completed all three of the transition events and had reported the date of each transition. Overall, 75.4% of the sample were classified on the temporal ordering variable. However, many men born from 1947 to 1952 were enrolled in school, not working, or unmarried at the time of the CPS/OCG-II survey. Only 37.2% of these youngest men could be classified on the temporal ordering variable. The percentage classifiable increased quickly with age, so that 69.2% of the cohorts of 1942–1946 could be assigned a transition ordering pattern. More than 75.0% of the men from any cohort born prior to 1942 were classifiable on the ordering variable. Thus, despite the severe data requirements, most respondents could be successfully assigned a rank on the temporal ordering scale. The cohorts of 1947 to 1952, for whom the transition process was censored, were the exception.

χ^2_{LR} is the likelihood ratio chi-square statistic.

df are the degrees of freedom.

p is the probability level that the chi-square statistic is due to chance.

Δ is the index of dissimilarity between the observed sample frequencies and the expected frequencies obtained with that model.

χ^2_H/χ^2_T is percent of the baseline (total) chi-square accounted for by the chi-square statistic of that model.

Note: This table is adapted from Hogan (1978b: Table 1).

The results of the analysis of the ordering of transition events for these youngest cohorts therefore must be interpreted with extreme caution.

SUMMARY

The data for this study were drawn from the March 1973 Current Population Survey and its adjunct, the Occupational Changes in a Generation II survey. The surveys provided the data needed to achieve the study's objectives: (*a*) to compare transition behaviors of cohorts of men born during the twentieth century; (*b*) to compare transition behaviors within cohorts of subgroups based on social class, ethnic ancestry, and size of community of origin; and (*c*) to identify effects of early life transitions on life course career and family achievements. This chapter has described the data provided by the survey and the definitions of key concepts made possible by these data. All the key variables were operationalized with these data, and rates of nonresponse were quite low.

A major portion of this chapter was concerned with the population coverage of the survey. Potential biases among the younger birth cohorts due to the exclusion of men on active duty in the Armed Forces were discussed. Potential biases in the representation of the transition behavior of the older cohorts due to the use of data from a sample of survivors were examined. Tests indicated that there is close correspondence between 1970 Census and CPS/OCG-II estimates of the age at marriage of single-year birth cohorts of men born from 1911 to 1944. The 1973 survey estimates of timing of marriage for the birth cohorts of 1917–1931 also correspond closely to those obtained with the 1962 OCG survey. In general, then, differential mortality does not appear to bias the results for the older cohorts, and the exclusion of persons in the military affects the transition rates almost only for cohorts of military service veterans born 1947 or later.

The censoring biases inherent in describing the transition behaviors of groups that include men who have not completed all transitions at the time of the survey were considered. Survival table techniques were adopted to resolve these censoring biases, and this chapter has discussed these techniques in considerable detail. The transition behavior of a group is described by its survival table-based age-specific transition rates. The study reported here uses the first, second, and third quartiles of age at transition implied by a group's survival table to summarize its behavior. Finally the study has examined the sequencing of early life transitions. For this purpose, a scale of the temporal ordering of events was developed and tested.

II

Intercohort Differences in the Transition to Adulthood

Over the course of the twentieth century there have been marked changes in the timing and sequencing of school completion, first job, and first marriage among American men. These historical changes have characterized men differentially, depending on the year in which they were born and on their age-specific experience of such historical events as the economic depression of the 1930s, World War II, the Korean War, and the Vietnam War. The continued urbanization and industrialization of the United States and the concomitant expansion of the educational system have been important factors structuring the school enrollment behavior and labor force behavior of cohorts of men as they have undergone the passage to adulthood.

Birth cohorts are the most appropriate units of analysis in the study of historical changes in age-dependent transitions (Ryder, 1965; Riley, 1976). Men born during a single calendar year are defined as members of the same birth cohort. Men in a birth cohort age chronologically at the same pace and experience historical events at the same age. All members of a birth cohort thus are characterized by the same history of social contexts. The constellation of variables determining the social history of birth cohorts differs markedly among the cohorts. A cohort-level analysis therefore is an appropriate method of discerning the effects of social structural conditions on the transition behavior of men.

The consideration of intercohort differences in the transition to adulthood begins (in Chapter 3) with a descriptive analysis of intercohort changes in the timing of school completion, first job, and first marriage for single-year birth cohorts of American men born from 1907 to 1952. The timing patterns for each transition event by each birth cohort are discussed, using descriptive transition parameters derived from single-decrement survival tables (as described in Chapter 2). The interrelations of the timing among the three transitions are described with particular attention to the sequential ordering in which the transitions were completed.

Previous research has demonstrated the extreme importance of the military service obligations faced by members of each birth cohort for understanding intercohort differences in transition behavior (Hogan, 1978a, 1978b). This analysis, therefore, divides the members of the birth cohorts into two groups: those men who served in the military and those who did not. Transition behaviors are described for men in these two types of single-year birth cohorts. The unique effect of period-specific, Armed Forces demands for manpower on the transition behavior of the cohorts thus is a major theme of Part II of this book.

Chapter 3 describes intercohort changes in the transition behavior of American males in order to identify crucial turning points at which intercohort changes in transition behavior occurred and to discern underlying, long-term trends in transition behavior. The intercohort changes in transition behavior that are identified are then related to unique historical events that may have affected the cohorts differentially, depending upon their ages at the occurrence of the events. The hypothesized relationship between social structural conditions and transition behavior is subjected to formal test in Chapter 4, where the transition behavior parameters presented in Chapter 3 are regressed on a set of independent variables that describe the social structural conditions experienced by each cohort at the time they were undergoing the passage from youth to adulthood.

3

Cohort Patterns in the Transition to Adulthood

This chapter describes the timing and sequencing of school completion; beginning of first, full-time job; and first marriage for single-year birth cohorts of American men born from 1907 to 1952. The transition behaviors of birth cohorts of veterans and nonveterans also are presented. The timing patterns for each transition are based on descriptive transition parameters drawn from single-decrement survival tables calculated for each transition for each birth cohort group. The age at which a cohort begins a particular transition is characterized as the age by which one-quarter of the cohort has completed that transition. The average age of cohort at a transition is indicated by the age by which 50% of the cohort completes the transition. A cohort is said to complete a transition by the age at which three-quarters of the men in the cohort have completed the transition. The interquartile range for each transition characterizes the duration of time required for the cohort to complete the transition. The years required by a cohort to complete the transition from youth to adulthood are defined as the difference between the ages at the third quartile of the marriage transition and the first quartile of the education transition for that cohort. Three patterns of the temporal ordering of transition events are identified:

1. Men with a normative ordering of events first, complete school; next, begin to work; lastly marry
2. Men with one inversion from the normative pattern begin a job before completing school, or marry before beginning work but

after completing school; such men have an intermediate, nonnormative ordering pattern

3. Men who marry before completing school have at least two inversions from the normative ordering pattern and thus an extreme, nonnormative ordering pattern[1]

INTERCOHORT CHANGES IN EDUCATIONAL ATTAINMENT

Remarkable intercohort improvements in level of schooling completed occurred in this century (Table 3.1). Among men born from 1907–12 only 40.6% achieved a high school diploma. This percentage increased very rapidly among later cohorts, reaching 60.2% completing high school among the cohort of 1918–22. The percentage of men completing elementary and secondary school educations improved steadily, but more slowly, thereafter reaching 84.8% among men born from 1948 to 1952. Among men born in the early part of this century, only 11% completed at least four years of college. Between the cohorts of 1913–1917 and 1928–1932 the percentage of men completing four years of college increased to about 20%. There were no intercohort increases in the percentage of men completing college between the cohorts of 1928–1932 and 1943–1947.[2] Among the 1907–1912 cohort, about 5% of men attended college after obtaining the bachelor's degree. This proportion increased gradually thereafter to reach 11% among the cohort of 1938–1942. The most dramatic intercohort upgradings in school attainments thus have obtained at the grade school and high school level.

[1]Winsborough (1978) has already presented the first, second, and third quartiles of ages at completion of schooling, beginning of first job, and first marriage for the same group of single-year birth cohorts. His calculations for the school completion and first job transitions used the same OCG-II data as this study. Indeed, the analysis presented in this chapter was inspired by Winsborough's work. However, the results of the analysis represent an elaboration and improvement on the earlier work of Winsborough in a number of ways. First, in order to represent the national population of males accurately, the OCG-II survey data have been properly weighted to reflect departures from simple random sampling. Second, the transition parameters I present are based on survival table procedures that resolve the truncation problem inherent in including cohorts that have not yet completed a given transition. Third, this chapter presents separate transition parameters for single-year cohorts of men who were in the military and for men who were not, something Winsborough did not attempt to do. Fourth, this chapter considers the ordering patterns in which individual men from the cohorts complete the transition events.

[2]The percentage of men completing college is artifactually low among the 1948–1952 birth cohorts, since these men were ages 20–24 at the time of the 1973 OCG-II survey and had not yet had time to complete the educational process; therefore, these percentages are not shown in Table 3.1.

Table 3.1
Level of School Completed by 5-Year Birth Cohorts of American Males Born 1907–1952

Birth Cohort	Level of Schooling					
	Elementary, 0–8	High School, 1–3	High School, 4	College, 1–3	College, 4	College. 5 or more
	(Percentage with this level of schooling or higher)					
1907–12	100.0	58.2	40.6	18.0	10.7	4.7
1913–17	100.0	69.9	52.3	20.4	10.9	5.1
1918–22	100.0	76.0	60.2	25.9	13.5	5.4
1023–27	100.0	79.9	61.6	27.3	16.7	7.5
1928–32	100.0	83.4	67.6	32.2	20.4	9.7
1933–37	100.0	86.3	71.8	35.2	21.1	10.6
1938–42	100.0	90.8	76.3	37.2	21.8	11.0
1943–47	100.0	93.0	81.7	42.3	22.3	--[a]
1948–52	100.0	95.9	84.8	46.2	--	--

[a] Percent undefined due to censored experience.

Although greatest among the early birth cohorts, these improvements have proceeded over the course of the century. Intercohort upgrading in college educations occurred between the cohorts of 1913–1917 and 1928–1932. The former group attended college primarily during the 1930s, whereas the latter attended college during the period immediately following World War II. Cohorts attending college during the 1950s and 1960s did not display any increases in the percentages completing college (although they did display intercohort increases in the percentage of men with one or more years of college).

AGE AT SCHOOL COMPLETION

The median age at the completion of schooling increased from less than 16.8 years for men born in 1907 to about age 18 for men born from 1914 to 1928 (Table 3.2; Figure 3.1), as more of the men from successive birth cohorts remained in school until the completion of high school. As greater proportions of the cohorts completed high school and continued on to college in the post-World War II period, the median age at school completion increased from 18.6 years for men born in 1929 to over 19 years for men born in 1942. Age at school completion continued to increase steadily among men born after 1942, reaching an apparent high of 20.2 years among men born in 1950.

Table 3.2
Measures of Age at School Completion for Single-Year Birth Cohorts of American Males Born 1907–1952, by Military Service Experience

Birth Cohort	Veterans				Nonveterans				Total			
	First Quartile	Median	Third Quartile	Inter-quartile Range	First Quartile	Median	Third Quartile	Inter-quartile Range	First Quartile	Median	Third Quartile	Inter-quartile Range
1907......	14.96	16.64	20.83	5.87	14.35	16.82	19.89	5.54	14.45	16.77	20.10	5.64
1908......	15.13	17.56	21.34	6.21	14.23	16.68	19.67	5.44	14.53	16.87	19.96	5.43
1909......	15.30	17.48	21.52	6.22	14.79	16.75	18.84	4.05	15.00	16.92	19.36	4.36
1910......	15.26	17.54	20.87	5.61	14.18	16.73	19.15	4.97	14.55	17.09	19.69	5.14
1911......	15.30	18.34	22.46	7.16	14.61	17.07	19.78	5.17	14.82	17.34	20.67	5.85
1912......	15.63	18.03	21.98	6.35	14.71	16.95	19.21	4.50	15.11	17.33	20.46	5.35
1913......	15.75	18.44	21.33	5.58	15.25	17.31	19.33	4.08	15.44	17.61	20.09	4.64
1914......	16.12	18.19	21.57	5.45	15.41	17.60	19.62	4.21	15.70	17.84	20.20	4.50
1915......	16.34	18.10	21.44	5.10	15.28	17.36	19.84	4.56	15.89	17.87	20.46	4.57
1916......	16.46	18.31	22.57	6.11	15.30	17.36	19.76	4.46	15.89	17.89	21.16	5.27
1917......	16.14	18.07	20.96	4.82	14.96	17.33	19.22	4.26	15.65	17.75	20.14	4.50
1918......	16.76	18.75	22.19	5.43	14.09	16.48	19.40	5.31	15.80	18.20	21.34	5.54
1919......	16.40	18.17	20.99	4.59	14.40	17.28	19.67	5.27	15.91	17.87	20.65	4.74
1920......	16.58	18.48	22.68	6.10	14.86	17.34	19.63	4.77	16.09	18.24	21.34	5.26
1921......	16.64	18.29	22.39	5.75	15.20	17.55	20.04	4.84	16.34	18.14	21.25	4.91
1922......	16.69	18.42	25.09	8.40	14.60	17.28	19.80	5.20	16.18	18.14	24.45	8.27
1923......	16.53	18.21	24.11	7.58	14.36	16.53	18.65	4.29	16.06	17.96	23.15	7.09
1924......	16.69	18.18	25.10	8.41	14.29	16.49	18.59	4.30	16.14	17.87	23.60	7.46
1925......	16.82	18.46	24.64	7.82	14.08	17.22	19.79	5.71	16.41	17.95	24.26	7.85
1926......	16.45	18.33	24.08	7.63	14.64	17.22	19.06	4.42	15.13	18.01	23.55	7.42

1927......	16.35	18.15	23.65	7.30	14.20	16.67	18.91	4.71	15.84	17.79	22.72	6.88
1928......	17.05	18.97	24.52	7.47	14.84	17.42	20.58	5.74	16.39	18.28	23.44	7.05
1929......	17.35	19.47	25.62	8.27	15.30	17.51	19.65	4.35	16.88	18.57	23.82	6.94
1930......	17.11	18.92	25.47	8.36	15.06	17.46	21.25	6.19	16.48	18.40	24.41	7.93
1931......	16.99	18.85	25.73	8.74	14.86	17.43	20.16	5.30	16.32	18.38	24.30	7.98
1932......	17.34	19.50	26.30	8.96	15.33	17.88	21.78	6.45	16.99	18.79	25.09	8.10
1933......	17.48	18.89	24.80	7.32	16.13	17.99	20.84	4.71	17.11	18.58	23.75	6.64
1934......	17.61	19.88	25.03	7.42	16.13	18.27	21.90	5.77	17.24	18.91	24.36	7.11
1935......	17.67	19.54	25.38	7.71	16.37	18.41	22.44	6.07	17.26	18.87	24.04	6.78
1936......	17.38	19.18	24.95	7.57	16.37	18.21	22.71	6.34	17.04	18.72	23.73	6.69
1937......	17.57	19.42	24.94	7.37	16.90	18.65	23.74	6.84	17.27	18.95	24.31	7.04
1938......	17.50	19.22	24.60	7.10	16.94	18.84	23.61	6.67	17.26	18.98	24.20	6.94
1939......	17.57	19.15	23.54	5.97	17.24	18.71	24.12	6.88	17.41	18.87	23.82	6.41
1940......	17.46	18.81	23.64	6.18	17.23	18.76	23.69	6.46	17.33	18.79	23.67	6.33
1941......	17.54	18.84	24.02	6.48	17.21	18.83	24.26	7.05	17.38	18.83	24.17	6.79
1942......	17.59	18.99	23.97	6.38	17.50	19.55	25.01	7.51	17.54	19.32	24.67	7.12
1943......	17.66	19.18	25.09	7.43	17.33	19.00	23.73	6.40	17.49	19.06	24.08	6.59
1944......	17.74	19.04	24.71	6.97	17.39	19.23	24.40	7.01	17.55	19.15	24.54	6.99
1945......	17.95	19.97	26.16	8.21	17.45	18.99	23.46	6.01	17.66	19.52	24.48	6.81
1946......	17.89	19.61	25.29	7.40	17.73	20.40	24.08	6.35	17.83	19.96	24.72	6.90
1947......	17.83	19.29	24.13	6.30	17.73	20.73	23.74	6.01	17.80	19.79	23.85	6.05
1948......	17.68	18.83	22.51	4.83	18.08	21.36	23.93	5.85	17.87	20.03	23.63	5.75
1949......	17.72	18.73	21.05	3.33	18.21	20.74	23.22	5.01	17.97	19.71	22.93	4.95
1950......	17.53	18.57	22.03	4.50	18.19	20.74	--	--	17.95	20.20	--	--
1951......	17.45	18.16	19.77	2.32	18.00	20.18	--	--	17.88	19.86	--	--
1952......	17.09	18.08	19.50	2.41	17.90	19.38	--	--	17.84	19.27	--	--

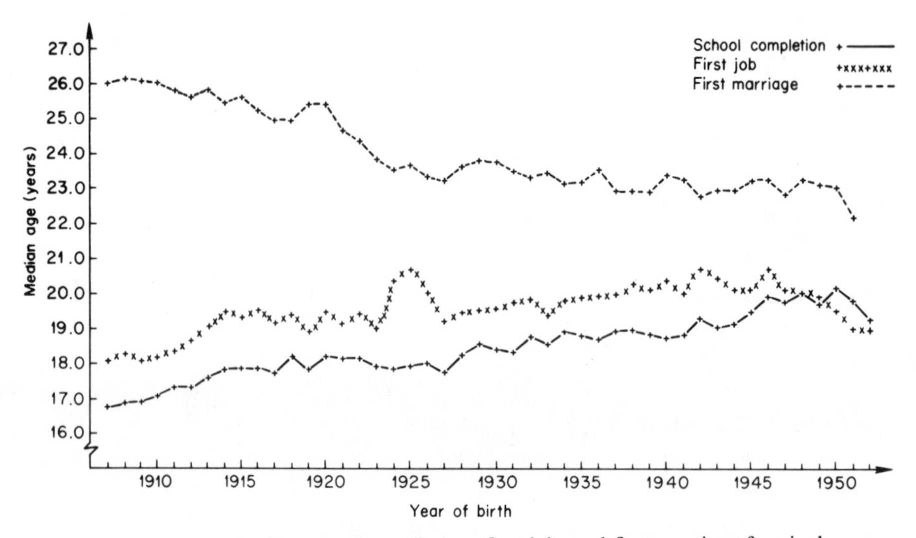

Figure 3.1. Median ages at school completion, first job, and first marriage for single-year birth cohorts of American males born 1907–1952.

The most consistent historical trend in age at school completion has been the increase in the age at which one-quarter of the birth cohort finished school. As compulsory school attendance has lengthened the time children must remain in school, the age at which a birth cohort began the school-leaving transition (as measured by the twenty-fifth percentile) climbed from less than fifteen years for men born prior to 1912 to over seventeen years for cohorts born after 1932 (and educated in the post–World War II period). During the 1960s, special government programs attempted to reduce the percentage of persons dropping out of high school prior to graduation. The effects of these programs were evident in the intercohort increases in percentage of men completing high school and in the slight increase in the first quartile of the school completion distribution from about 17.6 years for men born in the early 1940s to 17.8 years and above for men born after 1945 (and reaching age 16 in 1962 or later).

Unlike the rather steady rate of increase in the first and second quartiles of the school completion distribution, the third quartile was markedly erratic, increasing from about 20 for men born 1907 to 1915 to around 21 for men born 1916 to 1921. It jumped suddenly to 24.5 years for men born in 1922 and remained high for the birth cohorts born through 1946.

What factors accounted for this sudden, apparently permanent, increase in the age at which the birth cohorts finished the school exit transition? The cohorts of men born before 1922 were able to complete school prior to the military service call-ups of World War II. The college enrollment of men born from 1922 to 1926 were interrupted during the 1941–1944 period because of the wartime service demands of World War II. College attendance therefore was postponed until after the end of the war; one-quarter of the men still had not completed their schooling at the end of 1946. Because of their ages during World War II, the experiences of the cohorts of 1922 to 1926 thus were quite different from those of earlier cohorts. Cohorts born after 1926 did not have their schooling interrupted by World War II, but a greater proportion of these cohorts decided to attend college during the post-war expansion of the educational system. As more men attended college, the age by which three-quarters of the cohort finished their schooling increased.

As a result of the upward shift in the third quartile of the school completion distribution and a lesser increase in the first quartile, the size of the interquartile range increased from the 4.5–5.5 years it had been for cohorts born from 1907 to 1921 to 6.5–8.3 years among cohorts born later. For the youngest cohorts, it appears that the duration of the school completion transition has narrowed, but this may be due to gaps in population coverage.

The military service demands on cohorts thus were a critically important feature of their history. The proportion of men who served in the military was important, as was the timing of military service in the life cycle. The proportion of men serving in the armed forces varied markedly among the birth cohorts (Table 3.3). Less than half of the men born from 1908 to 1914 served in the military. The percentage of the birth cohort with military service experience jumped to 54.9 for men born in 1915, and increased steadily thereafter, reaching three-quarters of the cohort of 1920. Three-quarters of the cohorts of 1920 to 1926 served in the military (providing manpower for the armed forces during World War II). The proportion of men with military service experience declined beginning with the cohort of 1927 but remained above 50% until the cohort of 1936. For the cohorts of 1936 to 1948, between 40% and 50% of the men served in the armed forces.

These intercohort differences in proportions of men serving in the military reflected sudden historical changes in the manpower requirements of the armed forces. Following the World War I demobilization (1919–1920), the number of persons on active duty in the armed forces declined to less than one-half million and remained at this low level until 1941 (Table 3.4). The United States government began to expand the size of the armed forces in 1941 and 1942 in preparation for the battles of World War II. By 1943, more than nine million American men were

Table 3.3
Percentage of Men Serving on Active Duty in the Armed Forces for 6 Months or Longer for Single-Year Birth Cohorts of American Males Born 1907–1946

Birth Cohort	Percent in the Armed Forces	Birth Cohort	Percent in the Armed Forces
1907.........	24.3	1927.........	72.3
1908.........	25.3	1928.........	65.1
1909.........	26.7	1929.........	67.7
1910.........	28.6	1930.........	67.6
1911.........	31.7	1931.........	67.2
1912.........	36.0	1932.........	66.4
1913.........	36.4	1933.........	60.4
1914.........	43.4	1934.........	57.4
1915.........	54.9	1935.........	53.7
1916.........	56.0	1936.........	48.2
1917.........	59.0	1937.........	48.5
1918.........	68.4	1938.........	46.1
1919.........	70.3	1939.........	44.8
1920.........	75.6	1940.........	42.2
1921.........	77.2	1941.........	40.3
1922.........	76.3	1942.........	41.0
1923.........	78.7	1943.........	43.6
1924.........	76.6	1944.........	39.9
1925.........	76.0	1945.........	42.8
1926.........	79.5	1946.........	52.9

on active duty in the armed forces. This number grew to more than eleven million in 1944 and 1945. Following the end of World War II in 1945, rapid demobilization occurred. By 1946 only three million men were on active duty in the armed forces. The demobilization continued, with about 1.5 million men serving in the military from 1947 to 1950. The size of the armed forces doubled to more than three million in 1951 due to the outbreak of the Korean War. The number of men on active duty remained above three million through 1954. During the peacetime, cold war years (1955–1965) the size of the armed forces was between 2.5 and 3.0 million. Vietnam War requirements increased these figures to more than 3.0 million men from 1966 to 1970, with troop levels declining thereafter.

The experiences of cohorts of men who served in the military differed substantially from those of cohorts of men who had no military service experience (Table 3.2; Figure 3.2). The median age at school completion

Table 3.4
Number of Military Personnel on Active Duty, United States Armed Forces, 1935–1972

Year	Number on Duty (Thousands)	Year	Number on Duty (Thousands)
1935....	252	1955....	2935
1936....	291	1956....	2806
1937....	312	1957....	2796
1938....	323	1958....	2601
1939....	334	1959....	2504
1940....	458	1960....	2476
1941....	1801	1961....	2484
1942....	3859	1962....	2808
1943....	9045	1963....	2670
1944....	11451	1964....	2687
1945....	12123	1965....	2655
1946....	3030	1966....	3094
1947....	1583	1967....	3377
1948....	1446	1968....	3548
1949....	1615	1969....	3460
1950....	1460	1970....	3066
1951....	3249	1971....	2715
1952....	3635	1972....	2323
1953....	3555		
1954....	3302		

Source: U.S. Bureau of the Census. Historical Statistics of the United States, Colonial Times to 1970, Bicentennial Edition, Part 2, Series Y 904 and U.S. Bureau of the Census, Statistical Abstract of the United States, 1978, Table 602.

among civilian men showed no consistent trend between the birth cohorts of 1907 and 1931, remaining between 16.5 and 17.6 years. After 1937, the median age at school completion increased steadily to over 20.5 years for men born during the late 1940s. The first and third quartile of school completion distribution for civilian men showed the same lack of trend from 1907 to 1931, with a consistent upward trend thereafter. As a result, the duration of the school-leaving process fluctuated between 4 and 6 years for civilian men born before 1935, and increased by about 1 year thereafter. Among civilian men, therefore, only cohorts educated during the post-World War II period of educational expansion showed a trend toward later ages at school completion. The school-completion transition of the cohorts of men who avoided military service was not affected in

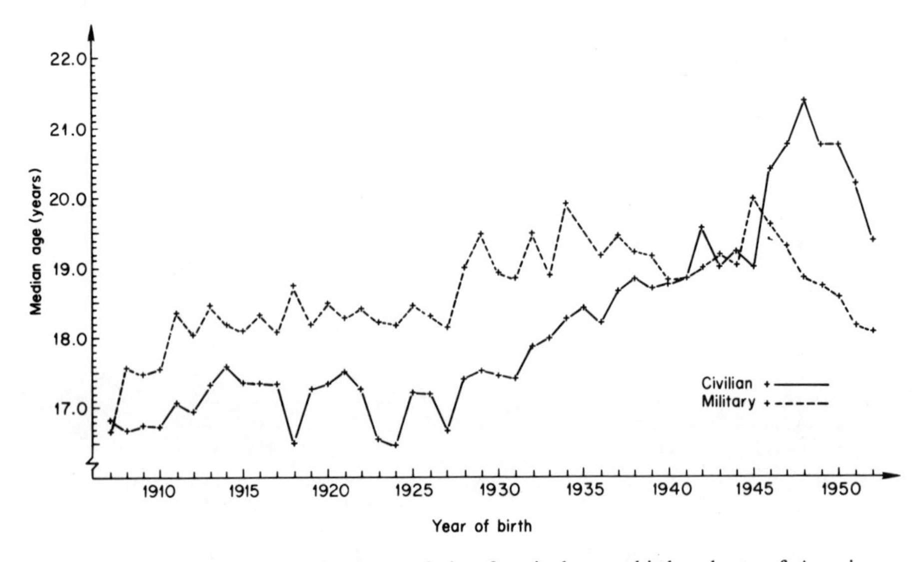

Figure 3.2. Median age at school completion for single-year birth cohorts of American males born 1907–1952, by military service experience.

any pronounced and consistent way by the economic depression of the 1930s or by World War II. (Annual fluctuations in transition behavior may have resulted from such factors, however, as discussed in Chapter 4.)

For all cohorts born from 1908 to 1939, men who had served in the military had later median ages at school completion than men who had not. The size of the differential fluctuated but tended to be about one to one-and-a-half years. Ages at school completion for the twenty-fifth and fiftieth percentiles were about the same for veterans and nonveterans born from 1940 to 1944. After 1946 the trend was toward a later median age at school completion for civilians than for veterans. This tendency may have resulted from the Selective Service policies of the early Vietnam War era, which provided military service deferments to men enrolled in college.

Among veterans born from 1907 to 1921, 75% completed their schooling by 20.8 to 22.7 years of age. The third quartile of the school-completion distribution increased suddenly to 25.1 years in 1922 and remained between 23.5 and 26.3 years through the birth cohort of 1947. This group, of course, comprises the men who served in the military during World War II and the subsequent cold war period. These men qualified for G.I. Bill benefits, which helped finance college attendance after military service. Enough of the veterans chose to continue their educations to raise the ages at which the cohorts typically finished their school transitions.[3,4]

Because of these differences in average ages at the beginning and end of the school-completion transitions, birth cohorts of veterans displayed greater variability in the duration of the school-completion transition. This difference amounted to about one-half to one-and-a-half years among the cohorts of 1908 to 1916, but it grew to two to four years for the cohorts of 1922 to 1935. After the 1937 cohort, there were only small differences between veterans and nonveterans in the length of the school-completion transition.

The overall shifts in the timing of school completion among birth cohorts was thus a complex intermixture of the behavior of men who were in the military and those who were not. Among the earlier birth cohorts, the principal trend in age at school completion was an upward shift in the age at which the cohort began the school-completion transition. This trend was associated with intercohort increases in the proportion of men finishing high school. This trend continued among the more recent cohorts. Among the more recent cohorts, more men also attended college, raising the median and third quartiles of the age at school-completion transition. The median age at school completion increased fairly steadily among civilian men born from 1928 to 1948 but displayed only a single increment between veterans born in 1927 or earlier and those born 1928 or later. This sudden jump in age at school completion among veterans was undoubtedly related to the availability and widespread use of G.I. Bill benefits among younger veterans during the post-war period.

[3]Federal funding for veterans' education and training began in 1945, with the expenditure of $9 million. This figure increased to $351 million in 1946 and $2,122 million in 1947. Expenditures on veterans remained at about $2 billion from 1947 to 1950, then declined to $1.3 billion by 1952. Expenditures on veterans' education remained below $1 billion from 1953 to 1970. (All figures are current dollars. Data are from U.S. Bureau of the Census, *Historical Statistics of the United States, Colonial Times to 1970, Bicentennial Edition*, Part 2, Series Y987.)

[4]The third quartile of the school-completion distribution of veterans appeared to decline substantially among men born after 1947. Such men were ages 20 to 24 at the time of the OCG-II survey. Since the survey population covered only the civilian population, men ages 20 to 24 who were in the military service but had not yet been discharged were not represented in the survey. Many of these men may have entered military service after the completion of one or more years of college, and may again attend college after discharge from the military. Others may enter college after discharge from the military service. The exclusion of the experiences of these men makes it impossible to make any conclusive statements about trends in age at school completion among veterans born 1948 to 1952.

AGE AT FIRST JOB

Median age at first job increased from about 18 years among men born 1907 to 1911 to around 19.0 to 19.5 years among men born 1912 to 1923 (Table 3.5; Figure 3.1). The median age at first full-time civilian job jumped to over twenty years for the birth cohorts of 1924 to 1926, as these cohorts faced immediate post-high school induction into the Armed Forces during World War II, and could not begin working until later. Men from earlier birth cohorts had some time to begin full-time civilian jobs prior to their wartime service. The median age at first job dropped to 19.2 years for the cohort of 1927 and remained below age twenty until the cohort of 1938. Median age at first job remained slightly above 20 for all cohorts from 1938 to 1948, displaying no consistent trend. Over the course of 40 years, between 1907 and 1948, the median age at beginning of first job has shown a gradual upward trend of about 2 years.

With the exception of the wartime transition cohorts born 1924 to 1926, the changes in the median age at first job have closely paralleled changes in median age at school completion. In general, the median age at first job has been one to one-and-a-half years older than the median age at school completion for the birth cohorts. Beginning with the birth cohorts of 1945, this historical difference appeared to narrow and, perhaps, reverse.

Intercohort changes in the age at which each cohort began the first-job transition (as indicated by the first quartile of the first-job distribution) have closely paralleled changes in the median age at first job. The first quartile of the age at first job distribution increased fairly regularly from about 15.5 years for the birth cohorts of 1907 to 1911 to more than 18 years for the cohorts born after 1942. The age at which each cohort began to undergo the transition to a full-time civilian job decreased slightly among the birth cohorts of 1925 to 1927, which began their first-job transitions during World War II (1942 to 1944), at a time when the demand for labor was strong.

The age at which each cohort completed the first-job transition (as indicated by the third quartile of the first-job distribution) was subject to rather large annual fluctuations. The long-term trend in the third quartile of age at first job was clearly curvilinear, however. Cohorts born 1907 to 1919 generally completed their first-job transitions by 22.6 to 23.2 years of age, whereas cohorts of men born 1918 to 1934 did not usually complete the first-job transition until 24.0 to 25.8 years of age. This change in the third quartile occurred suddenly between the cohorts of 1917 (22.8 years) and 1918 (24.6 years), with no consistent trends appearing to characterize the 1907 to 1917 or 1918 to 1934 cohorts. After this intercohort increase of about 2 years in the usual age at which the cohorts completed the first-job transition, the third quartile age at first job decreased beginning with the cohort of 1935. This decrease continued at an annual rate of about 0.12 years through the cohort of 1949, and appears to have accelerated thereafter.

What factors accounted for these changes in the age at which each cohort finished the first-job transition? The wartime demand for soldiers was obviously related to the sudden initial increase in the third quartile of the age at first-job transition between the birth cohorts of 1917 and 1918. Half of the 1917 birth cohort had finished the first-job transition by late 1936, but half of the 1918 cohort did not finish the first-job transition until late 1938. An additional one-quarter of the cohort of 1917 completed the first-job transition within 3.65 years (by mid 1940) compared with 5.18 years for the cohort of 1918 (by mid 1943). Clearly a major factor distinguishing the first-job transitions of the two cohorts was the sudden period demand for soldiers during World War II. Those cohorts that had not completed the first-job trasition prior to the beginning of World War II had to postpone the completion of the transition for a number of years. Thus, military service-related postponements of school completion and the beginning of first job help to explain the intercohort variations in transition timing patterns, as discussed further below.

The duration of each cohort's first-job transition (as indicated by the interquartile range) followed the same general pattern of change as the third quartile. The interquartile range was 6 to 7 years for the birth cohorts of 1907–1917, and increased by about 1 year for the cohorts of 1918 to 1932. The duration of the first-job transition showed steady intercohort declines from 1933 onward. The declines were large, with the first-job transition taking 7.61 years for the birth cohort of 1932 but only 4.61 years for the 1948 cohort. About three-quarters of this decline was accounted for by the downward shift in the third quartile.

The importance of military service for the first-job transition of the cohorts becomes apparent when cohorts of men with and without military service experience were examined separately (Table 3.5; Figure 3.3). The median age at first job was relatively constant for all the civilian cohorts born 1907 to 1935. Slight annual fluctuations in the median age at first job (especially the half-year increase for men born 1914 to 1916) probably related to economic conditions at the time of the transition (discussed in Chapter 4). Cohorts of civilian men born from 1936 to 1950 had a median age at first job about 1 year older than comparable men from earlier birth cohorts.

Cohorts of men who were in the military service reported median

Table 3.5
Measures of Age at First Job for Single-Year Birth Cohorts of American Males Born 1907–1952, by Military Service Experience

Birth Cohort	Veterans				Nonveterans				Total			
	First Quartile	Median	Third Quartile	Inter-quartile Range	First Quartile	Median	Third Quartile	Inter-quartile Range	First Quartile	Median	Third Quartile	Inter-quartile Range
1907......	15.24	17.49	21.95	6.71	15.38	18.22	22.51	7.13	15.33	18.07	22.31	6.98
1908......	15.84	18.81	25.21	9.37	15.50	18.06	21.58	6.08	15.61	18.27	21.93	6.32
1909......	15.83	18.35	23.56	7.73	15.50	18.03	21.89	6.39	15.60	18.11	22.37	6.78
1910......	16.11	19.16	22.87	6.76	15.11	17.95	21.82	6.71	15.38	18.17	22.22	6.84
1911......	15.81	18.99	24.89	9.08	15.40	18.08	21.62	6.22	15.51	18.34	22.56	7.05
1912......	16.45	20.33	24.00	7.55	15.62	18.10	22.26	6.64	15.94	18.68	23.09	7.15
1913......	16.77	19.69	23.81	7.04	16.01	18.72	21.71	5.70	16.29	19.06	22.43	6.14
1914......	17.57	19.84	24.74	7.17	16.15	19.22	22.49	6.34	16.87	19.49	23.54	6.68
1915......	17.18	19.38	23.02	5.84	16.56	19.26	23.09	6.53	16.93	19.33	23.06	6.13
1916......	17.22	19.93	23.42	6.20	16.19	19.12	22.54	6.35	16.70	19.54	23.11	6.40
1917......	17.45	19.36	22.90	5.45	16.43	18.81	22.70	6.27	17.07	19.16	22.81	5.73
1918......	17.44	19.73	27.24	9.80	15.26	18.30	22.41	7.15	16.90	19.39	24.57	7.67
1919......	17.15	19.06	25.64	8.49	15.99	18.52	21.99	6.00	16.90	18.93	24.01	7.11
1920......	17.44	19.59	26.17	8.73	16.00	18.79	22.57	6.57	17.12	19.48	25.87	8.75
1921......	17.45	19.28	24.91	7.46	16.23	18.73	22.89	6.66	17.16	19.17	24.72	7.55
1922......	17.44	19.78	26.19	8.75	16.44	18.62	22.58	6.14	17.24	19.44	25.79	8.55
1923......	17.36	19.60	24.73	7.37	16.09	18.19	20.68	4.59	17.11	19.02	24.45	7.34
1924......	17.41	21.43	25.22	7.81	14.96	17.60	21.34	6.38	17.01	20.37	24.84	7.84
1925......	17.11	21.21	25.31	8.20	15.86	18.01	22.14	6.28	16.81	20.70	24.91	8.10
1926......	17.13	20.39	24.41	7.28	16.02	18.39	23.37	7.35	16.81	20.07	24.29	7.47

1927......	16.99	19.65	23.85	6.86	15.39	17.69	21.56	6.17	16.53	19.24	23.39	6.86
1928......	17.68	20.20	25.45	7.77	15.75	18.35	21.71	5.96	17.16	19.49	24.37	7.21
1929......	18.02	20.95	26.44	8.42	15.95	18.16	21.09	5.14	17.34	19.54	25.42	8.08
1930......	17.68	21.19	26.05	8.37	15.91	18.07	22.30	6.39	17.17	19.62	25.43	8.26
1931......	17.61	20.95	25.72	8.11	15.85	18.46	22.26	6.41	17.09	19.76	25.10	8.01
1932......	17.56	21.03	25.73	8.17	16.40	18.70	22.88	6.48	17.29	19.83	24.91	7.61
1933......	17.90	21.02	25.61	7.71	16.91	18.52	21.88	4.97	17.47	19.40	24.47	7.00
1934......	17.97	21.21	25.25	7.28	16.93	18.64	22.30	5.37	17.55	19.80	24.65	7.10
1935......	17.95	21.46	25.15	7.20	17.02	18.80	22.44	5.42	17.41	19.89	23.89	6.47
1936......	18.26	21.43	24.92	6.66	16.98	19.15	22.95	5.97	17.53	19.94	23.86	6.33
1937......	18.55	21.62	25.66	7.11	17.18	19.10	22.76	5.58	17.80	19.98	24.23	6.43
1938......	18.39	21.20	24.90	6.51	17.30	19.44	23.38	6.08	17.86	20.28	23.96	6.10
1939......	18.58	21.20	24.84	6.26	17.17	19.20	23.49	6.32	17.88	20.10	24.16	6.28
1940......	18.36	21.35	25.63	7.27	17.58	19.61	23.53	5.95	17.90	20.39	24.21	6.31
1941......	18.11	21.34	24.01	5.90	17.57	19.37	23.84	6.27	17.78	20.04	23.94	6.16
1942......	18.57	21.37	24.25	5.68	17.85	20.04	23.81	5.96	18.14	20.71	23.95	5.81
1943......	18.58	21.69	24.79	6.21	17.61	19.60	22.96	5.35	17.99	20.49	23.72	5.73
1944......	18.70	21.69	25.14	6.44	17.47	19.26	23.21	5.74	18.01	20.13	23.84	5.84
1945......	18.33	21.07	24.62	6.29	17.89	19.67	22.79	4.90	18.07	20.11	23.39	5.33
1946......	18.35	21.04	23.50	5.15	18.01	20.41	23.27	5.26	18.20	20.73	23.40	5.20
1947......	18.22	20.05	22.86	4.64	18.00	20.19	22.94	4.94	18.11	20.13	22.90	4.79
1948......	17.96	19.50	22.07	4.11	18.25	20.53	22.93	4.68	18.10	20.08	22.72	4.61
1949......	18.14	19.36	22.23	4.09	18.22	20.26	22.59	4.37	18.18	19.93	22.46	4.28
1950......	17.92	19.09	21.88	3.96	18.29	19.68	21.84	3.55	18.11	19.56	21.85	3.74
1951......	17.63	19.07	21.11	3.48	17.61	19.05	20.75	3.14	17.62	19.05	20.80	3.18
1952......	17.42	19.06	20.18	2.76	17.68	18.91	20.23	2.55	17.67	18.92	--[a]	--

[a] Age undefined due to censored experience.

Figure 3.3. Median age at first job for single-year birth cohorts of American males born 1907–1952, by military service experience.

ages at first job about 1 year older than civilian men from the same cohorts among men born 1907 to 1923. The median age at first job rose from 19.6 years for veterans born in 1923 to 21.4 years among veterans born in 1924. This sudden increase in median age at first job among veterans was not accompanied by a similar increase among the civilian cohorts; the difference in median age at first job between veterans and nonveterans from the same cohort thus increased to over 2 years. This differential persisted until the cohort of 1945, after which veterans and nonveterans from the same cohort had similar median ages at first job.

There was a gradual upward trend in the age at which civilian cohorts finished their first-job transitions. Although the third quartile figures showed fairly large annual fluctuations, the overall increase in the third quartile of the age at first-job distributions for civilians was about 1 year—from about 22 for men born in 1910 to about 23 for men born in 1945.[5]

Cohorts of veterans displayed pronounced intercohort trends in the age at which they completed the first-job transition. As with the third quartile of the school-completion distribution for these men, the intercohort trends were curvilinear, with the youngest and oldest cohorts

[5]The cohorts born from 1946 to 1953 showed a sharp downward trend in age at first job, but this may reflect the effects of temporarily held first jobs being reported as full-time first jobs by men who will eventually return to school and begin their "true" first jobs (under the OCG-II definition) later.

completing the transition first. There was a pronounced jump between men born in 1917 and those born in 1918, with the former completing their first-job transition by mid 1940 and the latter having to wait until the beginning of 1946, after the post-war military demobilization. The relatively late age at completion of the job transition continued for the veteran cohorts as long as they displayed a tendency to delay the completion of their school transitions.[6]

As discussed above, intercohort changes in the duration of the first-job transition among birth cohorts of all men were curvilinear, with a sharp intercohort decline among men born from 1932 to 1948. This pattern was largely a result of changes in the first-job transition among veterans. Among civilian men, there was a gradual trend toward a somewhat shorter (about 1 year) duration for the first-job transition. Although the pattern was somewhat erratic, first-job transitions usually took 1 to 3 years longer for veterans than for civilians born in the same year. This difference largely disappeared among men born 1935 and later. Thus, the veterans showed a curvilinear intercohort change in the length of both school-completion and first-job transitions, whereas the civilians experienced a gradual intercohort increase in the length of the school transition and a decrease in the length of the first-job transition.

AGE AT FIRST MARRIAGE

There were steady intercohort declines in age at first marriage among males born from 1907 to 1927, with the median dropping about 2.7 years (26.0 to about 23.3) between 1907 and 1927 (Table 3.6; Figure 3.1). Average age at first marriage declined only gradually thereafter, remaining about twenty-three for men born from 1927 to 1950. The age at which a cohort began the marriage transition (the twenty-fifth percentile of the first-marriage distribution) remained steady at about 22.5 years for cohorts of men born 1907 to 1918, a period of substantial decline in the median age at marriage. Beginning with the cohort of 1918, the age at the beginning of the marriage transition began to decline, dropping from 22.4 for the cohort of 1918 to 20.9 for the cohort born in 1933. The cohorts born from 1933 to 1951 all began their marriage transitions at about age 21.

[6]Cohorts born after 1946 served during the Vietnam War. Men ages 20 to 25 who already had been discharged from the military service by 1973 were selectively drawn from the groups not attending school, and they have shown little proclivity to continue their schooling after military service. Instead, they appear to have directly entered or reentered the labor force after discharge from the Armed Forces.

Table 3.6
Measures of Age at First Marriage for Single-Year Birth Cohorts of American Males Born 1907–1952, By Military Service Experience

Birth Cohort	Veterans				Nonveterans				Total			
	First Quartile	Median	Third Quartile	Inter-quartile Range	First Quartile	Median	Third Quartile	Inter-quartile Range	First Quartile	Median	Third Quartile	Inter-quartile Range
1907......	25.38	29.93	38.72	13.55	21.88	25.22	29.60	7.71	22.25	26.02	32.28	10.04
1908......	23.94	30.06	37.21	13.27	22.21	25.58	29.52	7.31	22.58	26.12	32.15	9.57
1909......	24.83	29.39	36.14	11.31	22.34	25.29	29.14	6.80	22.92	26.09	30.96	8.03
1910......	24.65	30.29	36.81	12.16	22.38	25.25	29.29	6.92	22.78	26.03	31.24	8.46
1911......	23.82	28.74	33.43	9.61	22.30	25.02	28.81	6.50	22.61	25.80	30.50	7.89
1912......	24.13	28.54	33.70	9.56	22.20	24.53	28.08	5.88	22.71	25.61	29.90	7.19
1913......	24.49	28.51	34.49	10.00	21.85	24.69	27.16	5.31	22.52	25.82	30.25	7.73
1914......	23.80	27.30	31.81	8.01	21.83	24.31	27.30	5.47	22.36	25.48	30.06	7.70
1915......	24.20	26.85	30.94	6.74	21.60	24.03	27.55	5.95	22.77	25.61	30.36	7.58
1916......	24.02	26.07	30.62	6.60	21.70	23.88	27.42	5.72	22.50	25.24	29.82	7.32
1917......	23.36	25.77	30.18	6.83	21.73	23.81	29.28	7.55	22.62	24.99	29.90	7.28
1918......	22.89	25.66	29.00	6.11	21.31	23.56	28.01	6.70	22.35	24.99	28.97	6.61
1919......	22.60	25.94	28.55	5.95	21.64	24.26	30.26	8.62	22.26	25.43	28.85	6.59
1920......	22.28	25.42	28.34	6.06	21.73	25.39	32.50	10.77	22.16	25.41	28.78	6.62
1921......	21.84	24.55	27.38	5.55	21.85	25.08	30.79	8.94	21.84	24.64	28.22	6.38
1922......	22.03	24.33	26.95	4.92	21.59	25.08	30.72	9.13	21.91	24.39	27.88	5.97
1923......	22.07	23.94	27.13	5.05	21.12	23.57	28.73	7.61	21.82	23.88	27.29	5.48
1924......	21.66	23.44	26.58	4.92	21.60	24.57	30.60	9.01	21.65	23.58	27.39	5.74
1925......	21.38	23.57	27.11	5.73	21.19	24.00	29.28	8.09	21.34	23.68	27.49	6.14
1926......	21.21	23.25	26.42	5.21	21.49	23.89	29.45	7.96	21.25	23.36	26.73	5.48

1927......	21.07	23.41	26.74	5.67	20.99	22.76	28.07	7.07	21.05	23.25	26.92	5.87
1928......	21.78	23.96	27.34	5.57	20.36	22.64	27.70	7.34	21.30	23.63	27.44	6.15
1929......	22.11	24.40	27.57	5.47	19.97	21.99	27.14	7.17	21.29	23.81	27.46	6.17
1930......	21.80	23.82	26.82	5.02	20.47	23.75	27.22	6.75	21.46	23.80	26.92	5.46
1931......	21.45	23.73	26.35	4.90	19.98	22.68	28.53	8.55	20.94	23.53	26.73	5.79
1932......	21.46	23.57	27.12	5.66	20.01	22.69	28.81	8.80	20.84	23.34	27.43	6.59
1933......	21.61	23.77	26.68	5.06	19.83	22.50	26.74	6.91	20.90	23.44	26.70	5.80
1934......	21.95	23.79	27.11	5.16	19.99	22.28	27.13	7.14	21.05	23.17	27.11	6.06
1935......	21.98	23.76	27.10	5.11	19.83	22.03	26.55	6.72	20.80	23.19	26.87	6.06
1936......	22.14	24.31	26.90	4.76	20.29	22.72	27.12	6.83	21.16	23.54	26.97	5.82
1937......	21.73	23.80	27.15	5.42	20.33	22.32	26.20	5.87	20.94	22.95	26.86	5.92
1938......	21.39	23.34	26.66	5.27	20.50	22.58	26.20	5.70	20.90	22.91	26.47	5.57
1939......	21.57	23.69	26.97	5.40	20.28	22.20	26.01	5.73	20.72	22.90	26.61	5.89
1940......	21.98	24.44	26.91	4.93	20.60	22.56	26.09	5.49	21.08	23.40	26.51	5.43
1941......	21.54	23.90	25.87	4.33	20.63	22.79	26.14	5.52	20.99	23.25	25.99	5.00
1942......	21.00	23.28	25.72	4.72	20.35	22.42	25.91	5.56	20.58	22.78	25.80	5.22
1943......	21.52	23.80	26.22	4.71	20.29	22.30	25.88	5.59	20.72	22.99	26.08	5.36
1944......	21.59	23.59	26.12	4.53	20.21	22.19	24.97	4.76	20.62	22.95	25.66	5.04
1945......	21.70	23.73	26.35	4.65	20.26	22.70	26.08	5.83	20.79	23.24	26.22	5.43
1946......	21.40	23.29	26.05	4.65	20.76	23.19	26.87	6.10	21.16	23.25	26.38	5.22
1947......	21.23	23.09	25.39	4.16	20.35	22.58	--	--	20.84	22.85	25.64	4.80
1948......	21.04	22.92	24.93	3.89	21.04	23.50	--	--	21.04	23.22	--	--
1949......	21.05	22.98	--[a]	--	20.90	23.19	--	--	20.95	23.11	--	--
1950......	20.60	22.62	--	--	21.16	23.08	--	--	20.99	23.05	--	--
1951......	19.65	21.58	--	--	21.20	22.24	--	--	21.01	22.21	--	--
1952......	19.90	20.95	--	--	--	--	--	--	--	--	--	--

[a] Age undefined due to censored experience.

The third quartile of the age-at-marriage transition declined very rapidly from 1907 (32.3) to 1926 (26.7). This 5.6 year decline in the age at which birth cohorts finished the marriage transition thus occurred over a relatively brief 20-year interval. In the next 20-year period, for cohorts born from 1927 to 1946, age at the completion of the marriage transition declined by about one-half year overall, a much slower rate of decline.

For the birth cohorts of all men, therefore, the biggest changes in age-at-marriage behavior (the age at the beginning and end of the transition, and the average age at the transition) occurred among the birth cohorts born prior to 1930. Cohorts of men born after 1930 all experienced their marriage transition in the post-war period, and the nature of the transition varied little among men born from 1930 to 1947. The downward trends in age at marriage thus coincided with a period of economic depression and war. If anything, one would have expected each of these period events to cause the postponement of marriage rather than hasten its decline (see Ryder, 1969). (This apparent anomaly is analyzed systematically in Chapter 4.)

The intercohort declines in the third quartile of the first-marriage transition have been larger than the declines in the first quartile. Consequently, the duration of the marriage transition declined from 10 years for men born in 1907 to around 6 years for men born from 1922 to 1935. The duration of the marriage transition declined to less than 6 years for men born in 1936 and continued to decline gradually to about 5.0 to 5.5 years for men born in 1940 and later.

These dramatic intercohort changes in the marriage transition have differed substantially between veterans and nonveterans (Table 3.6; Figure 3.4). Median age at marriage among the veterans declined precipitously from a high of 30 years for the cohorts of 1907 to 1908 to a low of 23.4 years for men born in 1927. Median age at marriage then increased by about 1 year from the veteran cohort of 1925 to the veteran cohort of 1929, fluctuating between 23.3 and 24.4 for the next 18 cohorts.[7]

Older cohorts of veterans began and completed the marriage transition quite late, in addition to marrying late on average. This distinctive pattern disappeared by the cohort of 1927. Between the veteran cohorts of 1907 and 1927, the first quartile of age at marriage dropped from 25.4 to 21.1 years, and the third quartile declined from 38.7 to 26.7 years. There were no intercohort trends in the first quartile or median age at marriage among the veterans for the 20 cohorts born 1927 to 1946. There

[7]Median age at marriage may have declined slightly among military-experienced men born after 1948, but this apparent trend may be a result of the exclusion of younger men still in the military from the OCG-II survey.

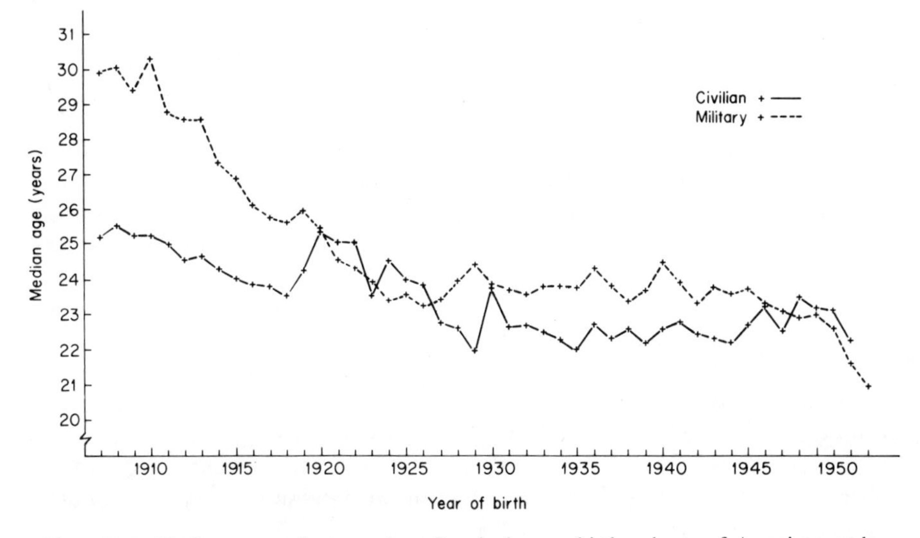

Figure 3.4. Median age at first marriage for single-year birth cohorts of American males born 1907–1952, by military service experience.

was a very gradual decline in third quartile age at marriage among these cohorts, of about .05 years per cohort.

These distinctive intercohort patterns of age at marriage among the veterans obviously were associated with the cohort-specific histories of the types of men who entered the military and the degree of control men held over the timing of their military service entry. The downward trends in age at marriage occurred as the men in the military service became less selective of late marriers. Among the oldest cohorts, relatively few men served in the military; those who did serve during the 1920s and 1930s were enlistees, many of whom were career soldiers. Men from these cohorts were in their thirties when World War II began, and wartime call-ups of these older men fell disproportionately on men who were not married or were married but had relatively few children. The cohorts born during the late 1910s and early 1920s were of prime military service age at the outbreak of World War II. These men were called upon to serve in the military in large numbers, regardless of their marital status. The veterans from these cohorts thus were not selective of late marriers, and the average age at marriage of veterans in these cohorts was lower than that of earlier veteran cohorts. Median age at first marriage among the veterans increased slightly beginning with the birth cohort of 1926. Following World War II the military service entrants once again were selective of late marriers.

The downward intercohort trend in age at marriage was much less pronounced among veterans than among the nonveterans. Median age at first marriage declined from 25.5 years among men born in 1908 to about 23.5 years among men born in 1918. The median age at marriage then increased by almost 2 years for men born in 1920, remaining at this level until the cohort of 1923, at which point marriage age declined to its previous level of about 23.5 years. The median age at marriage reached a low (22.0 years) in the nonveteran cohort of 1929, and with some fluctuations remained around 22.5 years through the cohort of 1947. Median age at marriage showed a tendency toward a later age (about 23.0 years) among cohorts born after 1947. Age at the beginning and the completion of the marriage transition among civilian men displayed the same intercohort tendencies as among the total population, although in somewhat reduced form. The duration of the marriage transition was subject to marked annual fluctuations, but the overall trend was toward a shorter duration of the marriage transition, beginning with the cohort of 1933.

Among the cohorts of 1907 to 1918, on the average, civilian men married 2 years or more younger than veterans. Beginning with 1920 and continuing through 1927, veteran and nonveteran men married at about the same age. Following World War II, a selectivity of late marriers in the military service was observed again. Among cohorts born from 1926 to 1952, on average, veterans married at about 1 year older than nonveterans. Exceptions were the cohorts that supplied manpower for the Korean and Vietnam Wars. Among these cohorts, nonveterans and veterans married at about the same median age.

For both veterans and nonveterans, median age at marriage remained later than the median ages at school completion and first job (Figures 3.5 and 3.6). The difference between median age at marriage and median ages at school completion and first job narrowed substantially between the veteran cohorts of 1907 and 1923 (from more than 12 years to less than 4 years), and remained at about 3 years thereafter. Among the nonveteran cohorts, the median ages at the three transitions displayed intercohort convergence, the differences declining from more than 8 years for men born before 1910 to less than 3 years among men born 1944 to 1952.

ORDERING OF EVENTS

This narrowing of the differences between median age at marriage and median ages at school completion and first job indicated an increasingly compact transition among members of more recent birth cohorts.

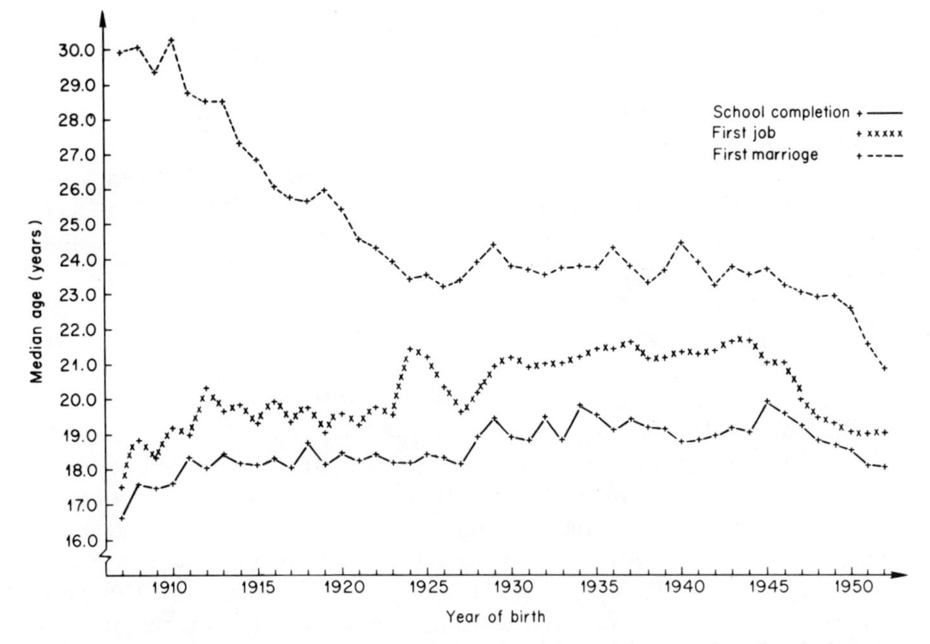

Figure 3.5. Median ages at school completion, first job, and first marriage for single-year birth cohorts of American males born 1907–1952, veterans.

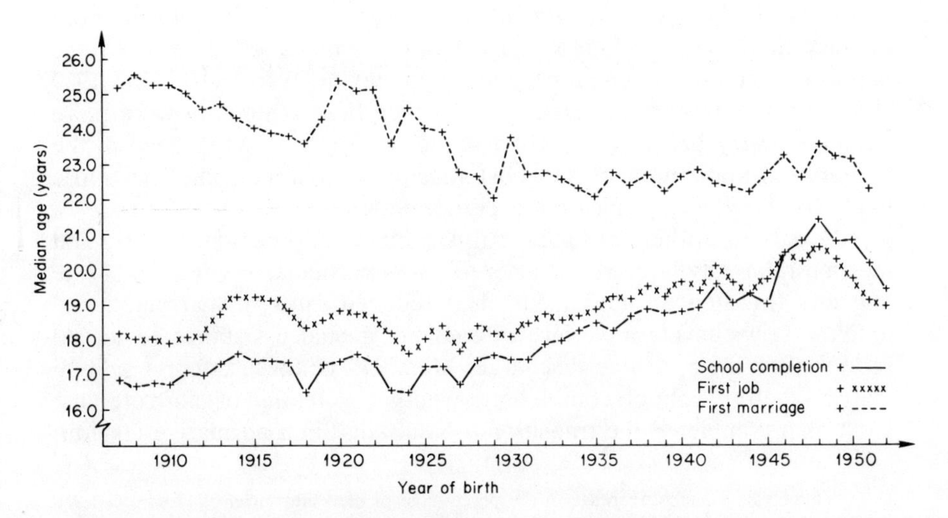

Figure 3.6. Median ages at school completion, first job, and first marriage for single-year birth cohorts of American males born 1907–1952, nonveterans.

Considering the military-experienced and civilian men combined, there was a strong pattern of intercohort decrease in the percentage of men who made the transition to adulthood by first completing school, then beginning work, and finally marrying (Table 3.7; Figure 3.7). The percentage of men with this orderly sequence of events declined from about 75% among the cohorts of 1909–1910 to about 70% for men born in 1916 and 1917, and about 60% for men born from 1924 to 1933. Fewer than 60% of the men in cohorts born from 1932 to 1952 completed the transition to adulthood in a normative fashion.

Conversely, the percentage of men marrying prior to completing school displayed a pronounced pattern of intercohort increases. Fewer than about 10% of the men born from 1907 to 1915 married prior to completing their schooling. Among men born from 1924 to 1947, 20% to 25% married before finishing their formal schooling.[8]

These temporal ordering patterns varied markedly between the veteran and nonveteran men (Table 3.7; Figure 3.8). Among the cohorts born from 1907 to 1915, the ordering patterns of the veterans and nonveterans fluctuated. Among men born 1916 to 1938, civilian men more frequently had normative orders. In many years during the 1920s and 1930s this difference amounted to 15 percentage points or more. Beginning in about 1939 the civilian and military men were about equally likely to have normative ordering patterns, although the rates fluctuated considerably.

These differences between military and civilian men resulted primarily from the fact that, among the cohorts of 1917 to 1934, more military men than civilians married before completing school (extreme nonnormative order). The birth cohorts of 1907 to 1916 and 1935 to 1939 showed no consistent pattern, whereas men born after 1939 were more likely to marry before completing school if they had never been in the military. Military men in the most recent years were somewhat more likely to show an intermediate ordering pattern.

Men born in the early part of this century finished school early and married relatively late. Military service was particularly selective of late marriers (or men on active duty had reduced rates of marriage), and military service veterans were offered no special assistance to attend school after their service discharge. Members of these cohorts seldom married before school completion, whether veterans or nonveterans; most men completed the transition to adulthood in a normative fashion.

[8]There was a sharp decrease in the percentage of men born after 1947 who ordered their transition events in a disorderly fashion, but this undoubtedly related to the fact that many of the men in these younger cohorts had not finished their schooling at the time of the OCG-II survey, and so could not be classified on the temporal ordering variable. A number of these men undoubtedly will marry before they complete school.

Table 3.7
The Temporal Ordering of Life-Course Events for Single-Year Birth Cohorts of American Males Born 1907–1952, by Military Service Experience

Birth Cohort	Veterans			Nonveterans			Total		
	Percent Norma-tive[a]	Percent Intermed. Nonnor-mative	Percent Extreme Nonnor-mative	Percent Norma-tive	Percent Intermed. Nonnor-mative	Percent Extreme Nonnor-mative	Percent Norma-tive	Percent Intermed. Nonnor-mative	Percent Extreme Nonnor-mative
1907....	78.3	17.4	4.3	72.2	20.3	7.6	73.8	19.6	6.7
1908....	71.3	16.1	12.6	71.5	20.5	8.0	71.3	19.3	9.4
1909....	79.1	12.1	8.8	75.3	19.9	4.8	75.4	18.5	6.2
1910....	73.6	22.6	3.8	75.7	18.1	6.3	75.6	19.2	5.3
1911....	63.5	23.0	13.5	77.3	15.7	7.1	72.5	18.3	9.2
1912....	66.0	18.4	15.6	68.8	22.3	8.9	68.1	20.9	11.0
1913....	72.6	17.8	9.6	74.6	17.7	7.8	73.9	17.6	8.5
1914....	71.7	17.6	10.7	68.4	21.8	9.8	70.3	19.9	9.8
1915....	73.9	14.1	12.0	71.2	22.0	6.8	73.1	16.9	9.9
1916....	66.9	20.9	12.2	72.5	16.1	11.4	70.0	18.7	11.3
1917....	67.8	18.4	13.8	74.4	18.2	7.4	70.5	18.3	11.2
1918....	67.1	16.6	16.3	69.9	19.9	10.3	67.7	17.4	14.8
1919....	68.8	17.2	14.0	70.8	20.5	8.7	69.4	18.3	12.3
1920....	65.0	16.3	18.7	73.5	18.9	7.6	67.1	16.4	16.5
1921....	61.3	17.2	21.4	74.8	17.1	8.1	64.1	17.6	18.3
1922....	57.0	20.2	22.8	70.8	24.1	5.1	60.1	20.8	19.1
1923....	61.9	17.9	20.2	69.1	20.9	10.0	63.8	18.8	17.4
1924....	59.6	16.1	24.3	76.9	16.4	6.7	62.5	16.3	21.2
1925....	52.6	20.7	26.7	71.9	16.5	11.6	56.9	19.4	23.7
1926....	59.4	16.3	24.3	78.7	11.5	9.8	62.9	16.2	20.9
1927....	60.0	15.7	24.3	73.5	19.2	7.3	62.9	16.8	20.2
1928....	57.8	22.0	20.2	67.7	16.7	15.6	61.2	20.0	18.8
1929....	51.0	21.6	27.3	73.6	14.4	12.1	58.1	19.3	22.6
1930....	52.5	18.9	28.6	69.3	16.6	14.1	58.2	17.8	24.0
1931....	58.3	16.0	25.7	71.5	15.1	13.4	62.1	15.7	22.2
1932....	52.7	18.5	28.8	69.4	13.1	17.5	57.7	17.0	25.3
1933....	53.0	23.0	24.0	67.5	16.7	15.8	58.5	21.0	20.5
1934....	52.2	19.9	27.9	62.8	19.0	18.2	56.0	19.5	24.5
1935....	54.2	22.3	23.5	58.3	20.0	21.7	55.6	21.4	23.0
1936....	58.2	18.1	23.7	64.9	13.8	21.3	61.0	15.6	23.5
1937....	58.9	19.0	22.1	59.2	15.8	25.0	59.0	17.7	23.3
1938....	56.0	20.5	23.5	66.4	12.5	21.1	61.1	16.3	22.6
1939....	57.7	19.8	22.5	58.5	18.3	23.2	58.1	18.9	22.9
1940....	58.0	22.4	19.6	62.2	13.6	24.2	60.1	16.8	23.1
1941....	55.6	25.8	18.7	58.8	17.4	23.8	57.8	20.8	21.4
1942....	54.5	27.1	18.4	55.5	17.5	27.0	54.5	21.9	23.6
1943....	53.4	29.7	16.9	62.2	16.1	21.6	57.5	21.7	20.7
1944....	60.7	19.2	20.1	57.7	18.6	23.7	57.1	19.0	23.8
1945....	55.3	26.0	18.7	64.8	16.0	19.3	59.7	20.2	20.1
1946....	58.5	21.8	19.7	59.5	16.1	24.3	58.1	19.2	22.7
1947....	62.1	20.6	17.3	57.1	14.8	28.1	59.3	17.7	23.1
1948....	65.5	22.0	12.6	56.8	18.8	24.4	59.8	20.3	19.9
1949....	54.1	36.5	9.4	58.5	21.8	19.7	56.3	27.6	16.0
1950....	66.7	24.1	9.2	62.2	22.3	15.5	63.2	22.9	13.9
1951....	43.2	38.6	18.2	56.8	30.8	12.4	55.7	30.4	13.9
1952....	72.0	20.0	8.0	59.3	28.3	12.4	59.2	27.8	13.1

[a]Normative ordering of events occurs when a man first completes school, next begins to work and lastly marries. The intermediate nonnormative pattern occurs when a man begins a job prior to finishing school or marries prior to beginning work, but after the completion of schooling. Extreme nonnormative ordering occurs whenever a man marries prior to the completion of his education.

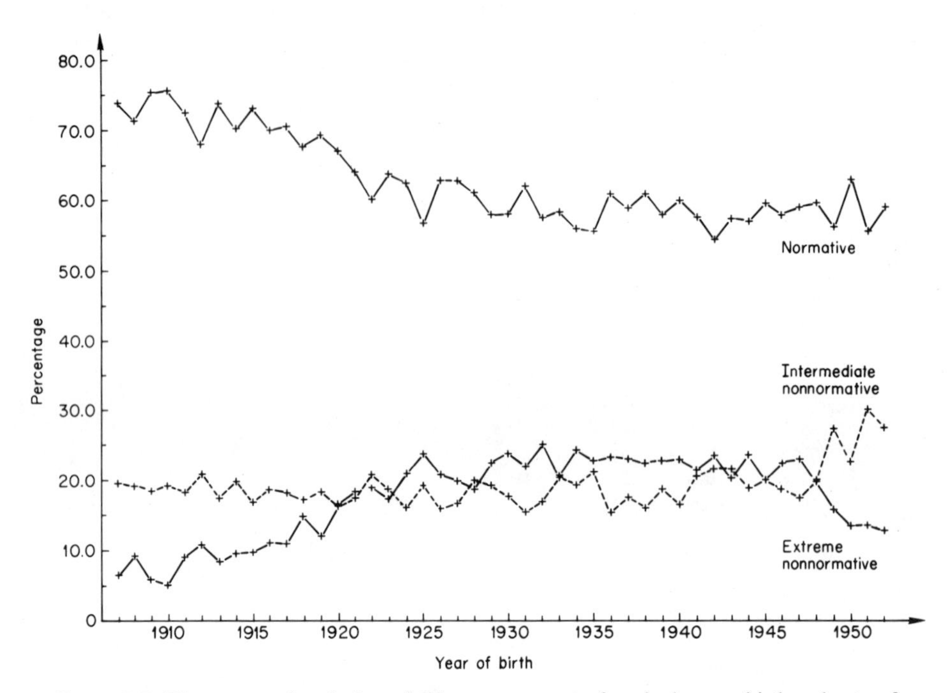

Figure 3.7. The temporal ordering of life-course events for single-year birth cohorts of American males born 1907–1952.

Among men born during the late 1910s and in the 1920s, military service requirements were heavy, and military service was not selective with regard to age at marriage. After World War II, the discharged veterans from these cohorts were offered G.I. Bill benefits to assist in continuing their educations, but few sources of aid existed for nonveterans to continue their schooling beyond the usual ages. Thus many more of the veterans completed their schooling following marriage, whereas relatively few of the civilians did so. The civilian men more commonly had normative ordering patterns. For cohorts of men in the late 1930s and after, fairly extensive government assistance was available to attend college. Many men did attend college but married prior to completing their educations. The Selective Service rules of the period tended to defer military induction for students and married men. Because of this selectivity, and because fewer veterans born in the late 1930s and after were using G.I. Bill benefits to attend college, civilians were more likely to report marrying before finishing school, whereas veterans more commonly reported an intermediate nonnormative order. The most likely sort of intermediate order among veterans probably was marriage after the com-

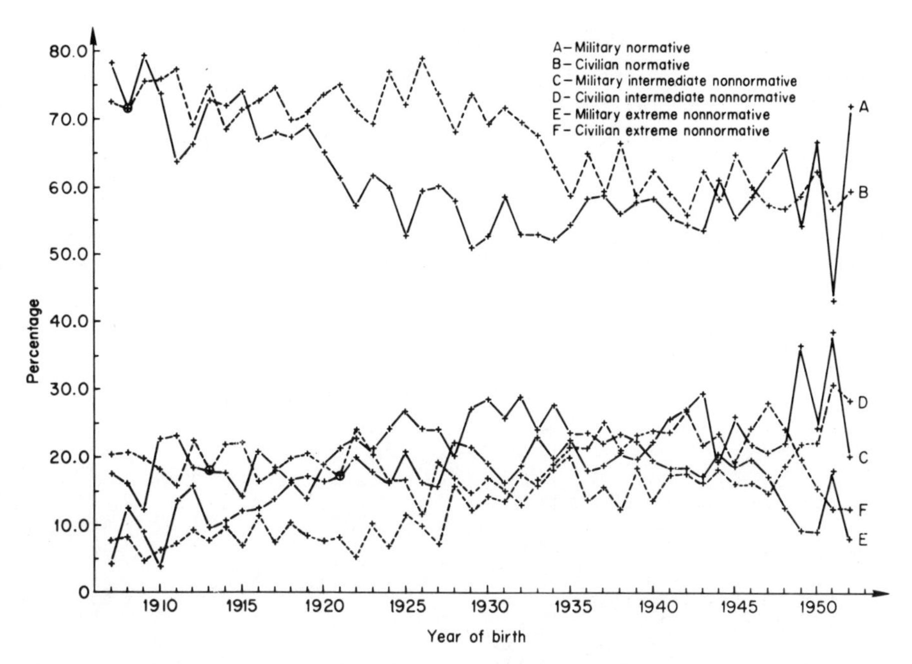

Figure 3.8. The temporal ordering of life-course events for single-year birth cohorts of American males born 1907–1952, by military service experience.

pletion of schooling while in military service—a marriage that might precede the first, full-time civilian job.

DURATION OF THE TRANSITION TO ADULTHOOD

In comparison with other parameters of the transition process, the duration of the overall transition to adulthood (defined as the difference between the third quartile of the marriage transition and the first quartile of the education transition) had a rather simple intercohort pattern (Table 3.8; Figures 3.9 and 3.10). Among all men, and among the veterans, there was a clear downward intercohort trend in duration of the transition to adulthood. Among the total population, the decline was ten years, from 17.8 years among men born in 1907 to 7.8 years among men born in 1947. The downward trend was sharper among the veterans, going from 23.8 years for the cohort of 1907 to 7.3 years for the cohort of 1948.

The civilian men showed an initial intercohort decline in the duration of the transition to adulthood from 15.3 in 1907 to 11.9 in 1913. The duration of the transition to adulthood then increased to a peak of 17.6 years in 1920, decreasing steadily thereafter to around 8.3 to 9.0 years

Table 3.8
The Duration of the Transition to Adulthood for Single-Year Birth Cohorts of American Males Born 1907–1952, by Military Service Experience

Birth Cohort	Duration to Adulthood[a]			Birth Cohort	Duration to Adulthood[a]		
	Veterans	Nonveterans	Total		Veterans	Nonveterans	Total
1907.....	23.76	15.25	17.83	1930.....	9.71	12.16	10.44
1908.....	22.08	15.29	17.62	1931.....	9.36	13.67	10.41
1909.....	20.84	14.35	15.96	1932.....	9.78	13.48	10.44
1910.....	21.55	15.11	16.69	1933.....	9.20	10.61	9.59
1911.....	18.13	14.20	15.68	1934.....	9.50	11.00	9.87
1912.....	18.07	13.37	14.79	1935.....	9.43	10.18	9.61
1913.....	18.74	11.91	14.81	1936.....	9.52	10.75	9.93
1914.....	15.69	11.89	14.36	1937.....	9.58	9.30	9.59
1915.....	14.60	12.27	14.47	1938.....	9.16	9.26	9.21
1916.....	14.16	12.12	13.93	1939.....	9.40	8.77	9.20
1917.....	14.04	14.32	14.25	1940.....	9.45	8.86	9.18
1918.....	12.24	13.92	13.17	1941.....	8.33	8.93	8.61
1919.....	12.15	15.86	12.94	1942.....	8.13	8.41	8.26
1920.....	11.76	17.64	12.69	1943.....	8.56	8.55	8.59
1921.....	10.74	15.59	11.88	1944.....	8.38	7.58	8.11
1922.....	10.26	16.12	11.70	1945.....	8.40	8.63	8.56
1923.....	10.60	14.37	11.23	1946.....	8.16	9.14	8.55
1924.....	9.89	16.31	11.25	1947.....	7.56	--	7.84
1925.....	10.29	15.20	11.08	1948.....	7.25	--	--
1926.....	9.97	14.81	10.60	1949.....	--[b]	--	--
1927.....	10.39	13.87	11.08	1950.....	--	--	--
1928.....	10.29	12.86	11.05	1951.....	--	--	--
1929.....	10.22	11.84	10.58	1952.....	--	--	--

[a]The duration of the transition to adulthood operationally is defined as the number of years between the ages at which one-quarter of the men in the birth cohort complete their schooling and three-quarters of the men first marry.

[b]Age undefined due to censored experience.

among the cohorts born after 1941. Temporary intercohort increases in the third quartile age at marriage for men born during the 1910s accounted for this lengthening of the duration of the transition to adulthood for those birth cohorts.

CONCLUSIONS

The most noteworthy long-term historical trend documented by this research is the intercohort decrease in the amount of time a birth cohort of men required to complete the passage from adolescence to adulthood. An intercohort prolongation of school enrollment was associated with a rise of mass public education at the secondary-school level. In addition, the age by which three-quarters of a birth cohort first married decreased

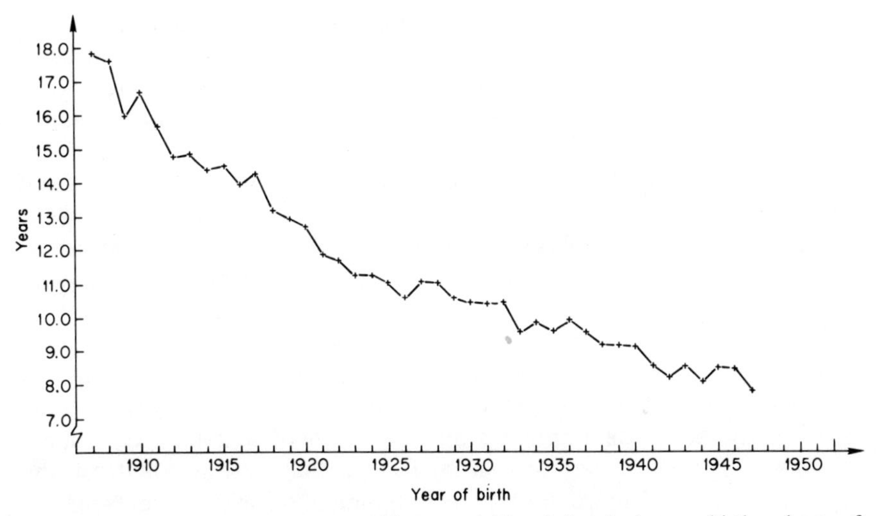

Figure 3.9. The duration of the transition to adulthood for single-year birth cohorts of American males born 1907–1952.

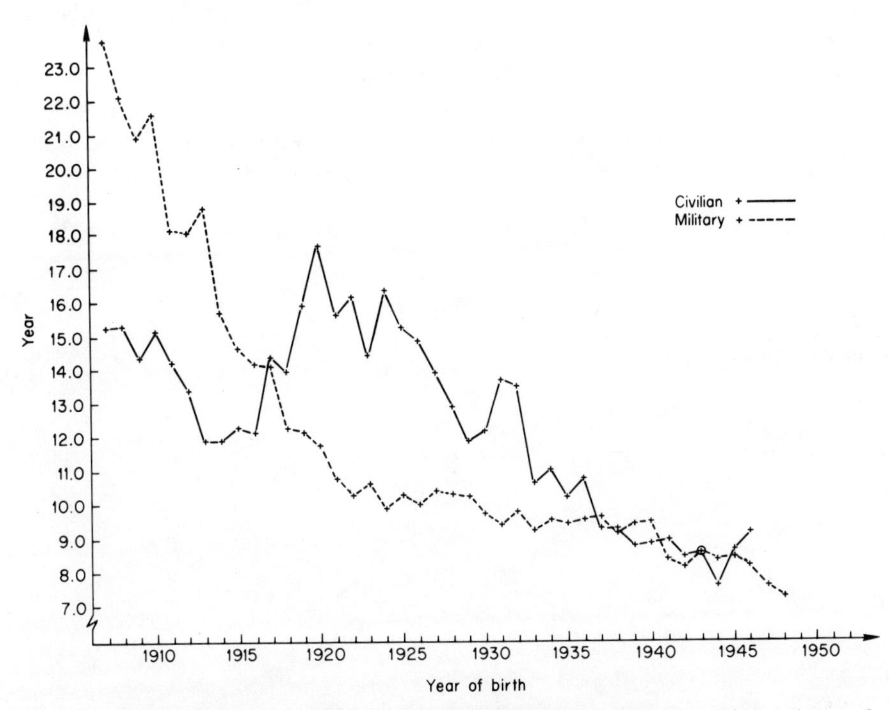

Figure 3.10. The duration of the transition to adulthood for single-year birth cohorts of American males born 1907–1952, by military service experience.

dramatically among cohorts. These trends produced a greater interspersing of transitions and a convergence of the median ages at school completion, first job, and first marriage. As a result, there was an intercohort decrease in the proportion of men experiencing the transition to adulthood in an orderly fashion; more recent cohorts of men were more likely to begin working and/or to marry prior to completing their formal schooling.

These broad intercohort trends were marked by systematic deviations in cohort transition behavior—deviations that seem to coincide with changes in the educational system and the economy and with the military service demands faced by cohorts. Military service was a crucial factor differentiating the life-course experiences of men in their passage to adulthood. Not only military service per se, but the selectivity of entrants into the military, the timing of military service, and the educational benefits available to veterans, were factors that may account for the different pattern of intercohort shifts in timing of transition events among the veterans.

The analysis of this chapter has been very suggestive of the types of social structural factors that may account for long-term trends in transition behavior, as well as the short-term fluctuations. In the next chapter, I attempt to systematize the results of this chapter by carrying out a structural equation analysis that relates changes in the transition behavior among birth cohorts to the shifting social structural conditions faced by the cohorts at the time of their transition to adulthood.

4

Social Structural Conditions and Intercohort Changes in the Transition Process

Chapter 3 provided a descriptive analysis of intercohort changes in the timing of school completion, first job, and first marriage for single-year birth cohorts of men born from 1907 to 1952. The analysis demonstrated that there were no uniform, simultaneous intercohort trends in the ages at transition for the various events. Although there was an overall tendency among the more recent birth cohorts toward a somewhat later age at school completion and age at first job, compared with earlier birth cohorts, these same men displayed a tendency toward a younger age at first marriage. The timing of the intercohort changes in median age at each transition vary among the school-completion, first-job, and first-marriage transitions. For any given transition event the dates of the intercohort changes in age at the first, second, and third quartile vary. There was an overall tendency toward a greater overlap in the transitions, with a narrowing of the overall time taken by a cohort to complete the transition to adulthood. Nonetheless, men born from 1922 to 1936, rather than men born after 1936, had the greatest tendency toward a disorderly sequencing of transition events.

These intercohort variations in the timing of the various transition events were interpreted with reference to a variety of period events that may have differentially affected the cohorts depending on their age at the time of the events. These events included the onset and persistence of the Great Depression, the sudden demands for military manpower during World War II, the rise of mass public education at elementary and secondary levels during the 1940s and 1950s, and the increase in college enrollments in the post-war era. These interpretations, while compelling, were *post hoc* and did not indicate the specific effects on transition behavior of particular types of events. While *post hoc* comparisons direct attention toward cases that are confirmations of an hypothesized effect of a variable, they systematically distract attention from cohorts among whom the transition behavior may not have reacted to a particular event in the hypothesized manner. The analysis of Chapter 3 shares this problem with the analyses of Uhlenberg (1978), Winsborough (1978), and Modell *et al.* (1976, 1978). All these researchers have engaged in *post hoc* interpretations of the effects of period events on the transition behavior of birth cohorts.

OBJECTIVE

In this chapter, I attempt to systematize the results of Chapter 3 by relating intercohort differences in the transition to adulthood to differences in the social structural setting at the time the cohorts were finishing school, beginning work, and first marrying. In this analysis, the 46 single-year birth cohorts of 1907 to 1952 are treated as the units of analysis in a cohort-level examination of the effects of social structural factors on transition behavior. The parameters of the transition process for each cohort (the quartiles and interquartile range of each transition, the ordering of events, and the duration of the transition to adulthood) are the dependent variables in the analysis. A variety of social structural factors hypothesized to influence the transition process are included as independent variables.

The lack of previous research in this area precludes the specification of exact hypotheses about which variables should significantly affect transition behavior and about the nature of their effects, but previous research (reviewed in Chapter 1) does suggest variables that may be important. The twentieth-century rise of mass public education at the secondary-school level and the post-World War II expansion of college enrollments have been key factors in the prolongation of school enrollment and the delay in beginning a first, full-time job. People delay their school exit and their entry into the labor force when the unemployment rate is high (Duncan, 1965). Marriage and first childbirth also appear to be postponed under conditions of high unemployment and slow economic growth (Ryder, 1969; Easterlin, 1978). Among males, military service is a variable of crucial importance for the timing of life-course transitions (see Chapter 3). Other research has suggested that the size of a birth cohort relative to the size of adjacent cohorts defines marriage-market chances affecting the cohort's age patterns of marriage (Riley, 1976,

1979; Hirschman and Matras, 1971). The relative size of a birth cohort may be of importance for other types of transition behaviors as well (Waring, 1975; Easterlin, 1978).

Fertility and mortality rates jointly help determine the size and composition of kinship networks, and these demographic factors vary on an intercohort basis (Riley, 1979). To the extent that family structure influences transition behavior, these demographic factors may have noteworthy effects on transition behavior (Elder, 1978b; Hogan, 1978a).

Any analysis of the effects of social structural conditions on the transition behavior of birth cohorts thus must include attention to such factors as the educational attainments of the cohort, the economic conditions and military service requirements faced by members of the cohort during the years they are undergoing the transition to adulthood, and such demographic characteristics as the birth and death rates of the population and the relative size of the cohort. The objective of the analysis reported in this chapter is to measure the direction and relative magnitude of the effects of these social structural variables on the transition to adulthood.

PROCEDURES

The procedures used in this analysis were selected on the basis of two considerations. First, each of the social structural conditions hypothesized to affect the transition behavior of a birth cohort can be measured by a variety of variables, each with a number of alternative specifications. Those alternative measures will ordinarily be highly correlated, although the correlations are unlikely to be perfect, due to measurement error. The analysis procedure must facilitate the selection among alternative measures, either by indicating which measure is superior, or by providing a composite measure for the underlying social structural condition.

Second, many of the social structural conditions are highly correlated, given the historical experiences of the birth cohorts. Indeed, many of the social structural conditions display a monotonic trend over the course of the twentieth century, with interannual deviations from the overall trend. To the extent that the transition behavior of the birth cohorts do display monotonic tendencies over time, correlations between social structural conditions and transition behavior will be artifactually high. The method of analysis chosen must be able to isolate deviations from the overall monotonic trends in the dependent and independent variables and calculate the degree of association between these deviations.

Based on these considerations, I decided to conduct the analysis in three steps. First, a wide variety of demographic data sources were examined to create indicators of the social structural conditions characterizing the birth cohorts during the period in which they were undergoing the transition to adulthood. Second, these indicators were subjected to a principal components analysis in order to provide summary measures of the key social structural experiences of the birth cohorts. Third, the effects of these social structural factors on the transition behavior of the birth cohorts were measured by means of a multiple regression analysis. In this regression analysis, the social structural factors were the independent variables, and the parameters of the transition process were the dependent variables. The 46 birth cohorts were the units of analysis.

THE MEASUREMENT OF SOCIAL STRUCTURAL CONDITIONS

The first step in the analysis was the identification of measures of the social structural conditions facing each birth cohort as it underwent the transition to adulthood. Appropriate measures were not always readily available since data were needed for cohorts born as long ago as 1907 and undergoing the start of the transition to adulthood as early as 1920.[1] This search culminated in a list of variables that could be measured for each birth cohort at key years of age. After identifying the social structural variables that could be included in the factor analysis, I attempted to operationalize them in such a way that they would be measured at that point in the life cycle of each birth cohort at which they might prove most instrumental in influencing transition behavior.[2] The resultant his-

[1]This research included a review of all variables reported in the *Historical Statistics of the United States*, the decennial U.S. Censuses, the *Statistical Abstract of the United States*, and the 1973 Occupational Changes in a Generation Survey.

[2]These decisions were necessarily judgmental. I first had to make decisions regarding the ages at which each social structural condition was likely to have its greatest impact. Then I had to decide what measures would be acceptable approximations, given the limited availability of relevant data. Where practical, I maximized the number of indicators of a given social structural condition, specifying a variety of ages at which its effects might prove important. For example, the demand for labor at the time each birth cohort was undergoing the first job transition was measured by four variables: the average percentage of the noninstitutionalized population in the labor force in the years the cohort was ages 16 and 17; the average percentage of the civilian labor force unemployed in the years the cohort was ages 16 and 17; the average percentage of the noninstitutionalized population in the labor force in the years the cohort was ages 18, 19, and 20; and the percentage of the civilian labor force unemployed in the years the cohort was ages 18, 19, and 20. These percentages represented the ages at which most members of the birth cohorts would be making decisions about whether to finish high school and attend college or to enter the labor force as a full-time employee. These measures of the labor force demand are based

torical file includes data on 42 different variables, including one or more measures of educational attainment, level of urban and industrial development, economic growth, unemployment, government social welfare expenditures, military service requirements, population vital rates, and relative cohort size. The variables measured, their operational form of measurement, and the data sources are presented in Table 4.1.

Exploratory data analysis confirmed that many of these indicators were highly interrelated, precluding their simultaneous inclusion in a causal model. In order to reduce the multicollinearity among these 42 independent variables and to achieve a parsimonious summary of the information contained therein, a principal components analysis was conducted. Principal components procedures were appropriate since no particular assumptions about the underlying structure of the variables was required. This type of analysis provided a method of transforming the given set of 42 independent variables into a new set of fewer variables that were based on those linear combinations of the original variables that account for the maximum amount of variance in those variables. In order to clarify the calculated principal component structure, an oblique rotation method was used. Factor scores corresponding to the extracted principal components were calculated for each birth cohort, for use as independent variables in the regression analysis.

These procedures produced a principal components solution with six factors, accounting for a total of 95.8% of the variation among the variables (Table 4.2). The first factor accounted for 56.0% of the variation, the second factor accounted for 19.5% of the variation, and the next four factors each accounted for 7.5% or less of the variation, explaining a total of only 20.2% of the variation collectively. The first six factors were statistically significant but additional factors were insignificant, with eigenvalues smaller than 1.0.

An examination of the factor patterns associated with the obliquely rotated principal components solution indicated that each of the six factors correspond to readily labeled, theoretically important variables. Factor 1 is scored high on percentage of men with high school, college, or graduate educations, percentage of the population in the labor force, average annual earnings, and life expectancy. The first factor is scored

---

on the entire population, rather than on the population of young persons, because the latter would, in part, result from decisions made by the cohort about labor-force entry, resulting in a false specification of the causal model to be estimated.

An examination of the correlations of alternative indicators of the social structural conditions indicated a high degree of congruence among the measures for the birth cohorts. This increases my confidence that the results of the analysis reported in this chapter are relatively robust.

Table 4.1
Definitions and Sources of Variables Measuring Social Structural Conditions of Birth Cohorts of American Males Born 1907–1952

Variable	Definition	Source
% with elementary school education	% of the birth cohort completing 0 to 8 years of schooling	OCG-II
% with one to three years high school	% of the birth cohort completing 9 to 11 years of schooling	OCG-II
% with four years high school	% of the birth cohort completing 12 years of schooling	OCG-II
% with one to three years of college	% of the birth cohort completing 1 to 3 years of college	OCG-II
% with four years of college	% of the birth cohort completing four years of college	OCG-II
% with five or more years of college	% of the birth cohort completing five or more years of college	OCG-II
% ever in Armed Forces	% of the birth cohort ever serving six months or longer on active duty in the Armed Forces	OCG-II
$\mathring{e}_o$ in year cohort is age 16	The expectation of life at birth for males in the year the birth cohort is age 16	HS, Series B-108
$\mathring{e}_o$ in year of cohort's birth	The expectation of life at birth for males in the year the birth cohort is born	HS, Series B-108
% change in $\mathring{e}_o$ between birth and age 16	% change in the expectation of life at birth between the year of the cohort's birth and the year of its sixteenth birthday	HS, Series B-108

IMR in year cohort is aged 16	Infant mortality rate in the year of the cohort's sixteenth birthday	HS, Series B-142
IMR in year of cohort's birth	Infant mortality rate in the year of the cohort's birth	HS, Series B-142
% change in IMR between birth and age 16	% change in the infant mortality rate between the year of the cohort's birth and the year of its sixteenth birthday	HS, Series B-142
Death rate of males 15-24	Death rate of males aged 15-24 in the year of the cohort's twentieth birthday	HS, Series B-185;1978 SA, Table 102
Youth dependency rate	(Population 0-14/population 15-64) in year cohort is age 10	HS, Series A-29, 30, 31, 37
% total population aged 16-20	% of the total population ages 16-20 in year cohort is age 18	HS, Series A-29, 39, 41
% size change between this and preceding cohorts	% difference in population size between the average size cohort aged 16-17 and the average size cohort aged 18-20 in the year the cohort is age 16	HS, Series A-39, 40, 41
% size change between this and succeeding cohorts	% difference in population size between the average size cohort aged 16-17 and the average size cohort aged 14-15 in the year the cohort is age 16	HS, Series A-38, 39, 40
Average annual earnings of employees	Average annual earnings of employees in the years cohort is aged 16-20, in 1972 dollars	HS, Series D-722, 723; Series E-135; 1978 SA, Table 792

Table 4.1 *(Continued)*

Variable	Definition	Source
% employed civilian labor force on farms, years cohort 18-20	Average percent of the employed civilian labor force on farms in the years the cohort is ages 18 to 20	HS, Series D-5, 6, 15, 16; 1975 SA, Table 558
% population in labor force, years cohort 18-20	Average percent of noninstitutionalized population in the labor force in the years the cohort is ages 18 to 20	HS, Series D-2, 13; 1975 SA, Table 558
% labor force unemployed, years cohort 18-20	Average percent of civilian labor force unemployed in the years the cohort is ages 18 to 20	HS, Series D-9, 87; 1975 SA, Table 571
Average annual change in Gross National Product	Average annual growth in the Gross National Product between the years the cohort is age 16 and age 20	HS, Series F-3, 31; 1975 SA, Table 616
% change in Consumer Price Index	Rate of change in the Consumer Price Index for all items between the years the cohort is age 16 to age 20	HS, Series E-135; 1975 SA, Table 687
% GNP spent on social welfare	Average annual percent of the Gross National Product spent on social welfare expenditures between the years the cohort is age 16 and age 20	HS, Series H-2; 1975 SA, Table 446
Per capita welfare expenditures	Average annual total social welfare expenditures per person in the population between the years the cohort is age 16 and age 20, in 1972 dollars	HS, Series A-6, 7; Series E-135; Series H-1; 1975 SA, Table 2, 1978 SA, Tables 517, 792

Expenditures on the aged	Average annual social insurance expenditures on persons age 65 and over between the years the cohort is age 16 and age 20, in 1972 dollars	HS, Series A-37; Series E-135; Series H-5; 1978 SA, Tables 517, 792
Immigration rate	Average rate of immigration during the years cohort is aged 16-20	HS, Series A-6, 7; Series C-89
% change in farm residents	% change in number of farm residents between the year cohort is age 16 and year cohort is age 20	HS, Series C-76; 1978 SA, Table 1164
% population on farms	Farm population as a percent of total population, in the year the cohort is age 16	HS, Series K-2
% employed civilian labor force on farms, years cohort 16-17	Average percent of the employed civilian labor force on farms in the years the cohort is age 16 and 17	HS, Series D-5, 6, 15, 16
% population in labor force, years cohort 16-17	Average percent of the noninstitutionalized population in the labor force in the years the cohort is age 16 and 17	HS, Series D-2, 13
% labor force unemployed, years cohort 16-17	Average percent of civilian labor force unemployed in the years the cohort is age 16 and 17	HS, Series D-9, 87
Elementary and secondary school expenditures	Average annual elementary and secondary school expenditures reported per person age 5 to 14 in the year the cohort is age 10, in 1972 dollars	HS, Series A-31; Series E-135; Series H-18; 1978 SA, Tables 516, 792
Higher education expenditures	Average annual higher education expenditures reported per person age 16 to 20 between the years the cohort is age 16 and age 20, in 1972 dollars	HS, Series A-39, 40, 41; Series E-135; Series H-19; 1978 SA, Tables 516, 792

Table 4.1 (*Continued*)

Variable	Definition	Source
Total education expenditure	Total education expenditure reported per person age 5 to 24 in the year the cohort is age 16, in 1972 dollars	HS, Series A-31, 32; Series E-135; Series H-17; 1978 SA, Table 792
Vocational and adult education expenditures	Average annual vocational and adult education expenditures per person age 16 to 20 between the years the cohort is age 16 and age 20, in 1972 dollars	HS, Series A-39, 40, 41; Series E-135; H-20; 1978 SA, Tables 516, 792
Total veterans expenditures	Average annual expenditures on veterans per person age 15 to 34 between the years the cohort is age 22 and age 26, in 1972 dollars	HS, Series A-32, 33; Series E-135; Series H-21; 1974 SA, Table 3; 1978 SA, Tables 516, 792; P-25 Series, #519, #643
Veterans education expenditures	Average annual expenditures on veterans' education per person age 15 to 34 between the years the cohort is age 22 and age 26, in 1972 dollars	HS, Series A-32, 33; Series E-135; Series H-24; 1974 SA, Table 3; 1978 SA, Tables 516, 792; P-25 Series #519, #643
Rate of persons on military duty	Average annual ratio of military personnel on active duty to men age 15 to 24 between the years the cohort is age 18 to age 25	HS, Series Y-904; 1978 SA, Table 602; P-25 Series, #311, #519, #643
Per capita housing expenditure	Average annual social welfare expenditures on housing per person in the population between the years the cohort is age 20 and age 24	HS, Series A-29; Series E-135; Series H-27; 1974 SA, Table 2; 1978 SA, Tables 516, 792; Series P-25, #643

Rate of new nonfarm housing units	Average annual number of new nonfarm housing units started per 1,000 persons in the population between the years the cohort is age 16 and age 20	HS, Series A-6, 7; Series N-156; 1973 SA, Table 1153; 1975 SA, Table 2

NOTES: HS--*Historical Statistics of the United States, Colonial Times to 1970*, *Bicentennial Edition*, *Parts 1 and 2*, U.S. Bureau of the Census, Washington, D.C., 1975.

OCG II--Occupation Changes in a Generation Survey.

P-25 Series--*Current Population Reports*, Series P-25, U.S. Bureau of the Census, Washington, D.C.; No. 311 (July 1965), "Estimates of the Population of the United States, by Single Years of Age, Color, and Sex: 1900 to 1959"; No. 519 (April 1974), "Estimates of the Population of the United States, by Age, Sex, and Race: April 1, 1960 to July 1, 1973"; No. 643 (January 1977), "Estimates of the Population of the United States, by Age, Sex, and Race: July 1, 1974 to 1976."

SA--*Statistical Abstract of the United States*: *1973*/*1974*/*1975*/*1978*, U.S. Bureau of the Census, Washington, D.C., 1973, 1974, 1975, 1978.

Table 4.2
Factor Pattern Coefficients of the Principal Components Analysis of Social Structural Conditions, Birth Cohorts of American Men Born 1907–1952

Variable	Factor 1	Factor 2	Factor 3	Factor 4	Factor 5	Factor 6
% with elementary education	-.693	-.398	-.171	-.065	-.147	.231
% with one to three years high school	-.321	-.378	.065	.225	-.162	.278
% with four years high school	.733	.249	.380	-.013	.196	-.242
% with one to three years college	.224	.912	.121	.135	.020	-.008
% with four years college	.604	.337	-.096	.058	.246	.003
% with five or more years college	.887	.083	-.133	.066	-.040	.037
% ever in Armed Forces	.251	-.644	.408	.352	.318	.028
Expectation of life at birth ($\mathring{e}_o$) in year cohort is age 16	.739	.265	-.076	.024	.178	-.050
$\mathring{e}_o$ in year of cohorts birth	.447	.152	-.030	.186	.034	-.588
% change in $\mathring{e}_o$ between birth and age 16	.014	.043	.001	-.270	.097	.902
Infant Mortality Rate (IMR) year cohort age 16	-.767	-.249	.026	-.072	-.102	.163
IMR year of cohort's birth	-.410	-.317	.412	.055	.170	.422
% change in IMR between birth and age 16	.048	.447	-.203	.012	-.020	-.628
Death rate of males 15-24	-.939	.010	-.104	.018	-.028	.150
Youth dependency rate	-.767	.689	.098	-.254	-.054	-.266
% total population aged 16-20	-.971	.493	.312	.251	-.003	-.104
% size change between this and preceding cohorts	-.121	-.071	-.033	-.383	.161	-.657
% size change between this and succeeding cohorts	-.289	-.195	.018	.529	-.115	.098
Average annual earnings of employees	.590	.435	-.050	-.007	.088	-.234
Immigration rate	-.400	.332	-.898	-.303	-.060	-.057
% change in farm residents	-.340	.010	.296	-.073	-.542	.277
% population on farms	-.624	-.414	.072	.063	-.012	.276
% employed civilian labor force on farms, years cohort 16-17	-.625	-.315	.180	-.034	-.023	.241
% population in labor force, years cohort 16-17	.775	.155	-.168	.209	-.117	-.022
% labor force unemployed, years cohort 16-17	-.182	.012	.749	-.251	.419	.174
% employed civilian labor force on farms, years cohort 18-20	-.607	-.314	.178	-.058	-.144	.213

% population in labor force, years cohort 18-20. . . .	.569	.155	-.174	.385	.180	-.127
% labor force unemployed, years cohort 18-20	-.047	-.004	.810	-.375	-.304	.066
Average annual change in Gross National Product. . . .	-.185	-.025	-.001	-.004	1.031	.060
% change in Consumer Price Index	.201	.275	-.100	.640	.372	.248
% GNP spent on social welfare	.003	.741	.032	-.466	.280	-.104
Per capita welfare expenditures.	.187	.746	-.213	-.146	.067	-.156
Expenditures on the aged	.234	.672	-.239	-.145	.013	-.222
Elementary and secondary school expenditures	.147	.798	.012	-.237	-.187	-.330
Higher education expenditures.	.200	.737	-.230	-.130	.001	-.169
Total education expenditures	.212	.693	-.216	-.184	.026	-.204
Vocational and adult education expenditures.	-.047	.932	-.169	.253	.023	-.084
Veterans expenditures.	.435	.003	-.185	.700	-.013	-.218
Veterans expenditures on education	-.096	.064	.018	.969	.167	-.105
Rate of persons on military duty	.185	-.390	.163	.531	.512	-.200
Per capita housing expenditures.	.077	.922	-.067	.193	.034	-.011
Rate of new nonfarm housing units.	.493	-.056	-.676	-.154	.099	.041
Eigenvalue	23.5	8.2	3.2	2.5	1.5	1.3
Percent of variance.	56.0	19.5	7.5	6.0	3.6	3.1
Cumulative percent of variance	56.0	75.5	83.0	89.1	92.7	95.8

low on percentage of the population with only an elementary school education, percentage of the population age 18 to 20 who are in the civilian labor force, percentage of the population living on farms and employed in agriculture, and age-specific death rate. The youth dependency ratio and percentage of the population aged 16 to 20 also are associated with a negative score on the first factor. Clearly, the first factor is a general indicator of degree of modernity, with a low score being associated with the early stage of modernization. A high score on the first factor indicates the cohort is growing up during an advanced stage of modernization, in a highly urban–industrial milieu. Many of the 42 variables included in the principal components analysis are closely related to level of modernity; it therefore is no surprise that the modernity factor accounts for 56% of the common variance of the variables.

The second principal component, accounting for 19% of the common variance of the variables, has a factor pattern with high scores on expenditures for all levels of education and for vocational and adult education programs, on average housing expenditures per person, on general measures of civilian welfare payments, and on welfare expenditures for the aged. This second principal component measures the extent of development of the modern welfare state, with a high score indicating a social milieu in which governmental social welfare expenditures are high.

The third principal component extracted accounts for an additional 7.5% of the common variation among the 42 independent variables. This factor results from high factor-pattern scores on the rate of unemployment among persons 16 to 17 and 18 to 20 and from low scores on numbers of new housing units constructed and the average rate of net international migration. The number of new housing starts commonly is used as an indicator of the condition of the economy. A high rate of immigration to the United States historically was associated with good economic conditions (acting as a "pull" factor in the migration decision), whereas a low rate of immigration was associated with a high rate of unemployment (Bogue, 1969: 806–810). A cohort with a high score on this third factor is one making the transition to adulthood during a period with high rates of unemployment and low rates of new housing starts and immigration. This third factor therefore was interpreted as a measure of the level of unemployment.

The fourth factor extracted in the principal components solution accounts for an additional 6% of the common variability among the 42 independent variables. This fourth factor has high factor-pattern coefficients on the rate of military personnel on active duty and on expenditures for veterans, especially expenditures on education. A positive coefficient is associated with a high rate of change in the Consumer Price Index. An increase in the Consumer Price Index usually occurs during and immediately following the military expenditures associated with wartime call-ups of military manpower. This fourth factor was interpreted as measuring the level of military service activities associated with the period when each birth cohort was undergoing its transition to adulthood.

The fifth factor pattern scored quite high on per capita change in the Gross National Product. The factor-pattern coefficients also are high, but less markedly so, on the percentage of change in number of farm residents and on the rate of available personnel on active duty in the armed forces. Wartime call-ups of manpower and the accompanying industrial demands are usually associated with high rates of economic growth. Declining numbers of farm residents are associated both with the push factors associated with an agricultural depression and the pull factors associated with high rates of economic growth in the urban, industrial sector of the economy. This fifth factor, accounting for 3.6% of the total variation in the 42 variables, was interpreted as a measure of the rate of economic growth during the period each cohort was undergoing its transition to adulthood.

While it accounts for only 3.1% of the total covariation among the 42 variables, the sixth factor produced by the principal components solution is of considerable interest to a demographer. This factor has a high score on the percentage change in life expectancy of males between birth and age 16 and a negative coefficient on the percentage change in the Infant Mortality Rate between birth and age 16. A negative coefficient also is associated with a low life expectancy at birth and with an increase in size between the cohort in question and the later cohorts. A cohort receives a high score on this variable if life expectancy is low at the time of its birth, but it experiences a decline in the Infant Mortality Rate and an increase in its life expectancy, and it is larger than birth cohorts that follow immediately (i.e., the crude birth rate was higher when it was born than when the succeeding cohorts were born). A high score on this variable was interpreted as indicating that the birth cohort grew up during the later part of the second phase of the demographic transition, a time of decline in the fertility and mortality rates (Matras, 1973). A low score on this variable indicates that the cohort grew up during the third phase of the demographic transition, a period with the modern pattern of low mortality and fertility rates.

The principal components analysis thus indicated that the 42 variables describing the historical conditions of the birth cohorts at the time of their transition to adulthood can be succinctly described with reference to six principal underlying variables:

1. Degree of modernity
2. Level of social welfare expenditures by the government

3. Rate of unemployment
4. Military service demands and expenditures associated with wartime
5. Rate of annual economic growth
6. Stage of the demographic transition

These factors correspond closely to my *a priori* theoretical expectations.

The factor score coefficients associated with this six-factor principal components solution were used to construct six factors, with unique scores on each factor assigned to each of the 46 birth cohorts. The summary factor scores then were transformed into standardized scores. These standardized variables constitute the independent social structural variables that were used in the regression analysis of changes in the transition behavior of American men.

SOCIAL STRUCTURE AND THE TRANSITION TO ADULTHOOD

The final step of the analysis involved the estimation of a series of ordinary least squares multiple regression models of the transition behavior of birth cohorts of American men making the passage from youth to adulthood. The six factor scores were independent variables in this analysis, describing the social structural conditions of the period during which a birth cohort was undergoing the transition to adulthood. The dependent variables of interest included the parameters of the transition process (first, second, and third quartile and interquartile range) for the school-completion, first-job, and first-marriage transitions, the percentage of the cohort with different ordering patterns for the three transitions, and the duration of time taken by the cohort to complete the transition to adulthood.

Birth cohorts were the units of analysis. The transition parameters estimated for the entire birth cohort were used as dependent variables instead of the transition parameters for cohorts of veterans and nonveterans, because the measures of social structural conditions apply to the entire birth cohort. Since the analysis included a control for the military service demands on the cohorts, the effects of the other independent variables were net of the effects of the military service histories of the cohorts.

For some of the more recent birth cohorts (1947–1952) selected transition parameters were not available because of truncation of the period of observation. (For example, the third quartile of age at school completion was not known for men born in 1952 and aged 20 at the time of the survey.) Complete transition data were available for all cohorts born 1907 to 1946; for cohorts born after 1946 the parameters of the transition process were to some degree unknown. The regressions reported here are based on the experiences of those 40 birth cohorts for which there was complete transition information (the cohorts of 1907 to 1946).[3]

Nonsignificant regression parameters were retained in the model for reasons of ease of presentation and interpretation. The deletion of nonsignificant variables from the regression equations did not affect the regression coefficients of the other variables since the correlations among the independent variables are low (the highest being −0.531 between the military service and social welfare expenditures variables). Standardized regression coefficients (beta weights) are shown in order to facilitate the evaluation of the relative magnitudes of the effects of each of the variables on a given transition.

The effects of each independent variable are most readily understood when they are considered in the context of the entire transition from youth to adulthood. Among persons within a cohort, the times at which transition events occur are interrelated, and the effect of any independent variable on the timing of any particular transition can be understood only in the context of its effects on the other transitions. Therefore, the discussion of the regression results proceeds by examining, in turn, the effects of each independent variable on all aspects of the transition to adulthood.

Modernity

The higher levels of educational attainment, better economic conditions, and urban social milieux associated with modernity have a major impact on each of the three transitions. An intercohort increase of 1

[3]Other regression models estimated included all of the birth cohorts for which a transition parameter was available. The results of these regressions did not differ importantly from the results of the regressions based only on the cohorts of 1907 to 1946. As an indicator of the similarity of the relative sizes and directions of the regression coefficients for the two models, the Pearson product moment correlation between the coefficients of the two regressions was calculated. Correlations averaged .95 for the education transition, .97 for the first-job transition, and 1.00 for the first-job, ordering-pattern, and duration regressions. Only one pair of regressions correlated at less than .95: the correlation of the coefficients of the regression models predicting the interquartile range of the education transition was .88. For this transition parameter, a regression model based on the birth cohorts of 1907 to 1949 showed a smaller effect of military service requirements and a larger effect of social welfare payments than a regression model based on the cohorts of 1907 to 1946. The estimate of the effects of social structural conditions on the other transition parameters did not vary by birth cohorts included.

standard deviation in degree of modernity delays the onset and median ages at the school transition by about .85 of a standard deviation (Table 4.3). Modernity produces somewhat smaller, but nonetheless substantial, increases in the third quartile of the education transition. Increased modernity also produces marked delays in the onset and median age of the first-job transition (Table 4.4). While degree of modernity is positively associated with age at school completion and first job, it is negatively associated with age at marriage (Table 4.5). A 1 standard deviation increase in degree of modernity results in three-quarters of a standard deviation decrease in age at marriage. More modern conditions lengthen the duration of the education transition, shorten the length of time taken by a cohort to complete the first-job transition, and substantially reduce the length of the marriage transition.

These upward shifts in the age at school completion and at first job and downward shifts in age at first marriage reduce the probability of a normative transition to adulthood and increase the likelihood of marriage prior to school completion (Table 4.6). The greater intermixing of these transitions associated with increased modernity is coincident with a substantial shortening of the duration of the transition to adulthood among the more recent birth cohorts.

Social Welfare Expenditures

Government expenditure on social welfare increases the average age at school completion. As discussed in Chapter 3, government expenditures at the primary and secondary education levels have tended to

Table 4.3
Regression Analysis of the Effects of Social Structural Conditions on Age at School Completion, Birth Cohorts of American Men Born 1907–1946

Social Structural Condition	Transition Parameter			
	First Quartile	Median	Third Quartile	Interquartile Range
Modernity	.862*	.847*	.686*	.393*
Social welfare	.057	.181*	.088	.096
Unemployment	.064	.127*	-.160*	-.313*
Economic growth	.145*	.103*	.198*	.202*
Military requirements	-.121*	-.139*	.272*	.544*
Demographic transition	-.185*	-.151*	-.102	-.010
Adjusted R^2	.961	.937	.905	.749

*$p < .05$. Standardized regression coefficients shown.

Table 4.4
Regression Analysis of the Effects of Social Structural Conditions on Age at First Job, Birth Cohorts of American Men Born 1907–1946

Social Structural Condition	Transition Parameter			
	First Quartile	Median	Third Quartile	Interquartile Range
Modernity	.822*	.675*	.404*	-.278*
Social welfare.	.053	.205	-.412*	-.515*
Unemployment.	.242*	.214*	.153	-.044
Economic growth	.219*	.108	.381*	.238
Military requirements	-.179*	.167	.131	.310*
Demographic transition.	-.173*	-.180*	-.046	.101
Adjusted R^2	.960	.771	.655	.569

*$p < .05$. Standardized regression coefficients shown.

universalize a grade school education and, more recently, a high school education among the cohorts. This produces delays in the median age of the school-completion transition. Government expenditures at the college level have tended to increase college enrollment, but the expenditures have been insufficient to pay for a man's entire college education. Consequently, fewer men have enrolled in college than in graded schooling, and the overall effect of changing government expenditures for education on age at completion of the school transition has remained

Table 4.5
Regression Analysis of the Effects of Social Structural Conditions on Age at First Marriage, Birth Cohorts of American Men Born 1907–1946

Social Structural Condition	Transition Parameter			
	First Quartile	Median	Third Quartile	Interquartile Range
Modernity	-.783*	-.772*	-.758*	-.678*
Social welfare.	-.016	-.116*	-.083	-.119
Unemployment.	.252*	.112*	-.037	-.217*
Economic growth	-.096*	-.115*	-.128*	-.137*
Military requirements	-.132*	-.258*	-.208*	-.239*
Demographic transition.	.153*	.096*	.203*	.217*
Adjusted R^2	.944	.959	.956	.879

*$p < .05$. Standardized regression coefficients shown.

Table 4.6
Regression Analysis of the Effects of Social Structural Conditions on Summary Measures of the Transition to Adulthood, Birth Cohorts of American Men Born 1907–1946

Social Structural Condition	Transition Parameter			
	Duration of the Transition to Adulthood	Ordering Pattern		
		Normative	Intermediate Nonnormative	Extreme Nonnormative
Modernity	-.810*	-.718*	-.069	.754*
Social welfare.	-.076*	-.003	.238	-.066
Unemployment.	-.047	.132*	-.100	-.112
Economic growth	-.137*	-.189*	-.036	.205*
Military requirements	-.098*	-.176*	-.060	.196*
Demographic transition. . . .	.201*	.157*	-.237	-.095*
Adjusted R^2	.981	.879	.033	.928

*p < .05. Standardized regression coefficients shown.

nil. Increases in government social welfare expenditures have not affected the duration of the school completion transition for the cohorts.

Expenditures on social welfare may have delayed the average age at the first-job transition somewhat but have had no effect on age at beginning of the first-job transition. Increased government expenditure on social welfare has decreased the age by which three-quarters of the men begin their first jobs. This change may have occurred because cohorts of men exposed to higher governmental expenditures on education and vocational training have brought better human capital skills to the job search. Overall, increased social welfare expenditures are the most important factor accounting for decreases in the length of the first-job transition.

Increases in social welfare expenditures reduce the median age at first marriage only slightly. Social welfare expenditures have relatively little effect on the overall duration of the transition to adulthood. They have no effect on temporal ordering patterns experienced by the cohorts. The primary effects of government social welfare expenditures thus are concentrated on the school-completion and first-job transitions.

Unemployment

Cohorts of men seem to delay the start of the school-completion transition in response to high rates of unemployment. Median age at school completion is delayed by a high rate of unemployment, but the third quartile of age at school completion is earlier rather than later. Apparently, when a cohort of young men faces a high rate of unemployment at the time they are considering leaving school, they delay leaving school in the hope that employment chances will improve. As a high rate of unemployment continues, the financial demands on the student may increase, and it will be more difficult to pay for advanced schooling. As a result, men appear to speed up their school exits, following their initial delays in school leaving. A high rate of unemployment thus shortens the duration of time a cohort requires to complete the school transition.

A high rate of unemployment causes men to delay the start of their first jobs. In part, this probably is voluntary, resulting from the decision of men to prolong their enrollment in school. However, these delays may also reflect an inability to secure employment following the completion of formal schooling. The entire first-job transition is delayed somewhat as a result of unemployment, but the length of the first-job transition remains unaffected by the rate of unemployment.

Men delay their first marriage in response to a high rate of unemployment. These delays are recorded in the first and second quartiles of the age at first-marriage transition of the cohorts. The third quartile of the age at first-marriage transition is unaffected by the rate of unemployment. It appears that men respond initially to high unemployment by delaying marriage. As delays in marriage become prolonged, men begin to marry at a higher age-specific rate than they otherwise would have, with the result that the marriage transition for the cohort is completed "on time," as compared with other cohorts.

A higher level of unemployment during later adolescence and early adulthood reduces the probability of marriage prior to the completion of schooling and enhances the probability of an orderly transition to adulthood. This results from the hastening of the school-completion transition and the delays in the beginning of the marriage transition associated with high levels of unemployment. Because unemployment has little effect on the age at completion of the marriage transition, it does not affect the overall duration of the transition to adulthood.

Economic Growth

Men making the transition to adulthood during a period of high economic growth delay the onset and average age of school completion somewhat. Economic growth produces rather substantial delays in the age at the completion of schooling, with a 1 standard deviation increase in the average rate of economic growth variable producing a .198 standard deviation increase in the age at completion-of-education transition. During periods of prosperity, economic resources are more readily available for human capital investment. During such periods men can afford to remain in school longer and apparently decide to do so. It is noteworthy that whereas high unemployment produces short-term delays in the completion of schooling, which men reversed by the third quartile of the transition, economic prosperity produces persistent delays in school completion. Cohorts of men adopt coping behavior in response to unemployment; in response to economic prosperity they act to maximize their good fortunes through prolonging human capital investment in their own educations.

A high economic growth rate has a strong delaying effect on age at first job, stronger even than its effect on age at school completion. A cohort making the transition to adulthood during a period of economic growth that is 1 standard deviation above average begins the first job .219 standard deviations later and completes the transition an average of .381 standard deviations later. These delays in first job are partly a result of later age at school completion, but it also appears that men are able to protract the period of nonemployment following school. It may be that the greater availability of economic resources associated with periods of economic prosperity not only allows men to remain in school longer, but also permits them to spend a longer amount of time searching for a suitable job after their schooling is completed.

Cohorts of men making the transition to adulthood during a period of economic prosperity marry at significantly earlier ages than other men. The onset of the marriage transition occurs earlier, and the age of the birth cohort at the completion of the marriage transition is younger. It appears that many men choose to expend part of the economic resources ordinarily available during a period of prosperity on the pleasures of marriage.

The combined effects of economic prosperity—prolonged schooling, postponed first jobs, and earlier first marriage—reduce the duration of time it takes a cohort to complete the transition to adulthood. Men undergoing the transition to adulthood during a period of economic prosperity are more likely to marry prior to completing schooling and less frequently order their transition events in a normative fashion. The economic resources available during periods of prosperity permit men to "purchase" a disorderly pattern of events by financing the married student life.

Military Service

The military service demands faced by a cohort of men have substantial effects on their overall transition behavior. Cohorts for whom the military service demands are greater experience an earlier beginning of the school completion transition and, on average, complete school at a somewhat earlier age. But high military service demands on a cohort also produce postponements in the school-completion transition for some members of the cohort. These postponements show up in a later, third-quartile age at school completion for men in these cohorts. Military service requirements interrupt the schooling process of a cohort. Many men who are forced to discontinue schooling because of military service requirements do not return to school after military service, reducing their age at school completion. Other men use the economic resources provided by the G.I. Bill for post-military schooling, finishing school at a later average age then would otherwise be the case. By causing interruptions in the schooling process, heavy military service demands lengthen the duration of the education transition.

Heavy military service demands on a cohort cause some members of the cohort to begin working at a younger age and cause other men to begin working at a relatively late age, lengthening the first-job transition. The men who begin working relatively late include men who complete their schooling and then begin working only after their military service. It may be the case that other men, seeing they will be drafted into the military, begin working at civilian jobs at a relatively young age, jobs that may not reflect their optimal career choices. If they do not continue their schooling after military service, these men are observed as having begun their first jobs relatively early.

In Chapter 3, we observed that military service ordinarily delays first marriage for individual men. However, at the cohort level and on average, those cohorts facing heavy military service demands marry at younger ages than other cohorts. The onset, average age, and age at completion of the first-marriage transition are all earlier in cohorts experiencing heavy military service demands. These seemingly contradictory results probably reflect a selectivity phenomenon. As military service demands on a cohort become pronounced, men may decide to marry in hopes of avoiding the draft (as could be done during the early 1960s). Other men, facing certain military service because of wartime, may choose to marry prior to leaving home. These phenomena would most commonly occur during periods of military draft. When military service demands are relatively light, there is a selectivity of military personnel from the late marriers. Single men entering the military find their marriage market prospects weakened and frequently are forced to delay marrying. Veterans consequently have later ages at marriage on average, even though the effect of heavy military service demands on a birth cohort is to hasten the marriage transition.

Heavy military service demands on a cohort thus cause postponements of the completion of schooling and a hastening of first marriage. The greater overlaps of the two transitions result in significantly fewer men completing the passage to adulthood in an orderly fashion, with more men marrying prior to completing their schooling and/or beginning work. Heavy military service requirements somewhat reduce the overall time needed to complete the transition to adulthood.

Demographic Transition

Birth cohorts of men living during the demographic transition experience earlier ages at school completion than cohorts of men who are born into a low-fertility and low-mortality population. The onset and average age at first job is also earlier, although the age at completion of the job transition is unaffected by the demographic factor. Age at first marriage, on the other hand, is later among men who are born prior to the onset of low mortality and low fertility. Men who are completing the passage to adulthood while the demographic transition is ongoing thus spend fewer years of their lifetime in school, more years working, and fewer years married. Given the relatively short life expectancies of these men, their married lives are particularly abbreviated.

These patterns may be related to the life expectancies of the parental generation. When a man's parents have rather short life expectations, they less frequently will survive to provide the financial assistance needed for prolonged attendance at college. Men more frequently will be forced to seek employment to support themselves. The lack of parental financial assistance could force the postponement of marriage until a man is completely self-supporting economically. Conversely, men undergoing the passage to adulthood during the post-demographic transition era ordinarily will have relatively young parents, with a father who is at his peak economic power. Fertility is relatively low, so such men will have fewer siblings to compete for the available resources. The family is able to provide more economic assistance during the passage to adulthood, enabling members of the more recent cohorts to remain in school longer, to postpone the beginning of economic self-sufficiency, and, more frequently, to marry prior to completing school and/or beginning work. The demographic transition thus has played a key role in producing modern changes in the transition to adulthood.

CONCLUSIONS

The analysis of this chapter has shown that six social structural variables characterizing the birth cohorts at the time they were undergoing the passage to adulthood can account for most of the intercohort variability in transition behavior. These social structural factors explain 90% or more of the intercohort variability in the ages of men at the school-completion and first-marriage transition. The models do somewhat more poorly with first job, explaining 96% of the intercohort variation in age at the onset of the transition, but only 77% of the median and 66% of the third quartile variability in age at first job. These factors account for 75% of the intercohort differences in duration of the school transition, 57% of the duration of the first-job transition, and 88% of the duration of the first-marriage transition. The models are quite successful in explaining intercohort changes in the duration of the overall transition to adulthood, accounting for 98% of the variation. Social structural conditions account for 88% of the variability in percent of the cohort with normative ordering patterns and 93% of the intercohort variability in percentage marrying prior to completing schooling. Only intercohort differences of the intermediate nonnormative ordering pattern are not responsive to changes in social structural conditions.

Of the six social structural variables, modernity is by far the most important in explaining changes in transition behavior. Increased levels of schooling are associated with modernity, and increased educational attainment necessitates prolongation of school enrollment. This has the consequence not only of increasing age at school completion but of delaying the first full-time job after schooling. While changes in school enrollments, and other factors associated with modernity, are by far the most important variables causing the intercohort changes in transition behavior, the inclusion of additional factors enabled the models to explain, on average, 16% more of the variance. The coefficients of these other variables are statistically significant. Several of these other variables fluctuate over time, and it is these fluctuations that help account for interannual variability in transition behavior.

The analysis of this chapter suggests that cohorts of men attempt to maximize their educational attainments and try to marry early. When social structural conditions are favorably inclined, men prolong their enrollment in school, but marry earlier than they otherwise would. This has the effect of intermixing the transition events, increasing the likelihood of marriage prior to school completion, and shortening the overall duration of the transition to adulthood. Favorable social structural events include periods of economic prosperity, low levels of unemployment, high government expenditures on education, and a population of low mortality and low fertility. The first three of these factors clearly have to do with the availability of the economic resources needed to purchase prolongations in school enrollments and early marriage. The demographic factor is indicative of a small family in which the parents are still living and at the peak of their earning power. I have interpreted this variable as indexing the economic resources potentially available from the family.

When social structural conditions are unfavorable to prolonged school enrollment and early marriage, cohorts of men appear to engage in coping behavior. They postpone marriage and attempt to remain in school. If the unfavorable conditions persist, they eventually are forced to complete their schooling at a younger age than they would otherwise have done. They have few resources for a prolonged job search and begin working sooner after school completion than do other men. Such men postpone the onset of the first-marriage transition but do not extend these postponements indefinitely. Rather than marry at a relatively late age, after the initial delays, these men tend to complete the marriage transition at a quicker pace. Unfavorable social structural conditions include periods of slow economic growth, high unemployment, and scarce government expenditures on social welfare programs (including educational aid). Periods of high mortality and high fertility also are unfavorable for men making the passage to adulthood. This may reflect the fewer potential economic resources available from the families of such men.

Heavy wartime military service demands on the cohorts prolong the length of the school-completion and first-job transitions. In large part, this probably results from the interruption of regular schooling by military service and from the availability of G.I. Bill benefits, which permit the resumption of schooling by some men. Although military service delays the marriage transition among individuals, high military service demands on a cohort cause an earlier marriage transition—a transition that is completed more quickly. I have interpreted this as a result of the selective drafting and enlistment of unmarried men into the military, with some men marrying prior to being drafted in the hope of avoiding military service. Also, during the massive wartime call-ups associated with World War II, many men married prior to departing for the battlefields of Europe, North Africa, and Asia.

This analysis has systematized our knowledge about the ways in which the social structural factors of modernity, social welfare expenditures, rate of employment, economic growth, wartime military service demands, and the demographic transition have affected the transition behavior of cohorts of men born from 1907 to 1946.[4] The effects of many

[4]The results of this analysis also obtain when the social structural conditions are measured somewhat differently. As a check on the robustness of the factor score-based regressions, I re-estimated all of the regression equations of this chapter, substituting a single indicator of each social structural condition for the factor-derived score. The per-

of these factors on the transition to adulthood are probably indirect, operating through their effects on the economic resources available to the cohorts during their passage to adulthood. In Part III, I explore this theme further, at the individual, instead of the cohort, level of analysis. That analysis of interindividual differentials in transition behavior confirms the importance of economic and social resources for the transition behavior of American males.

---

centage of the birth cohort with one or more years of college served as the indicator of modernity, total government expenditures on education in the year the cohort was age 16 was the measure of social welfare, the average annual percentage of the civilian noninstitutional population unemployed in the years the cohort was 18 to 20 was the measure of unemployment, average annual growth in per capita GNP between the years the cohort was aged 16 and 20 indicated economic growth, the average annual ratio of military personnel on active duty to men aged 15 to 24 between the years the cohort is age 18 to age 25 served as the measure of military service requirements, and the change in expectation of life at birth between the years the cohort was born and was age 16 served as a measure of the demographic situation.

There was a high correlation between the regression coefficients obtained with these independent variables and the coefficients of the analogous factor score-based models. For the education transition, the average correlation of the two sets of coefficients was .93, for age at marriage the correlation was .88, and for the ordering of events and duration of the transition to adulthood the average correlation was .81. These models thus agreed closely on the direction and relative magnitude of the effects of these six social structural conditions on transition behavior. The models agreed equally well for the first quartile and median of the age at first-job transition. However, the correlation between the factor-based and variable-based regressions was only .21 for the third quartile and .47 for the interquartile range of the first-job transition. Most of the coefficients for the third quartile age-at-first-job model were insignificant in the six-variable model; the major significant difference between the regressions was a much longer delay in first job associated with military service when it was measured by the ratio of men on active duty rather than by the factor-score military service variable. The effect of military service on the duration of the first-job transition was greater also when the ratio of men on active duty was used in place of the factor construct.

Although the two types of regressions produced roughly equivalent results, the factor score-based regressions were clearly superior. Of the 96 regression coefficients estimated for the transition parameters, 67 were significant with the factor-score variables compared to only 36 with the simple variables. The effects of economic growth, military requirements, and demographic conditions especially are more apparent with the factor-based models. The factor-constructed variables should be less subject to measurement error, and these regression results are in line with that hypothesis. It therefore seemed appropriate to present the regression results from the factor variable-based models.

III

Social Background Differentials in the Transition to Adulthood

> A cohort is said to be distinctively marked by the life stage it occupies when historical events impinge on it . . . , but exposure to an event is not likely to be uniform among its members. . . . The process [by which historical factors are expressed in the lives of youth] is shaped in part by what families and offspring bring to events, their cultural heritage and expectations, their material resources and social position. Class, ethnic, and residential variations may identify subgroups that differ in how they "work up" historically relevant experience [Elder, 1980:8].

This observation by Elder is the theoretical basis for the analysis described in Part III. In Part II, it was demonstrated that social structural conditions at the time a cohort is undergoing its transition to adulthood are important determinants of the timing and ordering of school completion, first job, and first marriage by members of the cohort. The results of the cohort-level analysis suggested that social structural conditions influence the transition behavior of members of the cohort by affecting the social and economic resources available. If this hypothesis is correct, the transition behavior of individual men should vary depending on their access to social and economic resources.

THEORETICAL DESIGN

In Part III, social class background, community size, and paternal ethnic ancestry differentials in the transition to adulthood are identified. These three social background characteristics have been shown to differentiate personal access to social and economic resources useful in the process of educational and occupational attainment (Blau and Duncan, 1967; Sewell, 1964; Sewell and Shah, 1968; Featherman, 1971; Kobrin and Goldscheider, 1978). These three background characteristics may each affect the timing and ordering of school completion, first job, and marriage by influencing normative regulations about the transitions or by affecting the control of resources that facilitate adherence to the relevant transition norms.

As discussed in Chapter 1, there exists almost no evidence about subgroup differentials in transition norms. It seems likely that most differentials among the groups in preferred age at school completion, first job, or marriage reflect intergroup differences in educational expectations. Men from groups with low educational aspirations thus would be expected to complete their schooling relatively early, whereas men from groups with higher educational aspirations would be expected to complete their schooling relatively late. Subgroup differentials in expected age at each transition event are likely to be quite small, controlling for level of education expected. Thus, if one asked persons from different groups at what age they would expect a young man to finish 4 years of college, the answer would be fairly invariant among the groups. Similarly, I expect that there are relatively few intergroup differences in preferred age at first job and first marriage, once controls are introduced for differences in educational expectations.

If this supposition is correct, intergroup differentials in actual transition behavior, *controlling for educational attainment*, result entirely from intergroup differences in social and economic resources that facilitate the transition to adulthood. The effects of social background on transition behavior probably are most pronounced among men at the post–high school levels of education. Differential financial resources should have little impact on age at completion of graded schooling since such schooling, in general, is publicly supported. It is at the post–high school levels of education, when private sources of funding are more important, that the differential resources of men from various social backgrounds should become significant. Men with access to relatively limited social and economic resources can be expected to encounter more difficulties in completing any given level of post–high school education. Such difficulties would appear in measures of age at school completion as a later median age at the completion of schooling and a wider variability in the age at which men finish schooling. Conversely, men with access to greater resources are expected to complete any given level of post–high school education at relatively early ages, with little variability about the median.

Average age at first job is closely associated with average age at school completion, with most men tending to delay the start of their first jobs until after the completion of schooling. This implies that, on average, men from social backgrounds that provide limited resources for school completion will begin their first full-time jobs later than men from more favorable backgrounds. But I also anticipate that the financial pressures associated with college enrollment will force many of the men from less favorable backgrounds to begin working prior to the completion of schooling.

Men display a pronounced tendency to delay marriage until after the completion of schooling (Chapter 2). However, men also tend to marry during a few modal years (Chapter 3). A man who delays marriage beyond the usual age for men of his cohort reduces his marriageability (by virtue of being "too old" for many potential mates). He also increases the risk of being forced to choose a relatively undesirable marriage partner from among the pool of women of suitable ages who have not yet found a spouse (or who have been previously married). Men thus face conflicting objectives to marry at a usual age but not to marry until after completing schooling and beginning work. These two objectives probably can be most readily fulfilled by men who complete a given level of schooling at a relatively early age. Men from social backgrounds that delay the completion of schooling are expected to display (*a*) a tendency toward a later age at marriage but (*b*) a greater probability of marriage prior to completing school.

ANALYSIS PLAN

These hypotheses about the effects of social background characteristics on the timing and ordering of school completion, beginning of first job, and first marriage are tested for social class background in Chapter 5. Chapter 6 reports differentials in transition behavior among men from different sizes of communities, and in Chapter 7 paternal ethnic ancestry differentials in transition behavior are examined. The analysis of each chapter begins with a description of the parameters of the transition process for men from different types of social backgrounds. Differences in transition behavior among the groups are interpreted as reflecting variations in educational aspirations and attainments as well as variability in access to social and economic resources that facilitate the transition to adulthood. The parameters of the transition process are examined also for men from different types of social backgrounds, controlling for their level of educational attainment. Intergroup differentials in transition behavior among men with the same level of completed education are interpreted as resulting entirely from variability in access to the social and economic resources that facilitate the transition to adulthood.

This descriptive analysis of the social background differentials in transition behavior is based on survival table estimates of the parameters of the transition process, with a separate survival table estimated for each transition for every combination of educational level and social background characteristic. The greatest strength of this approach is that it provides readily understood measures of transition behavior, while it resolves the problem of censoring in the case of incomplete transitions (see Chapter 2). Its primary disadvantage is that the number of sample cases do not permit simultaneous controls for such other potentially important factors as birth cohort and military service. The descriptive analysis section of each chapter thus assumes that there are no birth cohort or military service differentials in the effects of social background and educational attainment on transition behavior.

This assumption is relaxed in the second part of each chapter with the estimation of log-linear modified multiple regression models that measure the effects of social background characteristics on transition behavior, controlling for education level, birth cohort, and military service experience. The log-linear modified multiple regression framework requires categorical dependent variables. This presents no problems for the school-interruption and ordering-of-events measures. But the hypotheses tested in these chapters also concern the identification of men who are relatively early or late in their school-completion, first-job, and marriage transitions, compared to other men at the same level of education. Therefore, I decided to define these dependent variables by classifying men according to whether they were early, on time, or late in each transition, relative to other men at the same level of education. Operationally, this was done by estimating survival tables for each education group for each transition (tabulations not shown). Men completing a transition in the first quartile of their education group are classified as being relatively early in their transition; men making a transition during the fourth quartile are classified as relatively late. Men completing a transition during the second and third quartile are classified as being on-time in their transition. The on-time group is divided into those who are in the second-quartile and third-quartile age at transition in order to obtain a more refined measure of the dependent variable.

Only men who have completed a particular transition can be classified on the dependent variable. Censored observations (men still undergoing the transition process) therefore are excluded from this part of the analysis of each chapter. This is most problematic for the most recent birth cohorts, since they were still undergoing the transition process at the time of the survey. The analysis of each chapter includes a control for birth cohort. This birth-cohort control takes into account the truncation issue, while it also controls for the true effects of birth cohort on transition behavior. Since the control for birth cohort serves two purposes, the effect parameters of birth cohort are not readily interpretable. Since the primary goal in this part of the analysis is to examine the net effects of social class, community size, and ethnic origin on transition behavior, it is sufficient to control for birth cohort and military service in the models, even if the resulting cohort parameters are uninterpretable due to that variable's service as a proxy control for the truncation problem.

The log-linear analysis of each transition proceeds as follows. The multiway cross-classification of relative timing of a transition event by birth cohort by military service by level of education by one of the criterion variables (social class, community size, or ethnicity) is produced. There are five different dependent variables in the analysis—relative timing of school completion, of first job, and of marriage; a disruption in schooling lasting six months or longer; and temporal ordering pattern of transition events. In combination with the 3 criterion variables of interest, these 5 dependent variables result in 15 different matrices to be analyzed. The matrices are rather large. For example, the *timing of first marriage by birth cohort by military service by level of education by social class* matrix is a $4 \times 9 \times 2 \times 6 \times 5$ matrix with a total of 2160 cells. Although the matrices are large, the number of sample cases is also large, and the log-linear methods are designed to handle relatively sparse data and empty cells (see Goodman, 1971, 1972).

The appropriate hierarchical model that explains all of the statistically significant association of the criterion variable with the dependent variable is selected following the reverse stepwise model-fitting procedures discussed in Goodman (1971). This model is designed to allow for all association of the control variables (education, birth cohort, and military service experience) with the dependent variable and of the criterion variable with the control variables. The appropriate models of the effects of the criterion variables on the dependent variables, as well as of the differences in these effects as associated with levels of the control variables, are identified using these reverse stepwise model-fitting procedures. The effects parameters of the estimated model then are examined in order to identify the nature of the observed associations among the independent variables and transition behaviors. (These model-fitting procedures are analogous to reverse stepwise regression procedures for choosing the best fitting model in an ordinary least squares linear regression analysis.)

In general, the results of the log-linear analyses provide a confirmation of the descriptive analyses of the social background differentials in transition behavior. The log-linear analyses tend to confirm that social background affects the transition behavior of individuals differently according to their level of education. Relatively few differentials are found in the effect of social background among persons according to their military service or birth cohort histories. Based on these findings, and on the observed patterns of differentials among the social background by education groups, a final set of log-linear models are estimated that simultaneously examine the effects of social class, community size, and ethnicity on each type of transition behavior. The results of this analysis (reported in Chapter 8) indicate the net effects of each of the social background characteristics on transition behavior and identify a number of interesting interactions among the social background characteristics in their effects on transition behavior. Chapter 8 concludes with a discussion of the implications of the findings about social background differentiation in transition behavior for the intercohort changes in transition behavior discussed in Part II.

5

Social Class Background and the Transition to Adulthood

Social class background exerts a major impact on the educational and occupational attainments of American males. Men from blue-collar and farm origins complete fewer years of schooling than white-collar men. Men of lower social class origin have lesser occupational attainments than men of white-collar origin, in part because of their lesser educations, but also because of the direct effects of social class on first job and later career mobility (Blau and Duncan, 1967; Sewell and Shah, 1968; Sewell, 1971). Men from lower social class backgrounds complete school and enter the labor force earlier than men from better social origins, and they also form families of procreation earlier (Neugarten and Hagestad, 1976; Hollingshead, 1949). However, controlling for differentials in educational attainment, age at marriage varies remarkably little among men from different social status backgrounds (Hogan, 1978a). Almost nothing is known about social class differentials in age at school-completion and labor-force entry when the effects of educational attainment are controlled.

In this chapter, social class differentials in the timing and ordering of school completion, first job, and first marriage are identified. The total effects of social class on transition behavior, as well as its direct effects when educational attainment is controlled, are described by parameters from single-decrement survival tables calculated for each transition for men in each social class and education combination. Few social class differentials in transition behavior are expected among men with less than a college education. Among the college-educated men, those men who are from lower social class backgrounds, with access to relatively limited social and economic resources, are expected to experience a higher rate of interruption in schooling, and a later age at the completion of schooling. Such men may delay first job and first marriage slightly, but it is hypothesized that more frequently, they will marry prior to the completion of schooling. (For a complete discussion of the hypotheses and method af analysis of this chapter, see the introduction to Part III.)

Five levels of social class of family of origin are distinguished—upper white-collar, lower white-collar, skilled blue-collar, unskilled blue-collar, and farm (see Chapter 2). The analysis begins with a description of social class differentials in transition behavior based on survival table estimates of parameters of the transition process. The chapter concludes with the estimation of log-linear models of the effects of social class background on the transition behavior of men, controlling for their birth cohorts and military service experiences.

AGE AT SCHOOL COMPLETION

The total effects of social class background on age at the completion of schooling is, as hypothesized, positive (Table 5.1, bottom panel). The magnitude of the gradient is least for the first quartile of age at completion of schooling and greatest for the third quartile. This pattern is undoubtedly related to the equalizing effects on the first quartile for men from all social classes of nearly universal education at the grade school level and, more recently, the high school level. Few of the farm-background men complete college, so that three-quarters of those men complete school by 19.7 years of age. As the proportion of men attending college increases, the third quartile of age at school completion rises. Many of the white-collar origin men attend graduate or professional school; this raises the age at school completion to over 25 years for more than a quarter of such men.

Controlling for level of education, the direct effects of social class background on age at school completion can be assessed. As anticipated, the median age at the completion of graded schooling differs only slightly among men from different social class backgrounds. For example, median age at completion of high school varies between 18.1 and 18.4 years for the social classes. Age at the completion of high school is quite concentrated, with more than three-quarters of the men from each class finishing high school between 17.3 and 19.7 years of age. The interquartile range in age at the completion of graded schooling varies among the classes by no more than .4 years. (The only exceptions to these generalizations are at the elementary-school level, with a younger age at

Table 5.1
Measures of Age at School Completion by Social Class Background and Level of Schooling Completed, American Males Born 1907–1952

Educational Attainment	Social Class Background: High White Collar	Low White Collar	Skilled Blue Collar	Unskilled Blue Collar	Farm
Elementary, 0-8	13.07[a] 15.37 (4.68) 17.75	13.87 15.74 (3.54) 17.41	13.98 15.37 (2.82) 16.80	13.35 15.02 (3.07) 16.42	12.47 14.33 (3.51) 15.98
High School, 1-3	15.83 16.97 (2.58) 18.41	15.46 16.77 (2.82) 18.28	15.81 16.87 (2.10) 17.91	15.62 16.88 (2.41) 18.03	15.36 16.68 (2.77) 18.13
High School, 4	17.47 18.36 (2.21) 19.68	17.49 18.33 (1.95) 19.44	17.42 18.18 (1.80) 19.22	17.39 18.23 (1.97) 19.36	17.32 18.12 (2.03) 19.35
College, 1-3	19.00 22.66 (7.90) 26.90	19.95 22.46 (7.38) 27.33	19.54 22.41 (8.66) 28.20	19.44 21.76 (7.91) 27.35	19.31 21.06 (6.77) 26.08
College, 4	21.76 23.06 (3.96) 25.72	22.02 23.59 (4.55) 26.57	22.32 24.62 (6.06) 28.38	22.22 24.12 (6.28) 28.50	22.18 24.31 (5.91) 28.09
College, 5 or more	24.23 26.74 (7.29) 31.52	24.49 27.46 (8.60) 33.09	24.88 27.66 (9.37) 34.25	25.78 29.93 (11.65) 37.43	25.72 29.69 (10.31) 36.03
Total	18.63 22.16 (7.64) 26.27	18.03 20.97 (7.46) 25.49	17.25 18.61 (5.85) 23.10	16.64 18.20 (4.60) 21.24	15.05 17.46 (4.66) 19.71

[a] The first entry in each cell shows the first quartile (25th percentile), the second entry shows the second quartile (median), and the third entry shows the third quartile (75th percentile). The interquartile range is shown in parentheses.

school completion among men from farm backgrounds, and a larger interquartile range for men from high white-collar backgrounds.)

There appears to be a tendency among men with 1 to 3 years of college who are from unskilled blue-collar and farm backgrounds to discontinue their schooling at an earlier median age than do men from better social backgrounds. This may reflect the tendency of lower class men to drop out of college after fewer years of completed schooling or a greater tendency among the higher status men to reenter school after an initial interruption before dropping out for the final time. There is a great amount of variability in the age at completion of one to three years of college among men from all social classes. This undoubtedly reflects the tendency of some men to enter and drop out of college immediately after high school and of others to wait until after the completion of military service. Also, multiple college entries and exits among some men who never complete college would increase variability in age at school completion.

As hypothesized, social class has marked effects on age at school completion among college graduates (see Figure 5.1). Although the median age at completion of college is over 24 years of age for men from blue-collar and farm backgrounds, it is only 23.6 and 23.1 years of age for men from lower white-collar and upper white-collar occupations, respectively. Many more of the men from poorer social backgrounds are unable to complete college within the 4-year period following their high school graduations. Whereas only 36.4% of the college graduates from high white-collar backgrounds and 37.5% of those from low white-collar origins report discontinuing their schooling for 6 months or more, the percentages are 49.2, 44.7, and 48.6, respectively, among men with skilled blue-collar, unskilled blue-collar, and farm origins (χ^2 = 32.1 with 4 degrees of freedom, $p < .01$; see Figure 5.2). These interruptions probably represent periods of military service and/or employment at a civilian

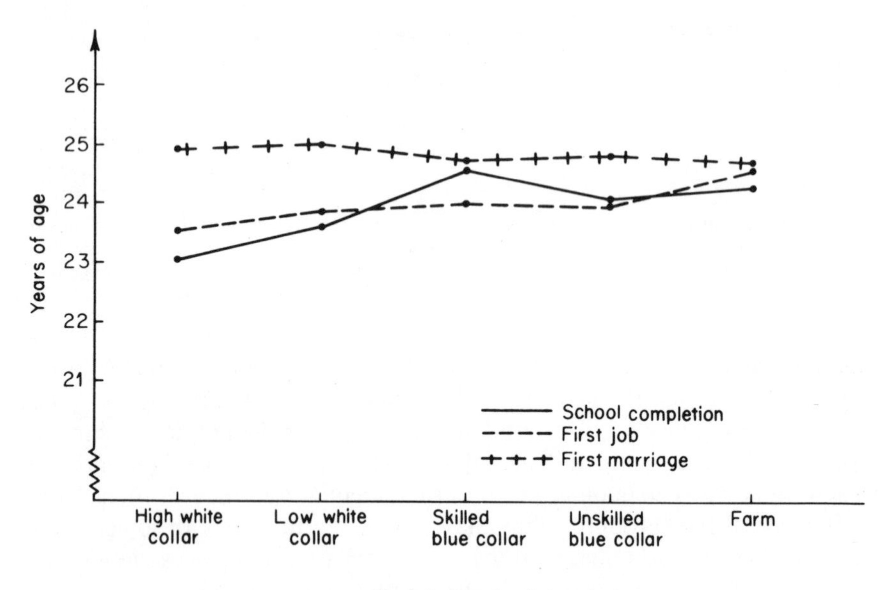

Figure 5.1. Median ages at school completion, first job, and first marriage by social class background, American males born 1907–1952, with 4 years of college.

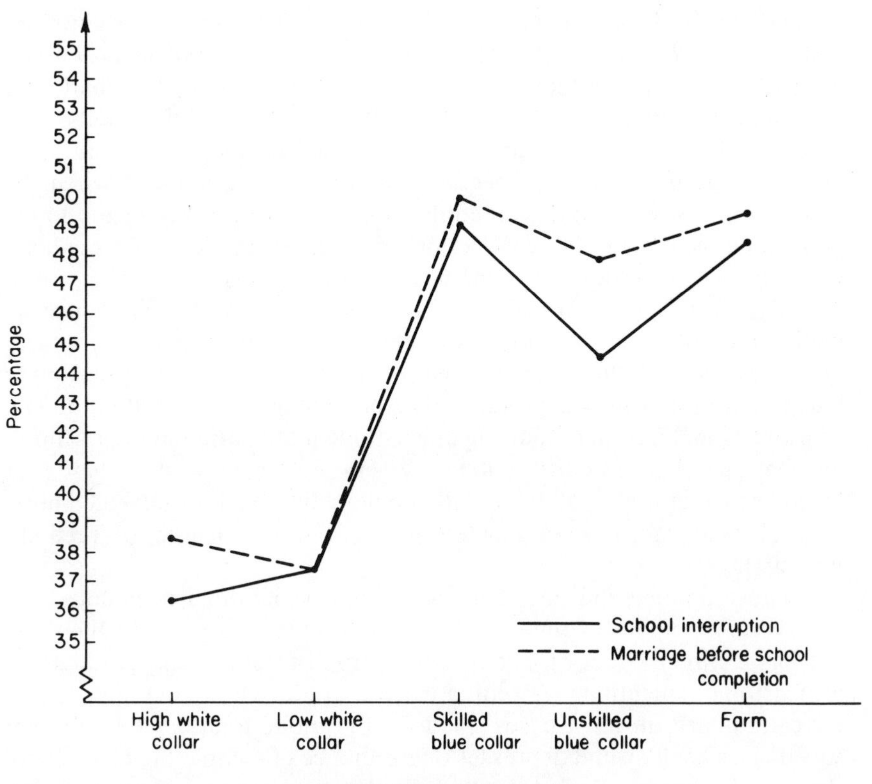

Figure 5.2. Percentages of men with one or more interruptions in schooling and marrying before the completion of schooling by social class background, American males born 1907–1952, with 4 years of college.

job in order to acquire the essential financial resources for a continued college education, but the OCG-II data do not permit a test of this hypothesis.

The more frequent interruptions in schooling experienced by men from lower status backgrounds result in a very late age at completion of schooling for some of the college graduates from such backgrounds. One-quarter of the lower status men are over age 28 when they complete college, whereas the third-quartile age is 26.6 among the lower white-collar men, and 25.7 among the upper white-collar men. A lower status social class background is positively associated with a wider interquartile range in age at completion of college.

Class differentials in the age at completion of schooling are most pronounced among the men with graduate or professional school training beyond the bachelor's degree. Among men of white-collar origin, 25% complete such schooling by 24.5 years of age, compared to 24.9 years of age for men whose fathers were skilled blue-collar workers and over 25.7 years for men from lower blue-collar and farm backgrounds. The inverse relationship between social class background and age at completion of graduate training becomes even more pronounced when the medians and seventy-fifth percentiles are examined. Many of the lower class men postpone the completion of their professional or graduate educations to well beyond their thirty-fifth birthdays.

Men from all social class backgrounds are likely to experience an interruption in their education before finishing a year or more of graduate or professional studies, but this risk is greatest among men from lower blue-collar and farm backgrounds. The percentage of men with graduate or professional training reporting at least one interruption in their schooling that lasted six months or longer is 46.4 for upper white-collar, 52.8 for lower white-collar, 50.9 for skilled blue-collar, 62.4 for unskilled blue-collar, and 58.0 for farm origin men ($\chi^2 = 23.7$ with 4 degrees of freedom, $p < .01$).

These findings indicate that social class background does not affect the average amount of time it takes men to complete graded schooling, but has a direct effect on age at completion of college and graduate or professional educations. As noted earlier, grade school and high school educations are, in most cases, paid for by public funds. While a lower social class background depresses one's chance of completing high school (Blau and Duncan, 1967; Sewell, 1971; Featherman and Hauser, 1978), it does not tend to produce age-grade retardation among those who remain in school. A lower social class background, on the other hand, not only reduces the chance that a man will enter college after high school and progress through the four years required for a bachelor's degree (Duncan, 1968); it increases the probability that a man who completes a given level of college will do so at a later than usual age. This pattern results partly from a higher rate of schooling interruption among men from the lower social classes, and it may result partly from a longer-than-average length of interruption among such men.

AGE AT FIRST JOB

Men from higher status social class backgrounds begin and complete the first-job transition at a later age than men from lower status origins (Table 5.2). The age at first job transition fairly closely follows the median age at school completion among each social class, but this difference is smallest among the men of white-collar origin. It appears that men who

Table 5.2
Measures of Age at First Job by Social Class Background and Level of Schooling Completed, American Males Born 1907–1952

Educational Attainment	Social Class Background: High White Collar	Low White Collar	Skilled Blue Collar	Unskilled Blue Collar	Farm
Elementary, 0-8	14.73[a] 17.27 (6.94) 21.67	15.36 17.20 (5.29) 20.65	14.95 16.74 (4.58) 19.53	14.76 16.52 (4.58) 19.34	13.63 16.43 (6.91) 20.54
High School, 1-3	16.08 17.71 (3.66) 19.74	16.18 17.83 (4.52) 20.70	16.32 17.71 (3.66) 19.98	16.20 17.65 (3.54) 19.74	15.79 17.75 (4.81) 20.60
High School, 4	17.74 18.99 (3.58) 21.32	17.80 18.92 (3.26) 21.06	17.67 18.82 (3.27) 20.94	17.70 18.86 (3.29) 20.99	17.55 18.97 (4.01) 21.56
College, 1-3	19.56 21.41 (4.80) 24.36	19.61 21.54 (4.32) 23.93	19.27 21.33 (5.14) 24.41	19.09 20.99 (4.81) 23.90	19.33 21.33 (5.47) 24.80
College, 4	22.13 23.56 (3.48) 25.61	22.37 23.92 (3.89) 26.26	22.35 24.03 (4.23) 26.58	22.12 23.95 (4.37) 26.49	22.60 24.58 (4.45) 27.05
College, 5 or more	24.01 26.14 (5.20) 29.21	23.84 26.13 (5.39) 29.23	23.79 26.29 (5.82) 29.61	23.78 27.06 (7.73) 31.51	24.38 27.54 (8.85) 33.23
Total	18.97 22.12 (6.43) 25.40	18.44 21.29 (6.20) 24.64	17.56 19.47 (5.54) 23.10	17.14 18.90 (5.07) 22.21	16.03 18.72 (6.70) 22.73

[a]The first entry in each cell shows the 25th percentile, the second entry shows the median, and the third entry shows the 75th percentile. The interquartile range is shown in parentheses.

prolong their schooling beyond about age 23 tend to begin working prior to finishing school, comparing the third quartiles of the school-completion and job-beginning transitions for men from white-collar origins. It is among such men, of course, that this contingency most commonly would arise because of enrollment in graduate or professional school.

Controlling for educational attainment, the median age at the beginning of the first full-time job held after the completion of schooling differs very little by social class for men at any level of schooling. Among men with one to three years of high school, and among high school graduates, the median age at first job differs among the social classes by less than .2 years. Among college graduates, men from farm backgrounds report slightly older median ages at first job, and men from high white-collar backgrounds have a slightly younger median age at first job (this pattern is illustrated in Figure 5.1). The farm and lower blue-collar background men with graduate or professional training report median ages at first job about one year older than the white-collar background men.

Among men with college educations, the seventy-fifth percentile of age at first job is later for men from lower status origins. This social class differential is most pronounced among men with 5 or more years of college completed. As with age at school completion, there is more variation in the age at first job among the lower status men, controlling for level of education. The higher social status men thus concentrate their school-completion and first-job transitions within a narrower band of a few modal ages.

Median age at first job is later than median age at school completion for men of all social classes at the elementary and high school levels. Within each social class, men with 0 to 8 years of schooling have median ages at first job 1.4 or more years later than age at school completion. This difference diminishes with increased levels of high school education, reaching a minimum of about .6 years among high school graduates. Interestingly, men with one to three years of college from every social class except farm background report a median age at first job that is .8 to 1.2 years earlier than median age at completion of schooling. Many of these men thus were working at their first, full-time jobs during part or all of their time in college. The ready availability of an outside job if they desired to quit school, and/or its constraints on students' allocation of time, are factors that may help explain why these men did not finish their college degrees. A median age at first job that precedes median age at school completion is reported among college graduates only for men from blue-collar backgrounds. Among those with 5 or more years of college, median age at first job is prior to median age at school completion for all men, but the difference tends to be larger among the lower social classes. A comparison of the third quartiles of age at school completion and age at first job represents the same pattern in even more pronounced form.

Thus, men who attend college and/or graduate or professional school tend to delay their school completion until a relatively late point in their life cycles. This rather prolonged period of school enrollment causes men from all social backgrounds to delay the beginning of their first job somewhat. As hypothesized, it appears that men from higher status social backgrounds more commonly delay the start of first job until after their schooling is completed, whereas men from lower status social backgrounds delay first job until a somewhat later age but not sufficiently to keep from beginning their first full-time jobs while still in school.

This pattern is in line with the hypothesis that a shortage of financial resources in family of origin will make it more difficult for men from lower class origins to complete any given level of schooling without interruption. The resulting prolongation of school enrollment forces the men from lower status origins to deviate from the statistically normative ages at school completion and beginning of work. Both because of the need for financial resources while in college and in response to possible normative pressures not to deviate greatly from the usual age at first job, the lower status men more frequently begin working prior to the completion of schooling, compared to men of higher status origin who complete the same level of schooling.

AGE AT FIRST MARRIAGE

Age at first marriage varies remarkably little by social class, given the very large differentials observed in age at school completion and age at first job (Table 5.3). Men from blue-collar backgrounds begin their first-marriage transition at about 21.1 or 21.2 years of age, compared with 21.9 years for men from white-collar backgrounds. The average age at first marriage is about 23.6 years for men of blue-collar and farm origin and 24.4 years for white-collar men. The average age at first marriage is thus greater than the average age at school completion and age at first job for men from all social backgrounds, but the difference is greatest among the lower status men. On average, men of higher status origin spend relatively more of their single years in school, and lower status men spend relatively more of their single years working.

Social class differentials in the average age at first marriage remain small, comparing men within each level of education. Men from lower white-collar backgrounds tend to have median ages at first marriage that are later than other men, but the differences are slight. Median age at marriage differs by less than one-half year between high white-collar and lower blue-collar men within each level of education. (Figure 5.1 illustrates these differences for men who have completed 4 years of college.)

The interquartile range of age at marriage does not differ systematically by social class background, controlling for level of education. Overall, men with 0 to 8 years of school completed display the greatest variability in age at marriage, with those from low white-collar origins showing the greatest degree of variation and those from farm backgrounds having the least variation. Class differentials in the size of the inter-

Table 5.3
Measures of Age at First Marriage by Social Class Background and Level of Schooling Completed, American Males Born 1907–1952

Educational Attainment	Social Class Background				
	High White Collar	Low White Collar	Skilled Blue Collar	Unskilled Blue Collar	Farm
Elementary, 0-8	20.83[a] 24.57 (10.36) 31.19	21.44 25.23 (14.14) 35.58	20.87 24.15 (9.18) 30.05	20.79 24.08 (9.60) 30.39	21.06 23.89 (7.76) 28.82
High School, 1-3	20.37 22.52 (5.71) 26.08	20.73 23.43 (6.76) 27.49	20.29 22.83 (6.30) 26.59	20.37 22.71 (6.03) 26.40	20.51 22.95 (5.89) 26.40
High School, 4	21.09 23.57 (6.38) 27.47	21.25 23.50 (5.61) 26.86	20.98 23.20 (5.38) 26.36	21.00 23.23 (5.63) 26.63	21.01 23.36 (5.62) 26.63
College, 1-3	21.89 24.39 (5.75) 27.64	22.31 24.45 (5.41) 27.72	21.71 24.12 (5.62) 27.33	21.70 23.91 (5.20) 26.90	21.29 23.79 (5.49) 26.78
College, 4	22.69 24.94 (5.56) 28.25	22.67 25.04 (5.55) 28.22	22.54 24.73 (5.41) 27.95	22.49 24.84 (6.07) 28.56	22.39 24.68 (6.33) 28.72
College, 5 or more	22.96 25.36 (6.07) 29.03	22.98 25.62 (6.88) 29.86	22.98 25.04 (5.99) 28.97	22.78 25.34 (6.29) 29.07	22.64 25.54 (7.26) 29.90
Total	21.94 24.41 (6.13) 28.07	21.95 24.33 (5.95) 27.90	21.27 23.62 (5.90) 27.17	21.06 23.53 (6.34) 27.40	21.08 23.65 (6.51) 27.59

[a]The first entry in each cell shows the 25th percentile, the second entry shows the median, and the third entry shows the 75th percentile. The interquartile range is shown in parentheses.

quartile range are 1 year or less among men with high school and college level educations. Among men with 4 or more years of college, those from farm origins tend to show slightly more variation in average age at marriage, as do men from lower white-collar origins with 5 or more years of college.

Median age at marriage has a curvilinear relationship with level of education; men who have elementary school or college educations report the oldest ages at first marriage. Most of the men with elementary school educations are from among the older cohorts, which had relatively later ages at marriage. Restricting our attention to men with more than an elementary school education, age at marriage is positively associated with level of schooling among each social class. Comparing college graduates to high school graduates, four years of college increases median age at marriage from 1.3 to 1.6 years in each of the social classes. An additional year of college thus increases median age at marriage by about .33 to .40 years.

Additional education clearly does not delay first marriage sufficiently to ensure that schooling is completed prior to marriage. As men remain enrolled in school at relatively advanced ages, they face the dilemma of postponing marriage until a relatively late age (substantially worsening their marriage-market situation) or of marrying before completing school. This problem is particularly severe for the men from blue-collar and farm backgrounds since they do not complete higher levels of schooling until relatively advanced ages.

ORDERING OF EVENTS

The median age at first job precedes median age at school completion among men from all social classes who completed 1 to 3 years of college. Median age at first job also is less than median age at school completion among college graduates from blue-collar and farm backgrounds. Average age at first marriage is nearly identical to average age at school completion among college graduates from blue-collar and farm backgrounds, but not among college graduates from white-collar backgrounds. Median age at first marriage is prior to both median age at school completion and age at first job among all men with graduate or professional school training.

These results suggest that a disorderly sequencing of school completion, first job beginning, and first marriage more frequently characterizes men from lower status social origins at any given level of education beyond high school. This hypothesis is tested in Table 5.4, which displays the crosstabulation of *temporal ordering pattern of transition events by social class background by level of education*. The results confirm that college-educated men from blue-collar and farm backgrounds are less likely to order events normatively than are men from white-collar backgrounds. Comparing the men from high white-collar backgrounds with men from unskilled blue-collar backgrounds, the differential is 6.3% among the college graduates and 9.9% among men with one or more years of graduate or professional training. The social classes do not vary greatly in the percentage of men with an intermediate ordering pattern. The major scource of the class differential in ordering pattern comes from the greater proclivity of men from blue-collar and farm backgrounds to marry prior to completing their formal education (Figure

Table 5.4
The Temporal Ordering of Life-Course Events by Social Class Background and Level of Schooling Completed, American Males Born 1907–1952

Educational Attainment	Social Class Background				
	High White Collar	Low White Collar	Skilled Blue Collar	Unskilled Blue Collar	Farm
Elementary, 0-8[b]	81.6[a] 14.2 4.2	75.1 17.8 7.1	83.7 12.3 4.1	83.9 13.5 2.6	75.4 21.4 3.2
High School, 1-3[c]	76.7 20.5 2.8	72.1 23.8 4.1	80.1 15.8 4.1	77.1 19.2 3.7	73.0 21.7 5.3
High School, 4[d]	67.3 22.4 10.3	70.4 22.1 7.5	69.3 22.2 8.5	70.2 21.5 8.3	67.3 22.7 9.9
College, 1-3[e]	45.6 24.3 30.1	49.3 18.9 31.8	44.5 20.2 35.3	42.2 23.8 34.0	50.6 20.8 28.7
College, 4[f]	47.1 14.4 38.5	46.7 15.7 37.6	36.3 13.6 50.1	40.8 11.2 48.0	39.1 11.3 49.6
College, 5 or more[g]	26.8 11.8 61.4	21.5 14.1 64.4	19.4 11.1 69.6	16.9 6.8 76.3	23.2 3.5 73.4
Total[h]	51.4 18.5 30.1	55.9 19.2 24.8	62.4 18.5 19.1	66.2 18.9 14.9	66.4 20.7 12.9

[a]The first entry in each cell shows the percentage of men with a normative ordering of events, the second entry shows the percentage with an intermediate nonnormative ordering pattern, and the third entry shows the percentage of men with an extreme nonnormative pattern. Normative ordering of events occurs when a man first completes school, next begins to work and lastly marries. The intermediate nonnormative pattern occurs when a man begins a job prior to finishing school or marries prior to beginning work, but after the completion of schooling. Extreme nonnormative ordering occurs whenever a man marries prior to the completion of his education.

[b]χ^2 = 33.2 with 8 degrees of freedom, $p < .01$.

[c]χ^2 = 12.6 with 8 degrees of freedom, $p > .12$.

[d]χ^2 = 7.8 with 8 degrees of freedom, $p > .45$.

[e]χ^2 = 13.0 with 8 degrees of freedom, $p > .11$.

[f]χ^2 = 23.1 with 8 degrees of freedom, $p < .01$.

[g]χ^2 = 27.5 with 8 degrees of freedom, $p < .01$.

[h]χ^2 = 433.5 with 8 degrees of freedom, $p < .001$.

5.2). Again comparing men of high white-collar origin with men from unskilled blue-collar origins, 9.5% more of the lower status men marry prior to completing 4 years of college, and 14.9% more of the lower status men marry prior to completing 5 or more years of college.

It is especially difficult for men who attend college, graduate, or professional school to maintain a normative ordering of events since an extended postponement of marriage until after the completion of schooling will result in making them "late" marriers relative to other members of their cohort. Such a postponement could, if strictly adhered to, result in the loss of a desirable marriage partner who is unwilling to be "late" on the marriage schedule of her cohort. It appears that as a result of the joint effects of the desirability of a college education and a preference for marriage at the right age, some men marry prior to completing their schooling, thereby violating any normative prescription that schooling should be completed prior to marriage.

There are no statistically significant social class differentials in temporal ordering patterns among men with 1 to 4 years of high school or among men with 1 to 3 years of college. Among men with elementary school educations there is a tendency for men from lower white-collar and farm backgrounds to deviate from a normative order of events more frequently than men from other social classes. In part, this relationship results from a greater percentage of farm origin men reporting that they began their first full-time civilian job prior to finishing school. These are primarily men whose first jobs were in farming (tabulation not shown).

DURATION OF THE TRANSITION TO ADULTHOOD

On average, men from unskilled blue-collar and farm backgrounds take longer than higher status origin men to complete the entire transition to adulthood (Table 5.5). These differences primarily are the result of the earlier ages at which the lower status men begin to complete their schooling.

The duration of the transition to adulthood varies sharply by level of education for men in every social class, ranging from more than 16 years among men completing 0–8 years of schooling to less than 5.5 years among men completing 5 or more years of college. As the level of completed education increases, men from all social classes tend to compress the school-completion, job-beginning, and first-marriage transitions into a narrower band of time. This results not only in an acceleration of the transition process, but in an increased probability of a disorderly transition pattern.

Among high school graduates, men of high white-collar origin have

Table 5.5
The Duration of the Transition to Adulthood by Social Class Background and Level of Schooling Completed, American Males Born 1907–1952

Educational Attainment	Social Class Background				
	High White Collar	Low White Collar	Skilled Blue Collar	Unskilled Blue Collar	Farm
Elementary, 0-8 . . .	18.12[a]	21.71	16.07	17.04	16.35
High School, 1-3 . .	10.25	12.03	10.78	10.78	11.04
High School, 4 . . .	10.00	9.37	8.94	9.24	9.31
College, 1-3	8.64	7.77	7.79	7.46	7.47
College, 4	6.49	6.20	5.63	6.34	6.54
College, 5 or more .	4.80	5.37	4.09	3.29	4.18
Total	9.44	9.87	9.92	10.76	12.54

[a]The duration of the transition to adulthood operationally is defined as the number of years between the ages at which one-quarter of the men in each of the social class and education groups complete their schooling and three-quarters of the men first marry.

relatively lengthy transitions to adulthood (10.0 years) and men of skilled blue-collar origin have relatively quick transitions (8.9 years). Among college graduates, men of skilled blue-collar origin again are found to have somewhat faster transitions (by about one-half year). Among men with 5 or more years of college, blue-collar and farm origin men experience especially quick transitions from adolescence to adulthood. As discussed above, these same men are especially subject to disorderly transition patterns.

LOG-LINEAR MODELS

Before drawing conclusions about the effects of social class background on transition behavior, it is necessary to confirm that the results of the descriptive analysis persist with the introduction of controls for birth cohort and military service. It also is important to discover whether the effects of social class background on transition behavior vary among the birth cohorts or between veterans and nonveterans. Answers to these questions are provided by log-linear modified multiple regression models of the effects of social class background on transition behavior.

The log-linear analyses confirm that social class differentials in transition behavior persist at particular levels of education, controlling for birth cohort and military service experience (Table 5.6). As observed earlier, there are direct effects of social class on age at marriage, effects that do not vary by level of education (i.e., the age-at-marriage model includes a *timing by social class* [TS] parameter but not a *timing by level of education by social class* [TLS] parameter). For all other transition variables, the expected interaction of social class, education, and transition behavior is observed (i.e., the models that fit incorporate a [TLS] parameter). There are two additional interactions among the variables not previously noted: The effects of social class background on school interruption vary by birth cohort (the *timing by social class by birth*

Table 5.6
Models of the Effects of Social Class Background on the Timing of Transition Events: American Males Born 1907–1952

Variables	Model[a]	χ^2_{LR} [b]	df[c]	p[d]	Δ[e]
Social Class Background					
School interruption	(TLMC)(LSMC)(TLS)(TSC)	302.8	376	>.5	2.8
Age at school completion. . .	(TLMC)(LSMC)(TLS)	975.2	1224	>.5	7.0
Age at first job.	(TLMC)(LSMC)(TLS)	1010.2	1224	>.5	7.3
Age at first marriage	(TLMC)(LSMC)(TS)	1097.3	1284	>.5	7.3
Temporal ordering of events .	(TLMC)(LSMC)(TLS)(TSM)	667.1	808	>.5	5.7

[a] Each model shown was selected using reverse stepwise procedures to include all statistically significant ($p \leq .05$) parameters in the model and to exclude all parameters not statistically significant ($p > .05$) from the model.

T = Timing variable. School interruption (no/yes), age at school completion, age at first job, age at marriage (first quartile/second quartile/third quartile/fourth quartile), temporal ordering of events (normative/intermediate nonnormative/ extreme nonnormative).

L = Level of education (0-8/9-11/12/13-15/16/17 or more).

M = Military service (no/yes).

C = Birth cohort (1948-52/1943-47/1938-42/1933-37/1928-32/1923-27/1918-22/1913-17/ 1907-12).

S = Social class (upper white collar/lower white collar/skilled blue collar/ unskilled blue collar/farm).

[b] χ^2_{LR} is the likelihood ratio chi-square statistic.

[c] df are the degrees of freedom.

[d] p is the probability level that the chi-square statistic is due to chance.

[e] Δ is the index of dissimilarity between the observed sample frequencies and the expected sample frequencies obtained with that model.

cohort [TSC] parameter of the school interruption model), and the effects of social class on temporal ordering patterns vary according to military service experience (the *timing by social class by military service* [TSM] parameter in the model fit for temporal ordering of events). These effect parameters are sufficient to account for all of the significant associations observed among the variables (p > .5).

In addition to producing chi-square tests of the existence of associations among the variables, the log-linear regression models produce parameters indicating the direction of the association. These odd probabilities (gammas) are greater than 1.0 when the probability of being in a particular category of the dependent variable is greater than average and less than 1.0 when the probability of being in that category of the dependent variable is less than average. A gamma coefficient equal to 1.0 means that membership in that category of the independent variable does not affect the likelihood of experiencing that category of the dependent variable.

The gamma coefficients for the odds probability of completing schooling relatively early or relatively late according to social class background and level of education completed are shown in Table 5.7. These

Table 5.7
The Net Odds Probability of Completing Schooling Relatively Early or Late by Social Class Background and Level of Schooling Completed: American Males Born 1907–1952

Educational Attainment	Social Class Background				
	High White Collar	Low White Collar	Skilled Blue Collar	Unskilled Blue Collar	Farm
	Net Odds Probability of Completing School Early				
Elementary, 0-8 . . .	1.362	0.724	0.672	0.948	1.591*
High School, 1-3. . .	0.677*	1.539*	0.783*	0.967	1.267
High School, 4. . . .	0.794*	0.769*	1.157	1.351**	1.048
College, 1-3.	0.712*	0.745*	1.516**	1.214*	1.024
College, 4.	1.374*	1.102	0.950	0.855	0.813
College, 5 or more. .	1.397*	1.422*	1.140	0.777	0.569*
	Net Odds Probability of Completing School Late				
Elementary, 0-8 . . .	1.411*	2.009*	1.032	0.674*	0.507**
High School, 1-3. . .	1.456*	1.114	0.734*	0.831	1.011
High School, 4. . . .	1.327*	1.181	0.772*	0.851*	0.971
College, 1-3.	0.845	0.873	1.101	1.125	1.095
College, 4.	0.668*	0.661	1.477*	1.333	1.151
College, 5 or more. .	0.650	0.656	1.053	1.396	1.596

*Standardized value greater than 1.0.

**Standardized value greater than 2.0.

coefficients are net of the effects of the other independent variables reported in the model of Table 5.6. The coefficients fluctuate quite a bit, but it appears that at the high school and some college levels of education the lower status men more commonly finish school relatively early (perhaps because of earlier dropout), whereas at the college and graduate school level the lower status men more commonly finish school relatively late. Thus, all 4 of the gamma coefficients for finishing college and graduate school relatively early are greater than 1.0 for the upper status men, whereas 5 of the 6 gamma coefficients for the lower status men are less than 1.0. Looking at the probability of completing graduate or professional school relatively late, all of the upper status gamma coefficients are less than 1.0 and all of the gammas of the lower status men are greater than 1.0. In the extreme, the odds of completing graduate school relatively late are .650 to 1.0 for the high white-collar men compared with 1.596 to 1.0 for the farm origin men. This indicates that the farm origin men are 2.46 times more likely than high white-collar men (1.596/.650 = 2.46) to finish graduate school relatively late.

The groups of men who have a higher probability of completing

Table 5.8
The Net Odds Probability of an Interruption in Schooling by Social Class Background and Other Selected Independent Variables: American Males Born 1907–1952

Independent Variables	Social Class Background				
	High White Collar	Low White Collar	Skilled Blue Collar	Unskilled Blue Collar	Farm
Educational Attainment					
Elementary, 0-8.	1.417*	1.283	0.903	0.760*	0.801*
High School, 1-3	1.024	1.142	0.957	0.884*	1.010
High School, 4	1.129*	0.974	0.948	1.033	0.928
College, 1-3	0.983	1.001	1.086	1.020	0.917
College, 4	0.783**	0.734*	1.313**	1.073	1.235*
College, 5 or more	0.793*	0.954	0.856	1.315*	1.175
Birth Cohort					
1948-52.	1.222	1.088	1.114	0.928	0.728
1943-47.	1.081	1.201	1.023	0.968	0.777*
1938-42.	1.131	1.145	1.003	0.909	0.848
1933-37.	0.761*	0.944	1.355**	1.108	0.928
1928-32.	0.987	0.955	0.821*	1.041	1.241*
1923-27.	0.991	1.027	0.973	0.939	1.076
1918-22.	0.919	0.917	0.988	1.077	1.116
1913-17.	0.835	1.006	1.058	0.979	1.150
1907-12.	1.172*	0.783*	0.773*	1.075	1.311*

*Standardized value greater than 1.0.

**Standardized value greater than 2.0.

college or graduate school relatively late also have a higher probability of experiencing an interruption in their schooling lasting 6 months or longer (Table 5.8, upper panel). At the elementary and secondary school level the patterns are mixed, but it seems lower status men may interrupt their schooling less frequently than the high status men. At the college and graduate levels the gamma coefficient for the probability of interrupting schooling is always less than 1.0 for men from white-collar origins. It is greater than 1.0 for men from blue-collar and farm origins, with the exception of skilled blue-collar graduates of 5 or more years of college. The probability of an interruption in schooling varies by social class more among some cohorts than among others, but the gamma coefficients present no clearcut pattern of intercohort change (Table 5.8, lower panel).

The effects of social class on the timing of first job varies by level of schooling. Men from farm origins are more likely to begin their first jobs relatively early, among men completing grade school and 1 to 3 years of high school (Table 5.9). This is due to the greater proclivity of farm origin men who enter farming as a first job to report their first job

Table 5.9
The Net Odds Probability of Beginning the First Job Relatively Early or Late by Social Class Background and Level of Schooling Completed: American Males Born 1907–1952

Educational Attainment	Social Class Background				
	High White Collar	Low White Collar	Skilled Blue Collar	Unskilled Blue Collar	Farm
	Net Odds Probability of Beginning First Job Early				
Elementary, 0-8.	0.925	0.832	0.785	0.800	2.070**
High School, 1-3	1.133	1.097	0.786*	0.899	1.138
High School, 4	0.933	1.015	1.128	0.974	0.961
College, 1-3	0.857	0.879	1.174	1.224*	0.923
College, 4	1.273*	1.043	1.009	1.091	0.684*
College, 5 or more . . .	0.938	1.177	1.212	1.069	0.699
	Net Odds Probability of Beginning First Job Late				
Elementary, 0-8.	1.746*	1.195	0.782	0.778*	0.787
High School, 1-3	0.751*	1.556*	0.957	0.878	1.019
High School, 4	1.201*	0.986	0.843*	1.005	0.997
College, 1-3	1.150*	0.894	1.191	0.863	0.947
College, 4	0.703	0.778	1.388	1.181	1.116
College, 5 or more . . .	0.786	0.785	0.959	1.429	1.184

*Standardized value greater than 1.0.

**Standardized value greater than 2.0.

as beginning (on a part-time basis) at a relatively early age (tabulation not shown). At the college and graduate school level of education, on the other hand, farm origin men delay the start of their first job compared with men from other class origins. At this highly educated level, men from white-collar backgrounds seldom begin their first jobs late, whereas blue-collar and farm origin men have high probabilities of a late first job. As with timing of education, the exception is men of skilled blue-collar background with 5 or more years of college, whose behavior is approximately average.

As described earlier in this chapter, age at marriage is earlier among farm origin men and tends to be slightly later among white-collar origin men. This tendency does not vary by level of education, and the pattern of effects persists with controls for birth cohort and military service history (tabulation not shown).

White-collar origin men less frequently marry before completing school than men from blue-collar or farm origins, controlling for birth cohort and military service experience (Table 5.10). The differences are fairly pronounced, with unskilled blue-collar college graduates having net rates of marriage before school completion fully 47% higher than high white-collar origin men (1.211/.822 = 1.47). Again the exception

Table 5.10
The Net Odds Probability of Normative and Extreme Nonnormative Ordering of Life-Course Events by Social Class Background and Level of Schooling Completed: American Males Born 1907–1952

Educational Attainment	Social Class Background				
	High White Collar	Low White Collar	Skilled Blue Collar	Unskilled Blue Collar	Farm
	Net Odds Probability of a Normative Ordering Pattern				
Elementary, 0-8.	0.979	0.604*	1.309*	1.446*	0.893
High School, 1-3	1.101	0.836	1.275*	1.133	0.752*
High School, 4	0.792*	1.282*	1.060	1.059	0.877
College, 1-3	0.874	1.323*	0.942	0.754*	1.217*
College, 4	1.153	1.350	0.733*	0.961	0.911
College, 5 or more . . .	1.162	0.865	0.818	0.795	1.531*
	Net Odds Probability of Marriage before School Completion				
Elementary, 0-8.	1.384	2.085*	0.956	0.626*	0.579*
High School, 1-3	0.810	1.157	1.040	0.860	1.193
High School, 4	1.489*	0.832	0.870	0.931	0.998
College, 1-3	1.001	1.067	1.126	1.090	0.764*
College, 4	0.822	0.677*	1.211	1.268*	1.171
College, 5 or more . . .	0.723*	0.691*	0.848	1.445*	1.624*

* Standardized value greater than 1.0.

Table 5.11
The Net Odds Probability of Normative and Extreme Nonnormative Ordering of Life-Course Events by Social Class Background and Military Service Experience: American Males Born 1907–1952

Military Service Experience	Social Class Background				
	High White Collar	Low White Collar	Skilled Blue Collar	Unskilled Blue Collar	Farm
	Net Odds Probability of a Normative Ordering Pattern				
Civilian	0.846*	0.963	1.023	1.050	1.143*
Veteran.	1.182*	1.038	0.977	0.952	0.875*
	Net Odds Probability of Marriage before School Completion				
Civilian	1.134	1.070	0.975	1.025	0.825*
Veteran.	0.882	0.934	1.026	0.976	1.212*

*Standardized value greater than 1.0.

is among the skilled blue-collar origin men who attend graduate or professional school—they have relatively low rates of marriage before school completion.

Among the white-collar origin men the probability of marriage before completing schooling is higher among the men without military service experience, and lower among veterans (Table 5.11). Among the blue-collar origin men there are only small differences between the veterans and the civilians. Among farm origin men, veterans are much more likely than civilians to marry prior to completing school.

SUMMARY

The analysis presented in this chapter has confirmed that social class background has important effects on the timing and ordering of school completion, first job, and first marriage. Social class differentials in transition behavior are relatively minor among men who have less than a college education, but they are much more marked among the college educated. These social class differences in transition behavior persist when controls are introduced for birth cohort and military service experience.

A higher status family background enhances the probability that a man will complete 4 or more years of college. Among men who complete 4 or more years of college, a higher status family background improves the chances that a man will finish his schooling without interruption and at a relatively early age. A lower status family background, on the other hand, is associated with a greater probability of an interruption in schooling and with a relatively late age at school completion.

It seems probable that this pattern results from the greater availability of financial assistance from family of origin for men of higher status backgrounds. Such financial assistance would facilitate a relatively expeditious completion of schooling. Completing school on time improves the prospect that a man can begin working and marry on time and in the normatively preferred sequence.

Men from blue-collar and farm backgrounds who attend college probably are more reliant on G.I. Bill benefits or on their own earnings to finance their educations. Thus, they more frequently begin working at their first full-time civilian jobs prior to completing school, despite a relatively late age at the beginning of that first job. Despite their relatively late age at school completion and beginning of first job, college-educated men from lower status backgrounds remain on time in the marriage transition. In so doing, men from lower status backgrounds more frequently have an out-of-sequence patterning of the three transition events. Thus, it is the prolongation of age at completion of schooling that accounts for the greater proclivity of men from lower status social backgrounds to work and/or to marry prior to completing their bachelor's, graduate, or professional degree.

6

Size of Community of Origin and the Transition to Adulthood

Men who grow up in rural communities and small towns complete fewer years of schooling than other men (Sewell, 1964; Blau and Duncan, 1967). Growing up in a rural community or small town is detrimental to the process of occupational attainment, as is post-schooling residence in such communities (Blau and Duncan, 1967). It seems probable that the process of transition to adulthood also varies among men from different types of community backgrounds (Elder, 1978a, 1980). For example, it probably is more difficult for men from a rural social milieu to complete college than it is for men in an urban environment, since geographic mobility will more frequently be required of the former. Small communities have less diversified labor markets than do large urban areas, and they offer fewer opportunities for employment and for occupational advancement. Men from small communities therefore may experience more difficulty in finding suitable first jobs than men from cities. Although geographic mobility permits men of small town and rural origin to move to more favorable labor markets, such geographic mobility may delay the beginning of the first, full-time job. Age-at-marriage norms may vary by community size, and it is likely that fewer single women are available for marriage in communities with small populations; these factors may affect the age at marriage of men with differing community origins.

The analysis of Chapter 5 confirmed that the level of family social and economic resources (as measured by father's occupational class) affects the transition to adulthood. In this chapter, I test the hypothesis that the timing and sequencing of school completion, beginning of first job, and first marriage vary among men according to the resources of the community in which they live. Community size is used as an indicator of community resources. As discussed in Chapter 2, five community size groups are used: large city, suburb of a large city, small city, rural nonfarm, and rural farm. In general, it is hypothesized that residence in large cities or in suburbs of large cities facilitates the transition to adulthood. Residence in small towns or rural areas is hypothesized to delay the completion of a given level of post-high school education and the beginning of first job, and to result in a nonnormative ordering of transition events.

The analysis of this chapter proceeds in the same fashion as that of Chapter 5. Descriptive parameters of the transition process (based on single-decrement survival tables) are presented for men from each size of community, and for men from each size of community controlling for educational attainment. Log-linear models of transition behavior are then estimated in order to confirm that the observed community-size differentials in transition behavior persist when controls are introduced for birth cohort and military service. Differences in the effects of community size on transition behavior among men from different birth cohorts or military service experiences are then discussed.

AGE AT SCHOOL COMPLETION

Size of community of residence at age 16 is positively associated with age at school completion, with the major difference occurring between men from rural areas and those from urban areas (Table 6.1). Males from urban origins do not begin the education transition until they are 17, compared to 16.3 for rural nonfarm men and 15.5 for farm origin men. By far the biggest difference is in the age at which males from different sized communities complete the education transition, with one-quarter of the urban men delaying the completion of schooling until they are 24, compared with 21.0 for rural nonfarm men and 19.8 for rural farm men. These differing age patterns produce a much longer duration for the education transition among men with urban origins.

These direct associations of the age at school completion and the length of the education transition with size of community of origin result from the higher levels of education achieved by men from urban backgrounds. Controlling for level of schooling completed, there are no community-size differences in the age pattern of school completion among males with high school educations. A direct relationship between community size and age at school completion persists in reduced form among

Table 6.1
Measures of Age at School Completion by Size of Community at Age 16 and Level of Schooling Completed, American Males Born 1907–1952

Educational Attainment	Community Size				
	Large City	Suburb of Large City	Small City	Rural Nonfarm	Rural Farm
Elementary, 0-8	13.41[a] 15.17 (3.47) 16.88	13.71 15.32 (2.94) 16.65	12.90 14.84 (3.53) 16.43	13.04 14.43 (2.86) 15.90	12.60 14.40 (3.39) 15.99
High School, 1-3	15.53 16.74 (2.51) 18.04	15.71 16.84 (2.20) 17.91	15.67 16.85 (2.31) 17.98	15.64 16.95 (2.70) 18.34	15.49 16.80 (2.67) 18.16
High School, 4	17.33 18.27 (2.29) 19.62	17.46 18.23 (1.80) 19.26	17.41 18.23 (2.04) 19.45	17.41 18.18 (1.68) 19.09	17.39 18.18 (1.85) 19.24
College, 1-3	19.85 22.54 (8.75) 28.60	19.84 22.79 (8.69) 28.53	19.57 22.02 (7.10) 26.67	19.31 21.18 (6.38) 25.69	19.30 21.18 (7.02) 26.32
College, 4	21.88 23.61 (5.52) 27.40	21.96 23.41 (4.65) 26.61	21.91 23.69 (4.90) 26.81	22.40 24.45 (5.48) 27.88	22.31 24.07 (5.97) 28.28
College, 5 or more	24.61 27.41 (8.85) 33.46	24.37 26.83 (7.33) 31.70	24.80 27.88 (9.24) 34.04	25.06 29.98 (11.96) 37.02	25.17 29.44 (11.18) 36.35
Total	17.27 19.28 (7.06) 24.36	17.38 19.01 (6.60) 23.98	17.15 18.87 (6.74) 23.89	16.30 18.11 (4.68) 20.98	15.53 17.70 (4.31) 19.84

[a]The first entry in each cell shows the first quartile (25th percentile), the second entry shows the second quartile (median), and the third entry shows the third quartile (75th percentile). The interquartile range is shown in parentheses.

males with elementary school education, but this may result from a greater number of years of grade school being completed by the urban origin men. A similar observation may be made about this relationship among men completing 1 to 3 years of college.

Among college graduates, the hypothesized inverse relationship between community size and age at school completion is observed (Figure 6.1). Urban origin men begin to complete their college educations at an age about one-third year earlier than rural origin men. This differential increases to one-half year or more when the median age at college completion is considered. Three-quarters of the men from suburbs of large cities and from small cities complete their college educations by 26.8 years of age. The comparable figure is 27.4 among men from large cities, 27.9 among rural nonfarm origin men, and 28.3 among rural farm origin

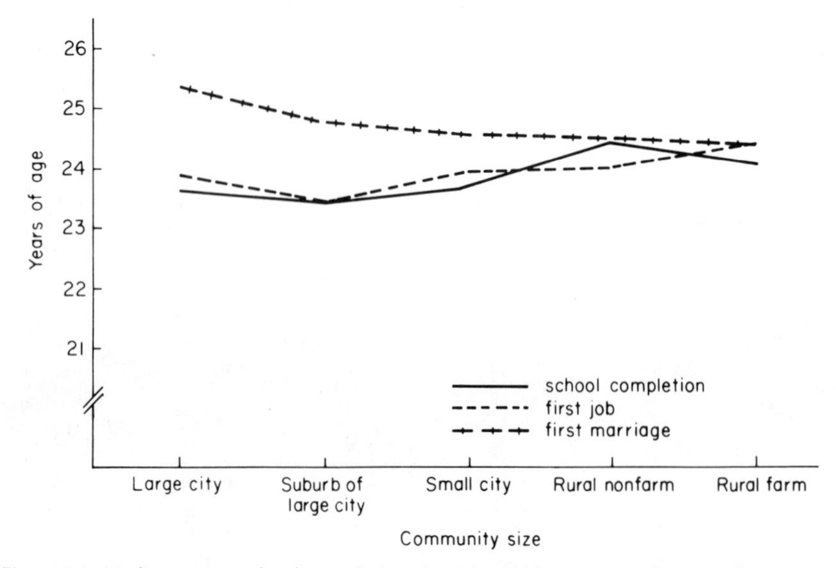

Figure 6.1. Median ages at school completion, first job, and first marriage by size of community at age 16, American males born 1907–1952, with 4 years of college.

men. The later ages at college completion characteristic of men from rural origins is in part a result of their greater propensity to interrupt schooling for 6 months or more, with 49.8% of the rural nonfarm origin men and 47.9% of the rural farm origin men reporting such interruptions compared to fewer than 41.6% of men from urban origins ($\chi^2 = 11.3$ with 4 degrees of freedom, $p < .025$; see Figure 6.2).

The inverse relationship between community size and age at school completion is even more pronounced among men with some graduate or professional school training. Among urban men, the average age at the completion of such advanced educations ranges from 26.8 years among men from suburban communities to 27.9 years among men from small towns. Rural men who complete 5 or more years of college have much later average ages at school completion (29.4 years among rural farm men and 30.0 among rural nonfarm men). Men from suburban communities are especially successful in finishing their graduate or professional schooling at a relatively early age; three-quarters of such men finish by 31.7 years of age compared to 33.5 years for men from large urban areas and 34.0 years for men from small town backgrounds. Men with rural origins often do not complete their graduate or professional education until well after their thirty-sixth birthdays. Men from rural areas consequently display a wider variation in the ages at which they complete 5 or more years of college.

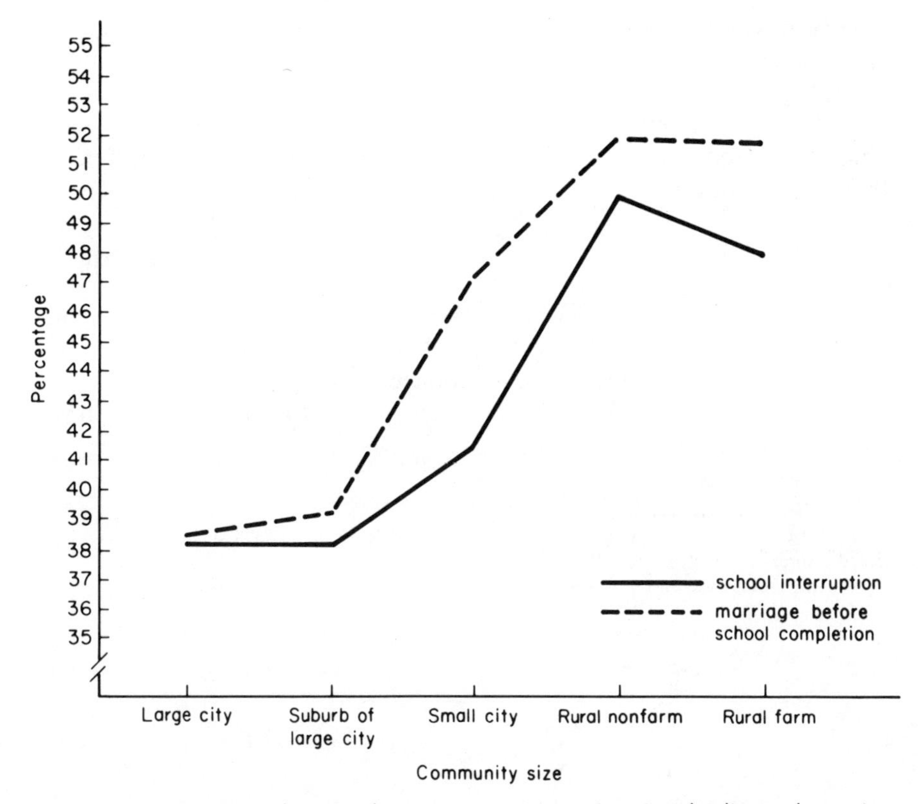

Figure 6.2. Percentage of men with one or more interruptions in schooling and marrying before the completion of schooling by size of community at age 16, American males born 1907–1952, with 4 years of college.

At this advanced level of education, men commonly experience one or more interruptions in schooling lasting 6 months or longer, especially men from small town and rural origins. (The percentage of men reporting such interruptions are 45.9 for those from large cities, 48.0 from suburban areas, 54.5 from small towns, 55.1 from rural nonfarm areas, and 63.5 from rural farm areas [$\chi^2 = 15.0$ with 4 degrees of freedom, $p < .01$].) The later age at college completion characteristic of the rural men may also be associated with more frequent repeat interruptions, longer interruptions, or a greater frequency of part-time rather than full-time school enrollments, possibilities that cannot be evaluated with the OCG-II data.

The findings to this point are largely consistent with the hypothesis that the broader opportunity structure provided by an urban environment facilitates an expeditious completion of schooling at the college level.

Men from rural environments commonly finish their college educations at an older age than men from urban environments, and they show a greater degree of variability in the age at which they complete their schooling. The slightly later age at college completion of men from large cities compared with men from the suburbs is an apparent exception to this generalization.

AGE AT FIRST JOB

Men from rural origins begin their first-job transitions more than one-half year earlier than men from urban areas, and their average age at first job averages about .7 years younger (Table 6.2). Men from rural origins complete their first-job transitions well before their twenty-third

Table 6.2
Measures of Age at First Job by Size of Community at Age 16 and Level of Schooling Completed, American Males Born 1907–1952

Educational Attainment	Community Size				
	Large City	Suburb of Large City	Small City	Rural Nonfarm	Rural Farm
Elementary, 0-8	14.52[a] 16.71 (6.14) 20.66	14.82 16.68 (5.69) 20.51	14.57 16.46 (4.48) 19.05	14.21 16.61 (6.03) 20.24	13.78 16.45 (6.44) 20.22
High School, 1-3	16.14 17.62 (3.85) 19.99	16.10 17.65 (3.84) 19.94	16.32 17.78 (3.65) 19.97	16.22 17.84 (3.85) 20.07	15.87 17.67 (4.15) 20.02
High School, 4	17.58 18.84 (3.54) 21.12	17.76 18.83 (3.08) 20.84	17.65 18.93 (3.75) 21.40	17.67 18.87 (3.30) 20.97	17.73 19.01 (3.64) 21.37
College, 1-3	19.18 21.29 (5.10) 24.28	19.30 21.30 (4.53) 23.83	19.53 21.54 (5.25) 24.78	19.44 21.14 (4.61) 24.05	19.47 21.27 (4.89) 24.36
College, 4	22.12 23.93 (4.26) 26.38	22.06 23.42 (3.52) 25.58	22.31 23.96 (3.90) 26.21	22.16 24.03 (4.69) 26.85	22.73 24.47 (4.49) 27.22
College, 5 or more	24.07 26.50 (5.99) 30.06	23.57 25.82 (4.68) 28.25	24.08 26.62 (6.21) 30.29	23.70 25.95 (7.65) 31.35	24.26 27.03 (6.63) 30.89
Total	17.57 19.93 (6.34) 23.91	17.70 19.81 (5.61) 23.31	17.54 19.94 (6.43) 23.97	17.07 19.12 (5.78) 22.85	16.53 18.85 (5.88) 22.41

[a] The first entry in each cell shows the 25th percentile, the second entry shows the median, and the third entry shows the 75th percentile. The interquartile range is shown in parentheses.

birthdays, whereas men from cities do not complete their first-job transitions until near their twenty-fourth birthdays. These differences in average age at first job are similar to size of place differentials observed in age at a school completion, with men from all types of communities reporting an average age at first job about one year older than their age at school completion. Among men of large city and suburban origin, the third quartile of the first-job transition is earlier than the third quartile of the education transition, suggesting that such men frequently begin working prior to their completion of schooling. Such a pattern would be consistent with the higher levels of education typically completed by such men.

Controlling for level of education, we observe the hypothesized differentials in age at first job among men with 4 or more years of college only among rural farm origin men. Among college graduates, men from urban and rural nonfarm areas begin work on average at 23.4 to 24.0 years of age compared to 24.5 years for men from rural farm origins (Figure 6.1). College graduates from the suburban areas show the earliest average age at first job and at the completion of the first job transition, whereas men from the rural areas are the latest. As anticipated, the duration of the first job transition is longer for college graduates from rural backgrounds; however, the interquartile range for residents of large cities is unexpectedly large.

Men with 5 or more years of college show the expected later age at first-job transition and longer duration of first-job transitions among the men from rural backgrounds. The differences are quite large, often amounting to two years or more. The average age at first job, as well as the age by which three-quarters of these highly educated men have begun working, is *earlier* than the average age as school completion for men from all community sizes, but differences are much more substantial among men from rural origins, as hypothesized.

AGE AT FIRST MARRIAGE

The age at which men begin the marriage transition is directly associated with size of place of residence, ranging from 20.9 years among rural farm origin men to 21.7 years among men from large urban communities (Table 6.3). Median age at marriage follows a similar pattern, with the maximum difference amounting to a 1-year earlier age at marriage among farm background men compared to those from large cities. Men from large urban communities have rather prolonged marriage transitions, with one-quarter of such men not married by age 28.6.

These community-size differences in age at first marriage charac-

Table 6.3
Measures of Age at First Marriage by Size of Community at Age 16 and Level of Schooling Completed, American Males Born 1907–1952

Educational Attainment	Community Size				
	Large City	Suburb of Large City	Small City	Rural Nonfarm	Rural Farm
Elementary, 0–8	21.44[a] 25.26 (11.21) 32.65	21.12 24.24 (8.73) 29.85	20.70 23.70 (8.12) 28.82	20.80 23.82 (8.86) 29.66	20.88 23.72 (7.74) 28.62
High School, 1–3	20.57 23.19 (6.68) 27.25	20.60 23.08 (6.28) 26.88	20.22 22.43 (5.63) 25.85	20.72 23.01 (5.83) 26.55	20.36 22.69 (5.72) 26.08
High School, 4	21.29 23.77 (6.55) 27.84	21.09 23.51 (5.64) 26.73	21.02 23.19 (5.49) 26.51	20.89 23.04 (5.16) 26.05	20.74 22.86 (5.17) 25.91
College, 1–3	21.88 24.41 (5.91) 27.79	22.06 24.43 (5.79) 27.85	21.79 24.10 (5.25) 27.04	21.62 23.69 (4.97) 26.59	21.18 23.54 (5.28) 26.46
College, 4	23.06 25.42 (6.23) 29.29	22.57 24.81 (5.71) 28.28	22.37 24.59 (5.27) 27.64	22.45 24.53 (6.12) 28.57	22.36 24.42 (5.12) 27.48
College, 5 or more	23.30 25.94 (6.71) 30.01	23.13 25.44 (6.28) 29.41	22.63 24.94 (5.93) 28.56	22.69 25.16 (5.54) 28.23	22.47 24.87 (6.61) 29.08
Total	21.70 24.35 (6.86) 28.56	21.55 24.02 (6.28) 27.83	21.29 23.63 (5.89) 27.18	21.11 23.49 (6.09) 27.20	20.88 23.30 (6.12) 27.00

[a]The first entry in each cell shows the 25th percentile, the second entry shows the median, and the third entry shows the 75th percentile. The interquartile range is shown in parentheses.

terize men completing each level of graded schooling and college. Although there are some inversions, in general, each of the parameters of the age-at-marriage transition (first quartile, median, third quartile, and interquartile range) are positively associated with community size. The previously observed positive association of age at marriage with size of *current* place of residence (Carter and Glick, 1970: Chapter 4) thus also holds among men classified according to the size of community of *origin*, controlling for level of education. These differentials in behavior quite possibly are the results of differences in preferred age at marriage, although we have no direct evidence concerning this.

Average age at the first-marriage transition is later than average age at school completion and first job among men from all community sizes, at every level of graded schooling, and among those with 1 to 3 years of college. Among college graduates, the marriage transition occurs after the school-completion and first-job transitions only among men from urban origins; men from rural origins experience the three transitions simultaneously. The marriage transition occurs prior to the school completion transition among all men completing 5 or more years of college, but the differential is largest among the rural origin men.

ORDERING OF EVENTS

These community-size differentials in the transition behavior of college-educated males are further manifested in the ordering patterns with which individual men complete the transition to adulthood (Table 6.4). Among men with 4 years of college, fewer than 40% of the large city and suburban men marry prior to completing school, compared to 47.3% of men from small towns and 51.7% of men from rural areas (Figure 6.2). Conversely, the college graduates from urban areas more commonly complete the transition to adulthood in the normatively preferred order. The majority of men with more than 5 years of college marry prior to completing their schooling, but the likelihood of doing so is greater among men with rural origins.

DURATION OF THE TRANSITION TO ADULTHOOD

Men from rural backgrounds experience a greater degree of overlap of the three transition regimes, and more commonly sequence their transition events in a disorderly fashion. These behaviors produce very pronounced size of community differentials in the length of the transition to adulthood among men at every level of education, with the length of the transition to adulthood being positively associated with community size at each level of education (Table 6.5).

LOG-LINEAR MODELS

Before drawing conclusions about the effects of size of community of origin on the timing and ordering of school completion, first job, and marriage, it is necessary to confirm that the results of this descriptive analysis persist when controls are introduced for birth cohort and military service. It also is useful to determine whether the effects of community size on transition behavior vary among the birth cohorts or between veterans and nonveterans. Answers to these questions are provided by log-linear modified multiple regression models of the effects of size of community of origin on transition behavior.

Table 6.4
The Temporal Ordering of Life-Course Events by Size of Community at Age 16 and Level of Schooling Completed, American Males Born 1907–1952

Educational Attainment	Community Size				
	Large City	Suburb of Large City	Small City	Rural Nonfarm	Rural Farm
Elementary, 1-8[b]	81.0[a] 14.4 4.5	82.1 15.4 2.5	82.0 14.6 3.5	78.4 19.0 2.6	76.4 20.8 2.9
High School, 1-3[c]	80.0 16.4 3.6	77.8 19.1 3.1	75.2 20.1 4.7	76.0 19.0 5.0	75.2 19.7 5.1
High School, 4[d]	68.0 22.2 9.8	70.6 20.9 8.5	69.1 22.0 8.8	70.6 21.3 8.1	67.3 23.7 9.0
College, 1-3[e]	41.3 23.7 35.0	43.1 21.3 35.6	47.7 22.7 29.6	49.4 21.8 28.7	49.4 19.7 30.9
College, 4[f]	46.3 15.2 38.5	44.3 16.5 39.2	41.5 11.2 47.3	37.6 10.6 51.8	36.6 11.7 51.7
College, 5 or more[g]	26.9 11.0 62.1	25.1 12.8 62.1	18.8 10.1 71.1	20.8 8.0 71.2	18.2 7.1 74.7
Total[h]	60.2 18.9 20.9	61.6 19.0 19.4	60.6 18.5 20.9	65.8 19.1 15.1	67.1 20.6 13.4

[a] The first entry in each cell shows the percentage of men with a normative ordering of events, the second entry shows the percentage with an intermediate nonnormative ordering pattern, and the third entry shows the percentage of men with an extreme nonnormative pattern. Normative ordering of events occurs when a man first completes school, next begins to work and lastly marries. The intermediate nonnormative pattern occurs when a man begins a job prior to finishing school or marries prior to beginning work, but after the completion of schooling. Extreme nonnormative ordering occurs whenever a man marries prior to the completion of his education.

[b] χ^2 = 18.8 with eight degrees of freedom, $p < .02$.

[c] χ^2 = 8.32 with eight degrees of freedom, $p > .4$.

[d] χ^2 = 6.2 with eight degrees of freedom, $p > .5$.

[e] χ^2 = 13.6 with eight degrees of freedom, $p < .10$.

[f] χ^2 = 22.5 with eight degrees of freedom, $p < .01$.

[g] χ^2 = 16.9 with eight degrees of freedom, $p < .03$.

[h] χ^2 = 112.9 with eight degrees of freedom, $p < .001$.

Table 6.5
The Duration of the Transition to Adulthood by Size of Community at Age 16 and Level of Schooling Completed, American Males Born 1907–1952

Educational Attainment	Community Size				
	Large City	Suburb of Large City	Small City	Rural Nonfarm	Rural Farm
Elementary, 0-8 . . .	19.24[a]	16.14	15.92	16.62	16.02
High School, 1-3. . .	11.72	11.17	10.18	10.91	10.59
High School, 4. . . .	10.51	9.27	9.10	8.64	8.52
College, 1-3.	7.94	8.01	7.47	7.28	7.16
College, 4.	7.41	6.32	5.73	6.17	5.17
College, 5 or more. .	5.40	5.04	3.76	3.17	3.91
Total	12.74	12.03	11.41	11.93	13.55

[a]The duration of the transition to adulthood operationally is defined as the number of years between the ages at which one quarter of the men in each of the social class and education groups complete their schooling and three-quarters of the men first marry.

The log-linear analyses confirm that the timing of school completion and first job vary significantly by size of community of residence at age 16, controlling for the effects of birth cohort and military service (Table 6.6). The likelihood of an interruption in schooling and the temporal ordering of transition events also varies by community size and level of education. As anticipated, the effects of community size on age at first marriage do not vary by level of education, although there are unanticipated differences between veterans and civilians. The effects of community size on school interruption differ by birth cohort, as well as by level of education.

The effects of community size on age at school completion fluctuate quite a bit from one level of education to the next, and from one size of place to the next (Table 6.7). There seem to be two consistent patterns. Men from small cities and rural communities who have elementary school educations finish their formal schooling earlier than men from large urban places. Among men with 4 years of college, urban origin men finish school relatively early and rural origin men are relatively unlikely to finish school early. Farm origin men are especially likely to finish college or graduate school relatively late. Despite the fluctuating pattern of exceptions, then, these results seem generally consistent with those of the survival table analysis.

Table 6.6
Models of the Effects of Size of Community at Age 16 on the Timing of Transition Events: American Males Born 1907–1952

Variables	Model[a]	χ^2_{LR}[b]	df[c]	p[d]	Δ[e]
Size of Community					
School interruption	(TLMC) (LPMC) (TLP) (TPC)	296.5	376	>.5	2.8
Age at school completion. . .	(TLMC) (LPMC) (TLP)	966.0	1224	>.5	6.8
Age at first job.	(TLMC) (LPMC) (TLP)	1005.9	1224	>.5	7.0
Age at first marriage	(TLMC) (LPMC) (TPM)	988.2	1272	>.5	6.6
Temporal ordering of events .	(TLMC) (LPMC) (TLP)	651.6	816	>.5	5.7

[a]Each model shown was selected using reverse stepwise procedures to include all statistically significant ($p \leq .05$) parameters in the model and to exclude all parameters not statistically significant ($p > .05$) from the model.

T = Timing variable. School interruption (no/yes), age at school completion, age at first job, age at marriage (first quartile/second quartile/third quartile/fourth quartile), temporal ordering of events (normative/intermediate nonnormative/ extreme nonnormative).

L = Level of education (0-8/9-11/12/13-15/16/17 or more).

M = Military service (no/yes).

C = Birth cohort (1948-52/1943-47/1938-42/1933-37/1928-32/1923-27/1918-22/1913-17/ 1907-12).

P = Size of place of residence (large city/suburb of large city/ small city/rural nonfarm/rural farm).

[b]χ^2_{LR} is the likelihood ratio chi-square statistic.

[c]df are the degrees of freedom

[d]p is the probability level that the chi-square statistic is due to chance.

[e]Δ is the index of dissimilarity between the observed sample frequencies and the expected sample frequencies obtained with that model.

These differences in the timing of school completion are tied closely to the prevalence of an interruption in schooling (Table 6.8). At the college level, the farm origin men much more frequently experience an interruption in schooling than men from urban places. Farm origin men were more likely to interrupt schooling if they were born in the early years of the century. Beginning with the cohort of 1918–1922 this pattern began to disappear. By the 1938–1942 birth cohort, the urban origin men were more likely to report an interruption in schooling lasting 6 months or more. These findings are net of the association of community size and birth cohort with level of education.

Table 6.7
The Net Odds Probability of Completing Schooling Relatively Early or Late by Size of Community at Age 16: American Males Born 1907–1952

Educational Attainment	Community Size				
	Large City	Suburb of Large City	Small City	Rural Nonfarm	Rural Farm
	Net Odds Probability of Completing School Early				
Elemementary, 0-8. . . .	0.778	0.605*	1.306	1.098	1.480*
High School, 1-3	0.962	1.016	0.817*	0.970	1.290*
High School, 4	1.542**	0.830*	0.884	0.977	0.905
College, 1-3	0.738*	0.977	0.941	1.213	1.214
College, 4	1.205	1.401*	1.251*	0.702	0.674*
College, 5 or more . . .	0.973	1.433*	0.899	1.128	0.707
	Net Odds Probability of Completing School Late				
Elementary, 0-8.	1.461*	1.436*	1.054	0.667*	0.678*
High School, 1-3	0.861	0.865	0.978	1.411*	0.973
High School, 4	1.047	1.022	1.172	0.899	0.886
College, 1-3	1.049	1.290	0.882	0.924	0.906
College, 4	1.036	0.843	0.964	0.898	1.323
College, 5 or more . . .	0.699	0.724	0.973	1.422	1.428

*Standardized value greater than 1.0

**Standardized value greater than 2.0.

The fluctuating pattern of timing of education by community size and level of education is carried over into the timing of first job (Table 6.9). Rural farm origin men with an elementary school education more frequently begin their first jobs relatively early, whereas the large urban and suburban origin men tend to begin their first jobs relatively late. Among men who are high school graduates or have some college, the men from large urban areas begin their first jobs relatively early. Farm origin college graduates tend to begin their first jobs relatively late.

The association of community size with the timing of first marriage does not differ by level of education, but it does vary according to military service experience. Among veterans, men from large cities tend to marry relatively early, whereas farm origin men tend to delay marriage until relatively late (Table 6.10). Among the civilians, the patterns are reversed, with men from large cities avoiding early marriage and the farm origin men more frequently marrying early.

Temporal ordering pattern is associated with community size differentially according to level of education. At the elementary school level, urban men are more likely to marry prior to completing their

Table 6.8
The Net Odds Probability of an Interruption in Schooling by Size of Community at Age 16 and Selected Independent Variables: American Males Born 1907–1952

Independent Variables	Community Size				
	Large City	Suburb of Large City	Small City	Rural Nonfarm	Rural Farm
Educational Attainment					
Elementary, 0-8	1.242*	1.104	1.102	0.831	0.796*
High School, 1-3.	0.980	0.819*	0.990	1.362*	0.925
High School, 4.	1.271**	1.056	1.038	0.776*	0.926
College, 1-3.	1.014	1.163*	1.006	0.930	0.906
College, 4.	0.792**	0.916	0.908	1.299*	1.168
College, 5 or more. . . .	0.805*	0.984	0.967	0.942	1.385*
Birth Cohort					
1948-52	1.221	0.931	1.388	0.877	0.722
1943-47	1.141*	1.158*	1.054	1.014	0.708*
1938-42	1.200*	1.134	0.946	0.931	0.834
1933-37	1.045	1.180*	0.965	0.795*	1.058
1928-32	1.002	0.893	1.035	1.003	1.077
1923-27	0.993	1.061	0.916	0.931	1.111
1918-22	0.805*	1.049	0.927	0.981	1.302*
1913-17	0.946	0.805*	1.008	1.170	1.114
1907-12	0.755**	0.866	0.845*	1.418*	1.276*

*Standardized value greater than 1.0.

**Standardized value greater than 2.0.

schooling than are men from rural areas (Table 6.11). The same is true of high school graduates and college dropouts, but not of high school dropouts. Among college graduates and among graduate students, persons from small cities and rural areas are more likely to marry before completing schooling than are men from large cities or their suburbs. Thus, the patterns of association of community size with temporal ordering pattern observed among men with four or more years of college persist when controls are introduced for the birth cohort and military service experiences of men.

SUMMARY

This analysis offers evidence in support of the hypothesis that size of community of origin affects the timing and ordering of school com-

Table 6.9
The Net Odds Probability of Beginning the First Job Relatively Early or Late by Size of Community at Age 16 and Level of Schooling Completed: American Males Born 1907–1952

Educational Attainment	Community Size				
	Large City	Suburb of Large City	Small City	Rural Nonfarm	Rural Farm
	Net Odds of Beginning First Job Early				
Elementary, 0-8	0.781	0.592*	1.015	1.218	1.751**
High School, 1-3.	0.946	1.069	0.824*	0.836	1.436**
High School, 4.	1.331**	0.869	1.034	0.952	0.878
College, 1-3.	1.163*	1.083	1.011	0.829	0.948
College, 4.	1.079	1.479*	1.185	1.052	0.503*
College, 5 or more.	0.810	1.137	0.965	1.184	0.950
	Net Odds of Beginning First Job Late				
Elementary, 0-8	1.172	1.378*	0.723*	0.938	0.913
High School, 1-3.	0.985	1.107	1.014	0.973	0.929
High School, 4.	0.963	1.057	1.155	0.799	1.064
College, 1-3.	0.954	1.121	1.141	1.011	0.811
College, 4.	0.918	0.663*	0.909	1.288	1.405
College, 5 or more.	1.027	0.836	1.139	1.053	0.972

*Standardized value greater than 1.0.

**Standardized value greater than 2.0.

Table 6.10
The Net Odds Probability of Marrying Relatively Early or Late by Size of Community at Age 16 and Military Service Experience: American Males Born 1907–1952

Military Service Experience	Community Size				
	Large City	Suburb of Large City	Small City	Rural Nonfarm	Rural Farm
	Net Odds Probability of Marrying Early				
Civilian	0.838*	1.040	1.049	0.998	1.095
Veteran.	1.193*	0.961	0.953	1.002	0.915
	Net Odds Probability of Marrying Late				
Civilian	1.128	1.000	1.084	0.914	0.895
Veteran.	0.887	1.000	0.923	1.094	1.117

*Standardized value greater than 1.0.

**Standardized value greater than 2.0.

Table 6.11
The Net Odds Probability of Normative and Extreme Nonnormative Ordering of Life-Course Events by Size of Community at Age 16 and Level of Schooling Completed: American Males Born 1907–1952

Educational Attainment	Community Size				
	Large City	Suburb of Large City	Small City	Rural Nonfarm	Rural Farm
	Net Odds Probability of a Normative Ordering Pattern				
Elementary, 0-8	0.895	1.095	1.101	0.979	0.947
High School, 1-3. . . .	1.239*	1.136	0.926	0.837	0.916
High School, 4.	0.871*	1.010	1.009	1.130	0.997
College, 1-3.	0.727**	0.814	1.089	1.164	1.332*
College, 4.	1.118	0.970	1.116	0.910	0.908
College, 5 or more. . .	1.274	1.008	0.800	1.018	0.957
	Net Odds Probability of Marriage before School Completion				
Elementary, 0-8	1.601*	1.023	1.028	0.793	0.749
High School, 1-3. . . .	0.882	0.828	0.987	1.267	1.095
High School, 4.	1.171	1.191	0.952	0.871	0.865
College, 1-3.	1.158	1.462*	0.809*	0.848	0.861
College, 4.	0.698*	0.793*	1.133	1.283	1.242
College, 5 or more. . .	0.748*	0.854	1.129	1.051	1.319

*Standardized value greater than 1.0.

**Standardized value greater than 2.0.

pletion, first job, and first marriage among American males born from 1907 to 1952. Size of community of origin is positively associated with the age at which groups of men begin and complete each of the three transition events; durations for each transition and for the overall transition to adulthood are longest for men from larger urban areas. These differentials are partly a result of the higher levels of education completed by men from the larger urban areas. Controlling for level of education, men from rural communities who complete 4 or more years of college are more likely to experience an interruption in their educations lasting 6 months or more, and take longer on average to complete a given level of schooling. Men from larger urban areas show a consistent tendency to finish their college education relatively early. Besides completing their education relatively late, the rural origin men show a greater variability in the age at which they typically complete 4 or more years of college.

The rural origin men with college degrees delay the beginning of their first job somewhat because of their later age at school completion.

These delays are insufficient to permit school to be completed prior to the beginning of work, for many of these men. Size of community of origin is positively associated with age at marriage. The rural origin men at each level of education thus marry at relatively early ages despite their later age at school completion and first job. A greater proportion of the rural origin men therefore marry prior to completing school and beginning work.

The rural nonfarm and rural farm origin men thus display transition behavior not unlike that of the lower social class background men. The behavior of men from cities of all sizes more closely resembles the behavior of white-collar origin men. Rural origins and lower social class families of origin are, of course, associated characteristics, and interpretation of the results of Chapters 5 and 6 must recognize this. Nonetheless, the correlation between community size and social class of origin is far from perfect. This analysis suggests that the social milieu in which men are raised has an important impact on their ability to achieve the transition to adulthood in an expeditious manner and in a normative fashion. Men who grow up in a *home* in which the father is employed in a blue-collar or farm occupation have a reduced probability of completing college, and lower status origins complicate the transition to adulthood of those men who complete college. Similarly, men who grow up in a rural *community* have a lower probability of completing college, and rural origins complicate the transition behavior of men who complete college. Thus, growing up in a community with a limited opportunity structure and growing up in a family with limited social and economic resources have similar effects on the timing and ordering of school completion, first job, and first marriage.

7

Ethnic Ancestry and the Transition to Adulthood

It is commonly believed that ethnic ancestry has important effects on the transition from adolescence to adulthood, but there is rather little empirical evidence for this hypothesis (Elder, 1978a, 1980). Ethnic ancestry is known to have direct effects on the level of schooling completed; blacks and Hispanics experience educational deficits and men of Jewish ancestry experience educational surpluses not accounted for by socioeconomic characteristics of family background. But nothing is known about the age at school completion of similarly educated men from different ethnic groups. Age at marriage is later among men of Irish birth and descent and earlier among first and second generation men from Southern and Eastern European nations, but these differentials do not persist among men who are third or later generation Americans (Carter and Glick, 1970; Hogan, 1978a). Nothing is known about the ordering of school completion, first job, and first marriage among American men of differing ethnic ancestry.

In this chapter, ethnic differentials in the timing and ordering of school completion, first job, and first marriage are examined. The total effects of ethnic ancestry on transition behavior, as well as the direct effects of ethnicity, controlling for educational attainment, are described. The issues of the persistence of these effects across birth cohorts and between military service veterans and nonveterans are then addressed by means of a log-linear analysis. Since relatively little is known about ethnic differentials in transition behavior, the analysis presented in this chapter is exploratory.

As described in Chapter 2, a man's ethnic ancestry is determined with reference to his responses to questions about his race and the original nationality of his family on his father's side. For men who mentioned more than one paternal ethnic ancestry, only the first response was coded in the OCG-II survey, and it is that response that is used in this analysis. Men who are not classifiable into one of the major ethnic groups are excluded from this analysis. Eight types of paternal ethnic ancestry are examined: British (English, Scottish, and Welsh); Irish; German; other Northern and Western European; Eastern European and Russian; Southern European; Hispanic; and black.

AGE AT SCHOOL COMPLETION

There are rather pronounced differentials in age at school completion among the ethnic groups, with Hispanics and blacks reporting a relatively early beginning, average, and completion age for the school transition and the English, Scottish, Welsh, Eastern Europeans, and Russians reporting relatively late ages for the school transitions (Table 7.1). The groups with the earliest education transition also report the shortest duration for that transition.

These ethnic differentials are only partially a result of differences in levels of schooling completed. Controlling for level of schooling, Hispanics and blacks have relatively late ages at the completion of graded schooling, and men of Eastern European and Russian ancestry report relatively early completion of graded schooling. Among men completing 2 to 3 years of college, the Southern Europeans, Hispanics, and blacks have average ages at school completion 1 year or more later than men with other ethnic origins. Delays in the completion of 1 to 3 years of college are especially characteristic of the Hispanics. Later-than-average ages at the completion of graded schooling or some college are associated with much-longer-than-average durations of the education transition.

Among the college graduates, there are no noteworthy differences in the average age at school completion among any of the Northern or Western or Central (i.e., German) European groups, all of whom begin the education transition at about 22 years of age, finish school on average at about 23.8 years of age, and complete the transition at about 27 years of age. The Southern and Eastern European men begin completing college about one-fourth year earlier on average and have a median age at college completion about one-half year earlier than the other European ethnic groups. The Southern European men complete the school transition at the same age as other European origin men, but the Eastern European and Russian men are about one-third older on average. Black and His-

Table 7.1

Measures of Age at School Completion by Paternal Ethnic Origin and Level of Schooling Completed, American Males Born 1907–1952

Educational Attainment	Ethnic Group							
	English, Scottish, Welsh	Irish	German	Other NW European	E. European & Russian	S. European	Hispanic	Black
Elementary, 0–8	13.42[a] 15.01 (2.98) 16.40	13.50 15.03 (2.84) 16.34	13.52 14.88 (2.83) 16.35	13.36 14.87 (2.80) 16.16	13.33 14.94 (3.30) 16.63	12.89 14.28 (2.89) 15.78	11.49 13.97 (4.54) 16.03	11.86 14.63 (4.88) 16.74
High School, 1–3	15.68 16.84 (2.29) 17.97	15.50 16.63 (2.28) 17.78	15.59 16.71 (2.21) 17.80	15.49 16.72 (2.45) 17.94	15.39 16.62 (2.56) 17.95	15.68 16.62 (2.03) 17.71	15.54 16.89 (3.06) 18.60	15.80 17.34 (3.03) 18.83
High School, 4	17.42 13.22 (1.92) 19.34	17.42 18.28 (2.12) 19.54	17.40 18.13 (1.75) 19.15	17.38 18.14 (1.70) 19.08	17.23 17.91 (1.74) 18.97	17.21 18.09 (1.92) 19.13	17.48 18.62 (2.84) 20.32	17.42 18.51 (2.58) 20.00
College, 1–3	19.65 22.09 (7.42) 27.07	19.70 22.34 (7.74) 27.44	19.72 22.18 (7.56) 27.28	19.71 21.76 (6.65) 26.36	19.50 22.00 (7.70) 27.20	19.93 23.40 (8.57) 28.50	20.11 24.44 (12.77) 32.88	19.85 23.09 (10.89) 30.74
College, 4	22.00 23.73 (4.88) 26.88	21.92 23.65 (5.12) 27.04	22.02 23.70 (5.02) 27.04	22.09 23.88 (4.84) 26.93	21.78 23.41 (5.52) 27.30	21.68 23.15 (5.25) 26.93	22.04 25.42 (10.45) 32.49	22.29 24.23 (9.14) 31.43
College, 5 or more	24.67 28.18 (9.72) 34.48	24.67 27.57 (9.74) 34.41	24.65 27.77 (8.25) 32.90	24.79 27.42 (7.95) 32.74	24.30 26.35 (7.54) 31.84	24.74 27.02 (7.84) 32.58	23.85 26.73 (10.30) 34.15	26.26 32.33 (14.34) 40.60
Total	17.45 19.47 (7.23) 24.68	16.96 18.61 (5.93) 22.89	17.23 18.75 (6.25) 23.48	17.11 18.64 (6.06) 23.17	17.21 19.44 (7.41) 24.65	16.59 18.44 (6.20) 22.79	14.73 17.59 (6.23) 20.96	15.74 18.15 (5.33) 21.07

[a] The first entry in each cell shows the first quartile (25th percentile), the second entry shows the second quartile (median), and the third entry shows the third quartile (75th percentile). The interquartile range is shown in parentheses.

panic college graduates begin the college transition at about the same age as other men, but the median age at college completion is about one-half year older among the blacks and one-and-a-half years older among the Hispanics, compared to men from other ancestral origins.

There are no statistically significant ethnic differences in the prevalence of one or more interruptions in regular schooling among college graduates ($\chi^2 = 10.9$, with 7 degrees of freedom, $p > .10$). The later age at college completion of blacks and Hispanics may arise from a pattern of more prolonged interruptions in regular schooling among the blacks and Hispanics, more frequent repeat interruptions, or from a greater reliance on part-time school enrollment. However, the OCG-II data do not permit a test of these possibilities.

The patterns of age at school completion are somewhat different among men with 5 or more years of college. The various European ancestry groups begin the school completion transition at roughly the same ages, but the Eastern European and Russian men have a median age at school completion about one year younger than the other men. They also enjoy a somewhat earlier age at the completion of the education transition. The Hispanic origin men with 5 or more years of college complete school at about the same age as other European ancestry men. A pattern of later age at school completion persists among the blacks who have a median 4 or more years later than the other ethnic groups. The black men with professional or graduate training display a grater degree of variability in the age at which they complete schooling.

The only major differences among the ethnic groups in the probability of having had an interruption in schooling lasting 6 months or longer is between the English, Scottish and Welsh who are prone to such interruptions (58.2% versus 53% for the population of college graduates overall), and the Southern and Eastern Europeans who less frequently are subject to such interruptions (42.5%; $\chi^2 = 15.9$, with 7 degrees of freedom, $p < .05$). Therefore, the later age at the completion of graduate and professional education of blacks cannot be attributed to higher risk of an interruption in schooling but must be a function of some other characteristic of their school enrollment behavior.

Very few blacks and Hispanics achieve advanced levels of education, so the results reported here are subject to rather large sampling errors. In general, it appears that the major differences in school completion are between the Hispanics and blacks, on the one hand, and the other European ethnic groups on the other; the former have relatively late ages at the completion of each level of schooling, especially at the college level, and a somewhat longer duration of the education transition. Among ethnic groups, blacks and Hispanics control the fewest economic resources. The social class composition of the ethnic groups probably accounts for some of the observed ethnic differentials.

Among the nonblack, non-Hispanic ethnic groups, an Eastern European or Russian ancestry facilitates the education transition at every level of schooling, especially the college level. This is a rather mixed ethnic group, including Catholic Poles as well as Eastern European Jews. Eastern European Jews attain higher levels of education than can be accounted for by their social origins (see Featherman, 1971). It may be that the same factors that cause such men to excel in educational attainment may also facilitate their expeditious completion of school.

AGE AT FIRST JOB

Men of Hispanic and black ancestry begin their first-job transitions at relatively early ages, as do men of Southern European ancestry (Table 7.2). The median age at first job occurs earlier among these three groups, in particular for the Hispanics. Blacks also complete the first-job transition at a relatively early age. Conversely, the men of English, Scottish, Welsh, Eastern European, and Russian ancestry have an average age at first job about one year older than other ethnics, and they finish the first-job transition at a relatively late age (24.3 years).

These patterns are related to the different levels of schooling completed by the various ethnic groups. The parameters of the first-job transition fluctuate somewhat among the ethnic groups for men at different levels of graded schooling. The most consistent pattern is for men who are of Hispanic or black ancestry to begin their first jobs at a later average age than other men and to complete their first-job transitions at a relatively late age. This pattern persists among men with 1 to 3 years of college.

There are no consistent patterns in first-job transition behavior among the ethnic groups with 4 or more years of college. In part, this may result from the sampling variability to which the Hispanic and black calculations are subject. Among the college graduates the age at which men begin the first-job transition varies rather little, ranging from 21.7 among the Southern European group to 22.5 among the men of other Northern and Western European origin. The median age at first job is relatively late for the English, Scottish, Welsh, other Northern and Western European, and Hispanic men compared to men of all other ethnic ancestries. The age at completion of the first-job transition is relatively late for these three ethnic groups and for the blacks.

Among men with 5 or more years of college, the blacks stand out as having quite late average ages af first job (29.0 years) compared to

Table 7.2

Measures of Age at First Job by Paternal Ethnic Origin and Level of Schooling Completed, American Males Born 1907–1952

	Ethnic Group							
	English, Scottish, Welsh	Irish	German	Other NW European	E. European & Russian	S. European	Hispanic	Black
Elementary, 0-8	14.36[a]	14.93	14.22	14.36	14.28	14.23	13.70	14.02
	16.61 (5.93)	16.59 (4.66)	16.40 (5.44)	16.08 (4.68)	16.75 (6.05)	16.13 (6.47)	16.48 (7.44)	16.74 (5.89)
	20.29	19.59	19.66	19.04	20.33	20.70	21.14	19.91
High School, 1-3	16.13	16.06	15.92	16.04	16.25	16.09	16.31	16.24
	17.54 (3.59)	17.61 (4.21)	17.42 (3.37)	17.69 (3.58)	17.82 (4.37)	17.35 (3.78)	18.07 (4.71)	18.01 (4.08)
	19.72	20.27	19.29	19.62	20.62	19.87	21.02	20.32
High School, 4	17.73	17.75	17.55	17.57	17.59	17.44	17.67	17.92
	18.91 (3.34)	18.98 (3.59)	18.72 (3.23)	18.75 (3.15)	18.81 (3.63)	18.67 (3.41)	19.24 (4.15)	19.40 (3.82)
	21.07	21.34	20.78	20.72	21.22	20.85	21.82	21.74
College, 1-3	19.34	19.32	19.41	19.49	18.99	19.24	19.11	19.77
	21.45 (5.20)	21.42 (4.66)	21.23 (4.70)	21.23 (4.48)	21.10 (4.66)	21.39 (5.80)	21.88 (7.07)	22.12 (5.03)
	24.54	23.98	24.11	23.97	23.65	25.04	26.18	24.80
College, 4	22.43	22.29	22.14	22.47	22.03	21.73	21.28	22.26
	24.17 (4.12)	23.68 (3.67)	23.79 (3.70)	24.15 (4.07)	23.40 (3.89)	23.69 (4.42)	24.48 (6.49)	23.88 (5.14)
	26.55	25.96	25.84	26.54	25.92	26.15	27.77	27.40
College, 5 or more	24.07	23.64	24.04	23.93	23.80	23.22	23.70	24.80
	26.68 (5.89)	25.90 (5.33)	26.05 (5.24)	26.58 (5.74)	26.04 (5.48)	26.18 (6.49)	26.43 (6.48)	28.96 (8.46)
	29.96	28.97	29.28	29.67	29.28	29.71	30.18	33.26
Total	17.90	17.38	17.50	17.42	17.75	17.06	15.98	16.62
	20.43 (6.49)	19.63 (5.71)	19.58 (5.82)	19.51 (5.94)	20.47 (6.55)	19.70 (6.25)	18.65 (7.05)	18.96 (5.67)
	24.39	23.09	23.32	23.36	24.30	23.31	23.03	22.29

[a]The first entry in each cell shows the 25th percentile, the second entry shows the median, and the third entry shows the 75th percentile. The interquartile range is shown in parentheses.

men from other ethnic groups (25.9 to 26.7 years). Black men also begin and complete the first-job transition relatively late, looking at men with advanced levels of education. As among college graduates, the first-job transition among Hispanic, English, Scottish, Welsh, and other Northern European groups is relatively late, but not as late as this transition is among blacks.

AGE AT FIRST MARRIAGE

Men of English, Scottish, Welsh, Irish, German, and other Northern and Western European ancestry all begin the marriage transition at about 21.3 years, and marry on average at about 23.6 years of age (Table 7.3). The Irish have a somewhat later age at the completion of this first-marriage transition, perhaps as a result of a pattern of very delayed marriage among a minority of the men of Irish ancestry. The blacks have an age-at-marriage pattern similar to that of their European ethnic groups, although the third quartile of the age-at-marriage transition is 28.8 years—more than one year later than that of the Irish. Hispanic marriage patterns resemble those of the blacks. The only groups with distinctively different marriage transitions are composed of men of Eastern European, Russian, and Southern European ancestry who do not begin the marriage transition until about 1 year later than other men. The median age at marriage of these groups is about 1.7 years later, and the third quartile of their marriage transition is more than 2 years later.

This pattern of ethnic differentials persists largely when controls are introduced for education. The only major ethnic differential in age at marriage among men with less than a college education is the much later age at marriage characteristic of the men of Southern and Eastern European and Russian ancestry. Among all men with more than a high school education, the men of Southern and Eastern European ancestry begin the marriage transition relatively late and marry at a later average age than other European men. A later average age at marriage also characterizes the black and Hispanic men. The Irish display some signs of delayed marriage compared with other men of Northern and Western European ancestry only at the professional and graduate school level of education. However, the age at marriage of Irish men does not exceed that of the Southern and Eastern European, Hispanic, or black men at any level of education.

Men of Southern and Eastern European ancestry thus have relatively early ages at school completion and relatively late ages at marriage, whereas men of Northern, Western and Central European ancestry (i.e., the British, Irish, Germans, and men of other Northern and Western

Table 7.3
Measures of Age at First Marriage by Paternal Ethnic Origin and Level of Schooling Completed, American Males Born 1907–1952

Educational Attainment	Ethnic Group							
	English, Scottish, Welsh	Irish	German	Other NW European	E. European & Russian	S. European	Hispanic	Black
Elementary, 0-8	20.72[a] 23.66 (7.01) 27.73	20.86 23.88 (7.92) 28.78	21.30 24.07 (7.43) 28.73	21.17 24.23 (9.16) 30.33	22.70 26.73 (11.41) 34.11	23.15 26.61 (8.38) 31.53	20.72 24.03 (8.27) 28.99	20.60 23.87 (9.99) 30.59
High School, 1-3	20.36 22.77 (5.56) 25.92	20.41 22.64 (5.71) 26.12	20.45 22.67 (5.84) 26.29	20.53 22.72 (5.31) 25.84	21.46 24.55 (8.33) 29.79	21.50 24.44 (6.67) 28.17	20.34 23.11 (6.32) 26.66	20.77 23.59 (6.91) 27.68
High School, 4	20.82 23.06 (5.13) 26.13	20.99 23.31 (5.95) 26.94	21.06 23.20 (5.19) 26.25	21.17 23.27 (5.13) 26.30	22.11 24.66 (6.98) 29.09	21.92 24.63 (7.02) 28.94	21.07 23.98 (6.64) 27.71	21.14 23.53 (6.64) 27.78
College, 1-3	21.62 23.79 (5.29) 26.91	22.01 24.44 (5.23) 27.24	21.59 23.89 (5.32) 26.91	21.44 23.44 (5.04) 26.48	22.75 25.07 (5.50) 28.25	22.92 25.21 (5.22) 28.14	22.11 25.48 (7.46) 29.57	21.86 24.94 (6.08) 27.94
College, 4	22.48 24.60 (5.39) 27.87	22.54 24.65 (5.61) 28.15	22.40 24.35 (4.83) 27.23	22.46 24.59 (5.12) 27.58	23.28 26.26 (6.59) 29.87	23.09 25.70 (6.17) 29.26	24.68 28.14 (7.39) 32.07	22.79 25.25 (6.16) 28.95
College, 5 or more	22.55 24.75 (5.91) 28.46	22.90 25.44 (8.80) 31.70	22.69 24.95 (6.11) 28.80	22.89 24.87 (5.59) 28.48	23.91 26.29 (6.22) 30.13	23.85 27.05 (6.23) 30.08	24.71 26.71 (5.96) 30.67	23.67 26.32 (5.88) 29.55
Total	21.31 23.66 (5.66) 26.97	21.30 23.77 (6.27) 27.57	21.37 23.60 (5.55) 26.92	21.36 23.62 (5.80) 27.16	22.62 25.46 (7.23) 29.85	22.37 25.26 (6.78) 29.15	21.02 24.18 (7.61) 28.63	21.14 23.91 (7.65) 28.79

[a] The first entry in each cell shows the 25th percentile, the second entry shows the median, and the third entry shows the 75th percentile. The interquartile range is in parentheses.

European ancestry) have relatively late ages at school completion and relatively early ages at marriage. A comparison of average age at school completion with average age at first marriage demonstrates that the differences are largest among the men of Southern and Eastern European origin, among men at each level of education from grammar school to college graduate. Among those men with 5 or more years of college, average age at marriage is less than average age at school completion for all men of Northern, Western, and Central European ancestry; only for those of Southern, Eastern European and Russian, and Hispanic ancestry do age at school completion and marriage coincide. Among men with college education, the Hispanics follow a transition pattern similar to that of the Southern and Eastern European ancestry men.

ORDERING OF EVENTS

Men with Eastern European or Russian paternal ethnic ancestry more frequently order their school completion, beginning of first job, and first-marriage transitions in a normative fashion, controlling for level of education (Table 7.4). Conversely, men of Eastern European and Russian origin less frequently marry prior to completing school. Men of Southern European ancestry also tend to delay marriage until after the completion of schooling, but this pattern is less pronounced than among men of Eastern European and Russian ancestry. The patterns among blacks and Hispanics vary across levels of education. There are no differences in temporal ordering patterns among the groups of Northern, Western, and Central European ancestry.

DURATION OF THE TRANSITION TO ADULTHOOD

Men of Eastern and southern European ancestry, as well as Hispanics and blacks, have relatively long transition times, with more than 12.5 years elapsing between the time they begin to complete school and the time they finish the first-marriage transition (Table 7.5). Men from the groups of Northern, Western, and Central European ancestry complete the transition to adulthood in 9.5 to 10.6 years. These patterns persist within education groups. The only exception is that black men who reach the college-degree level of schooling complete the transition to adulthood relatively quickly. The data provide no evidence of a prolonged duration of the transition to adulthood among the Irish, except among those men with 5 or more years of college. At such an advanced level of education, the Irish have a late third quartile for the marriage transition, producing a prolongation of the transition to adulthood.

Table 7.4
The Temporal Ordering of Life Course Events by Paternal Ethnic Origin and Level of Schooling Completed, American Males Born 1907–1952

Educational Attainment	Ethnic Group							
	English, Scottish, Welsh	Irish	German	Other NW European	E. European & Russian	S. European	Hispanic	Black
Elementary, 0-8[b]	76.7[a]	83.9	77.4	82.3	78.7	81.1	80.8	75.3
	19.4	13.2	20.8	14.2	18.6	16.2	14.3	20.1
	4.0	2.9	1.9	3.5	2.7	2.8	4.9	4.7
High School, 1-3[c]	78.7	74.1	77.8	80.5	81.0	83.2	72.1	72.2
	16.7	21.3	18.6	17.6	16.0	16.3	18.6	20.4
	4.6	4.6	3.6	1.9	3.1	0.5	9.3	7.4
High School, 4[d]	69.0	67.9	69.6	71.3	75.6	72.8	62.0	69.0
	21.7	21.3	22.9	19.4	18.4	21.4	21.9	20.5
	9.3	10.8	7.6	9.3	6.0	5.8	16.1	10.5
College, 1-3[e]	45.8	47.1	43.2	47.4	46.7	46.0	41.6	36.1
	20.4	21.1	23.2	22.9	23.9	20.5	22.8	29.9
	33.8	31.8	33.6	29.7	29.4	33.4	35.5	34.0
College, 4[f]	41.6	42.8	38.0	43.5	53.4	40.2	40.4	51.1
	14.9	12.2	15.3	10.5	14.1	18.3	20.5	8.8
	43.5	45.0	46.7	46.0	32.6	41.5	39.0	40.0
College, 5 or more[g]	19.9	25.0	23.1	19.4	31.3	16.9	39.7	11.3
	9.8	8.5	8.5	7.9	15.4	20.9	12.6	10.4
	70.3	66.6	68.5	72.7	53.2	62.2	47.7	78.4
Total	57.6	63.3	60.7	63.5	63.3	65.0	67.4	66.0
	18.4	18.5	20.2	17.2	18.0	19.4	18.2	20.4
	24.1	18.2	19.1	19.4	18.7	15.5	14.5	13.7

[a]The first entry in each cell shows the percentage of men with a normative ordering of events, the second entry shows the percentage with an intermediate nonnormative ordering pattern, and the third entry shows the percentage of men with an extreme nonnormative pattern. Normative ordering of events occurs when a man first completes school, next begins to work and lastly marries. The intermediate nonnormative pattern occurs when a man begins a job prior to finishing school or marries prior to beginning work, but after the completion of schooling. Extreme nonnormative ordering occurs whenever a man marries prior to the completion of his education.

[b]$\chi^2 = 18.6$ with fourteen degrees of freedom, $p > .15$.

[c]$\chi^2 = 29.7$ with fourteen degrees of freedom, $p < .01$.

[d]$\chi^2 = 36.5$ with fourteen degrees of freedom, $p < .01$.

[e]$\chi^2 = 9.8$ with fourteen degrees of freedom, $p > .5$.

[f]$\chi^2 = 19.5$ with fourteen degrees of freedom, $p > .14$.

[g]$\chi^2 = 35.0$ with fourteen degrees of freedom, $p < .01$.

[h]$\chi^2 = 106.8$ with fourteen degrees of freedom, $p < .001$.

Table 7.5
The Duration of the Transition to Adulthood by Paternal Ethnic Origin and Level of Schooling Completed, American Males Born 1907–1952

Educational Attainment	Ethnic Group							
	English, Scottish, Welsh	Irish	German	Other NW European	E. European & Russian	S. European	Hispanic	Black
Elementary, 0-8	14.31[a]	15.28	15.21	16.97	20.78	18.64	17.50	18.73
High School, 1-3. . . .	10.24	10.62	10.70	10.35	14.40	12.49	11.12	11.88
High School, 4.	8.71	9.52	8.85	8.92	11.86	11.73	10.23	10.36
College, 1-3.	7.26	7.54	7.19	6.77	8.75	8.21	9.46	8.09
College, 4.	5.87	6.23	5.21	5.49	8.09	7.58	10.03	6.66
College, 5 or more. . .	3.70	7.03	4.15	3.69	5.83	5.34	6.82	3.29
Total	9.52	10.61	9.69	10.05	12.64	12.56	13.90	13.05

[a]The duration of the transition to adulthood operationally is defined as the number of years between the ages at which one-quarter of the men in each of the social class and education groups complete their schooling and three-quarters of the men first marry.

LOG-LINEAR MODELS

Before we can draw conclusions about the effects of paternal ethnic ancestry on the timing and ordering of school completion, first job, and marriage, we must confirm that the results of the descriptive survival table analysis persist when controls are introduced for birth cohort and military service. It is also useful to determine whether the effects of ethnic ancestry vary among the birth cohorts or between veterans and nonveterans. Answers to these questions are provided by log-linear modified multiple regression models of the effects of paternal ethnic ancestry on transition behavior.

The effects of ethnic ancestry on transition behavior vary according to the level of education only for the school-completion transition (Table 7.6). The effects of ethnic ancestry on age at first marriage differ among birth cohorts but not by level of education. There are direct effects of ethnic ancestry on age at first job, the likelihood of an interruption in schooling, and the temporal ordering of events, but these effects do not interact with the other independent variables. There are no higher-order (i.e., four-way or five-way) interactions among the independent variables and transition behavior.

The net effects of ethnic ancestry on the relative timing of school completion by level of education are shown in Table 7.7. Net of the effects of military service and birth cohort, men from English, Scottish, Welsh, Irish, and German ancestry relatively rarely complete high school early, whereas men of Southern European and black ancestry frequently complete high school at a relatively early age. The Irish men more frequently complete high school relatively late, but the other ethnic groups do not display any tendency toward a late age at completion of high school. The Hispanic and black men also tend to complete their graded schooling relatively early. This early completion of graded school is probably associated with fewer years of elementary school completed, but it is difficult to offer a satisfactory interpretation of the earlier age at completion of high school that is characteristic of the ethnic groups of lower socioeconomic status.

The results of the analysis for persons with 4 or more years of college are only partially consistent with the findings of the survival table analysis. The men of Eastern European and Russian ancestry have a pronounced tendency to avoid a late age at the completion of graduate school. Blacks are especially unlikely to complete their college educations relatively early. The other ethnic groups display no pronounced patterns, and the Eastern European and Russian men tend to complete 4 years of college at an average age. The Northern and Western European

Table 7.6
Models of the Effects of Paternal Ethnic Origin on the Timing of Transition Events: American Males Born 1907–1952

Variables	Model[a]	χ^2_{LR} [b]	df[c]	p[d]	Δ[e]
Ethnic Ancestry					
School interruption	(TLMC)(LEMC((TE)	553.3	749	>.5	4.2
Age at school completion. . .	(TLMC)(LEMC)(TLE)	1598.0	2142	>.5	9.7
Age at first job.	(TLMC)(LEMC)(TE)	1653.5	2247	>.5	10.2
Age at first marriage	(TLMC)(LEMC)(TEC)	1497.2	2079	>.5	8.8
Temporal ordering of events .	(TLMC)(LEMC)(TE)	1088.9	1498	>.5	7.9

[a]Each model shown was selected using reverse stepwise procedures to include all statistically significant ($p \leq .05$) parameters in the model and to exclude all parameters not statistically significant ($p > .05$) from the model.

T = Timing variable. School interruption (no/yes), age at school completion, age at first job, age at marriage (first quartile/second quartile/third quartile/fourth quartile), temporal ordering of events (normative/intermediate nonnormative/extreme nonnormative).

L = Level of education (0-8/9-11/12/13-15/16/17 or more).

M = Military service (no/yes).

C = Birth cohort (1948-52/1943-47/1938-42/1933-37/1928-32/1923-27/1918-22/1913-17/1907-12).

E = Paternal ethnic ancestry (English, Scottish, Welsh/Irish/German/Other Northwest European/Eastern European and Russian/Southern European/Hispanic/Black).

[b]χ^2_{LR} is the likelihood ratio chi-square statistic.

[c]df are the degrees of freedom.

[d]p is the probability level that the chi-square statistic is due to chance.

[e]Δ is the index of dissimilarity between the observed sample frequencies and the expected sample frequencies obtained with that model.

ethnic groups tend to avoid a late completion of college, but often experience a late completion of graduate school.

While the ethnic differences in the timing of school completion vary according to level of education, the ethnic differences in the probability of an interruption in schooling are constant across levels of education (Table 7.6). The Irish, Hispanics, and blacks more frequently experience interruption in school (the gammas are 1.097, 1.231, and 1.077, respectively; tabulations not shown), whereas the men of Eastern European and Russian ancestry, the Germans, and the Southern Europeans have

Table 7.7
The Net Odds Probability of Completing Schooling Relatively Early or Late by Paternal Ethnic Origin and Level of Schooling Completed: American Males Born 1907–1952

Educational Attainment	Ethnic Ancestry							
	English, Scottish, Welsh	Irish	German	Other NW European	E. European & Russian	S. European	Hispanic	Black
	Net Odds Probability of Completing School Early							
Elementary, 0-8.	0.900	0.746	0.597	0.831	0.738	1.074	1.936*	1.960*
High School, 1-3	0.957	1.099	1.203	1.105	0.941	0.669*	0.978	1.162
High School, 4	0.721**	0.764*	0.815*	0.825	1.031	1.348*	1.146	1.695**
College, 1-3	1.174	1.097	1.262*	1.206	1.108	0.718	0.665	0.964
College, 4	1.185	1.142	1.216	1.021	1.070	1.417	0.635	0.618*
College, 5 or more	1.158	1.274	1.114	1.073	1.177	1.016	1.090	0.435*
	Net Odds Probability of Completing School Late							
Elementary, 0-8.	1.213	1.262	1.311	1.102	1.850*	0.642	0.500*	0.761
High School, 1-3	1.120	0.819	0.795*	1.175	1.291	0.802	0.961	1.175
High School, 4	1.108	1.286*	0.952	0.989	0.893	0.857	1.146	0.849
College, 1-3	0.753	0.795	1.042	0.826	0.874	1.947*	1.121	1.017
College, 4	0.710	0.846	0.836	0.880	1.098	1.048	2.284*	0.861
College, 5 or more	1.242	1.119	1.158	1.074	0.489*	1.111	0.708	1.505

*Standardized value greater than 1.0.

**Standardized value greater than 2.0.

lower rates of schooling interruption (gammas of .816, .920, and .858, respectively). The lower rates of school interruption among the men of Eastern European and Russian ancestry probably account for their less frequent completion of graduate school at relatively late ages. The more frequent interruptions in schooling among the blacks and Hispanics are probably related to their later ages at the completion of advanced schooling. The patterns, however, are complex and not amenable to straightforward summarization.

Ethnic ancestry has direct effects on the timing of first job net of the other independent variables, but this effect does not vary by level of education (Table 7.6). The English and Irish men less frequently begin work early (tabulation not shown; gammas are .851 and .876, respectively). Southern European men more frequently begin working relatively early compared to other ethnic groups (gamma = 1.232). Men of German and Northern and Western European origin avoid late job beginnings (gammas are .779 and .747, respectively). Black and Hispanic men often delay their job beginning until relatively late ages (gammas are 1.519 and 1.681, respectively). These results are consistent with the findings of the survival table analysis.

Ethnic differences in age at first marriage differ by birth cohort but not by level of education. As discussed in Chapter 5, the birth-cohort variable both acts as a proxy for truncation of experiences and represents true birth-cohort differences. The cohort differentials in age at marriage are statistically significant but display few obvious patterns (Table 7.8). The Germans display an intercohort increase in the likelihood of an early marriage, whereas the blacks show an intercohort decrease in rates of early marriage. The English, Scottish, and Welsh, and other Northern and Western European men show a curvilinear trend in the probability of an early marriage, with the tendency toward an early marriage peaking among men born in the late 1920s and 1930s. Generally, opposite patterns are observed for the probability of a late marriage. There are few readily interpretable patterns, however.

The temporal ordering of events varies by ethnic ancestry, but this effect is statistically constant among the different levels of education (Table 7.6). While the tabulations are not shown, the results are consistent with those reported in Table 7.4. Men of Eastern European and Russian ancestry are more likely to have a normative ordering pattern (gamma = 1.369) and less likely to marry prior to completing school (gamma = .643). Men of Southern European ancestry also display low rates of marriage before school completion (gamma = .760). Hispanics and blacks, conversely, less frequently report normative ordering patterns (gammas are .753 and .797, respectively) and more frequently marry

Table 7.8
The Net Odds Probability of Marrying Relatively Early or Late by Paternal Ethnic Origin and Birth Cohort: American Males Born 1907–1952

Educational Attainment	Ethnic Ancestry							
	English, Scottish, Welsh	Irish	German	Other NW European	E. European & Russian	S. European	Hispanic	Black
	Net Odds Probability of Marrying Early							
1948-52	0.842	0.875	1.635	0.799	1.412	1.403	0.956	0.549
1943-47	0.785*	0.988	1.723**	1.066	0.953	1.483	1.026	0.485*
1938-42	1.093	0.753*	1.085	1.172	1.311	1.477	0.989	0.499*
1933-37	1.505*	1.238	1.385*	1.099	1.297	0.612	0.543*	0.818
1928-32	1.076	0.919	0.861	1.476*	1.052	0.721	0.989	1.060
1923-27	1.122	0.971	1.174	0.966	0.768	0.998	1.040	1.017
1918-22	0.721*	1.294	0.760	0.867	0.885	0.727	1.274	1.983*
1913-17	1.139	1.031	0.570*	0.821	0.811	0.985	1.262	1.807
1907-12	0.927	1.042	0.540*	0.899	0.754	1.032	1.148	2.387*
	Net Odds Probability of Marrying Late							
1948-52	0.940	1.126	0.641	1.512	0.864	0.951	1.499	0.792
1943-47	1.814*	1.297	0.591*	0.957	1.030	1.011	0.673	1.071
1938-42	0.984	0.999	1.164	0.807	0.691	1.379	1.051	1.082
1933-37	1.047	0.949	1.046	1.138	0.614*	0.788	1.083	1.614*
1928-32	1.020	0.978	1.190	1.070	0.934	1.006	0.915	0.917
1923-27	0.823	1.443*	0.984	0.622*	1.618*	0.794	0.679	1.578*
1918-22	1.072	0.681*	1.190	0.896	1.326	1.413	0.769	0.892
1913-17	0.809	0.893	1.292	1.010	1.293	0.891	1.326	0.695
1907-12	0.783	0.841	1.204	1.249	1.023	0.951	1.377	0.754

*Standardized value greater than 1.0.

**Standardized value greater than 2.0.

before completing school (gammas are 1.487 and 1.206, respectively). Men from other ethnic ancestries do not differ from the average for all men.

SUMMARY

There are no substantial differences in transition behavior among men of English, Scottish, Welsh, Irish, German, and Northern and Western European ancestry. Despite the extensive attention that has been devoted to the topic, it does not appear that the delayed-marriage pattern characterizing the Irish in Europe has persisted among men of Irish ancestry in the United States in the twentieth century except perhaps among a small number of Irish men who complete five or more years of college. In fact, the Irish, along with these other groups of Northern, Western, and Central European ancestry, are characterized generally by relatively late average ages at school completion and first job and relatively early marriages. Many of these men marry prior to completing their schooling, especially those with 4 or more years of college.

Men of Eastern European, Russian, and Southern European ancestry complete any given level of schooling relatively early and marry for the first time relatively late. They marry prior to completing schooling less frequently than men of other European ancestry, and they take a longer time to complete the transition to adulthood. These patterns are more pronounced among the Eastern European and Russian men than among the Southern Europeans. These two groups of men differ in that the former begin their first jobs relatively late, whereas the latter begin working relatively early.

Among men of black and Hispanic ancestry the age at school completion was relatively late, the age at first job relatively early, and the age at first marriage relatively late. Despite their delayed marriages, it appears that men of black and Hispanic ancestry marry prior to completing schooling more commonly than other ethnic groups, although the results fluctuate across the education groups due to sampling variability.

These distinctive ethnic patterns may arise from different causes. Blacks and Hispanics commonly come from families with limited financial resources and more frequently grew up in rural communities. Their distinctive pattern of transition behavior is of the sort anticipated for men from these poorer socioeconomic origins. Therefore, it seems likely that the distinctive transition behaviors of blacks and Hispanics are a product of these groups' socioeconomic origins and not of their particular ethnic ancestry. This hypothesis is tested in Chapter 8.

The Southern and Eastern European origin men also come from

relatively depressed social origins. However, they more frequently grew up in urban communities. A poorer social class background would be expected to delay the age at school completion, but these men display the opposite tendency. It may be that growing up in an urban community counteracts the effects of social class background. It seems likely that neither their social class background nor size of community of origin can account for the later age at marriage characteristic of these men. Featherman (1971) has shown that men of Eastern European and Russian ancestry (but not of Southern European ancestry) achieve high levels of education that cannot be accounted for by their social backgrounds. The same may prove true for their distinctive pattern in the transition to adulthood. Tests of the hypotheses that these ethnic differentials do persist when controls are introduced for social class background and size of community of origin are reported in Chapter 8.

8

Social Class, Community Size, Ethnic Ancestry, and Transition Behavior

The independent effects of social class, community size, and ethnic ancestry on the timing and ordering of school completion, first job, and first marriage were described in Chapters 5, 6, and 7. The basic assumption underlying these analyses has been the argument that family-background characteristics affect the timing of transition events indirectly through years of schooling completed and directly through accessibility to resources that facilitate the completion of advanced levels of education. Men from social backgrounds that offer limited access to resources experience a later age at the completion of schooling, a higher prevalence of one or more interruptions in schooling, and more variability in the age at which they complete schooling.

Delays in the completion of schooling are accompanied by delays in the beginning of first, full-time job held after the completion of schooling, but the delays are insufficient to prevent the beginning of first job from preceding the completion of schooling for many of these men. Delays in the completion of schooling and beginning of first job do not appear to force postponements in marriage beyond the usual age for men at the same level of schooling. Men whose social backgrounds are an impediment to the completion of schooling thus are much more likely to marry prior to completing their schooling. Considered together, these characteristics of transition behavior result in a shorter duration of time to complete the transition to adulthood for men from poorer social and economic backgrounds.

The characteristics of a man's father and of the community in which he grew up are both important factors differentiating the transition to adulthood. The effects of social class are probably primarily economic in character, and result from the lesser economic assistance that a blue-collar or farm family can provide to help its son complete college. Men from lower social class backgrounds more freqently provide financing for their own college educations. Aside from academic scholarships and loans (about which we have no evidence), the primary sources of such resources would be G.I. Bill benefits and/or employment prior to the completion of schooling, both of which entail interruptions in regular schooling. Marriage prior to the completion of schooling may facilitate the completion of schooling if the wife supports herself and her husband while the husband is enrolled in school. Men from lower-status social class backgrounds appear to make more frequent use of each of these nonparental sources of economic support.

Men from rural communities of origin tend to have lower-status social class backgrounds than men from urban communities. At least part of the effects of community of origin on transition behavior probably are accounted for by this association. But it seems likely that, independent of its association with social class, growing up in a rural community is an impediment to the transition to adulthood. Rural communities provide a social milieu with a narrower range of educational services than that found in urban communities. Men of rural origin more frequently will have to migrate to an urban community in which a college is located in order to attend college, whereas men of urban origin more frequently will be within commuting distance of a college. Men of urban origin frequently will have the option of reducing college costs by living in their parents' home while attending college, whereas men of rural origin rarely will have that option. Such a method of reducing costs would be especially important for men from families with few economic resources.

These interpretations are based on the supposition that a rural community of origin delays the completion of advanced levels of education, net of the effects of social class. It seems probable that the higher prevalence of interruptions in schooling and later age at the completion of advanced schooling associated with a lower social class background may be greater in rural areas and small towns than in urban areas. These two hypotheses are empirically tested in this chapter.

Men who are black or Hispanic experience delays in school completion, more frequently have one or more interruptions in their schooling, begin their first jobs somewhat later, and complete their transitions in a relatively short period of time because of the disorderly sequencing of the school-completion, first-job, and first-marriage transitions. Blacks and Hispanics generally have access to relatively few family or community resources since they more freqently come from blue-collar or farm origins and from rural communities. This suggests that the effects of a black or Hispanic ancestry on transition behavior will disappear when social class and community origins are controlled. This hypothesis is tested in this chapter.

Although they tend to come from lower status social class backgrounds, men whose paternal ethnic ancestry is Southern or Eastern European (including Russian) have earlier ages at school completion, fewer interruptions in their schooling, a later age at first marriage, and a more orderly pattern of transition behavior. This pattern is most pronounced among the men of Eastern European and Russian ancestry. This appears to be an effect of ethnicity on transition behavior which will persist net of controls for social class origin and community size, a hypothesis tested in this chapter.

It is difficult to assess the precise meaning of these findings about ethnic differences in transition behavior. Featherman (1971) has shown that Jewish men from all ethnic groups attain about 1.5 years more schooling than other men, controlling for social background characteristics, whereas Catholics from all ethnic ancestries attain one-third to one-half year less education than other men. Featherman suggests that these religio-ethnic differences in educational attainment may be related to motivational or personality variables influencing educational attainments. If the findings about ethnic differentials in transition behavior had applied only to the men of Eastern European and Russian ancestry, it would have been tempting to infer that the finding reflected the behavior of Jews and extend Featherman's argument about motivational factors for educational attainment to issues of the timing of school completion. However, the applicability of our findings to the Southern European men renders such an argument inappropriate.

The Southern and Eastern European men are among the most recent migrants to America. It may be that the ethnic differences in transition behavior result from their retention in America of Old World norms about transition behavior. This would help account for the later age at marriage and the less frequent pattern of marrying prior to school completion that characterizes these men. Such an explanation would also account for the finding of no differences in transition behavior among the other European immigrant groups who migrated to America in the eighteenth and nineteenth centuries, and who would be more thoroughly assimilated to American norms for the transition to adulthood.

Neither social class, community size, nor ethnic ancestry display any marked effects on overall transition behavior among men with elementary or secondary levels of education. Rather, the effect of each of these family-background characteristics is limited to men with a college education and is most pronounced among those men with 4 or more years of college. It is at these levels that a poorer social background (in terms of either social and economic resources or opportunity structure) acts as an impediment in the transition to adulthood. Controls for the birth-cohort and military-service compositions of the educational and social background groups do not explain these effects of background characteristics on transition behavior at different levels of education.

ANALYSIS

In this chapter, the unique effects of each social background variable on transition behavior, controlling for the other two background variables, are identified. In order to reduce the size of the matrices to be analyzed, the social background variables have been recategorized by combining categories that displayed no significant differences in behavior in the analysis conducted thus far. The three categories of social class background are white-collar, blue-collar, and farm. Size of community of residence at age 16 distinguishes large-city residents and suburban residents; small-city and town residents; and rural residents. Four groups of paternal ethnic ancestry are used: Northern, Western, and Central European (i.e., English, Scottish, Welsh, Irish, German, and other Northern and Western Europeans); Eastern European and Russian; Southern European; and Hispanic and black. The level-of-education variable is unchanged except that elementary and some high school groups are combined. In order to reduce further the size of the matrices to be analyzed, controls for birth cohort and military experience are not included. Since the introduction of these controls did not alter the effects of the social background variables on transition behavior, their exclusion from this analysis should not create any difficulties.

Each of the five transition variables is examined in turn. Each matrix subjected to log-linear analysis is thus a *transition behavior by level of education by social class by size of community of residence by paternal ethnic ancestry* cross-tabulation. Reverse stepwise procedures are used to identify the model that includes all statistically significant ($p \leq .05$) parameters and excludes all parameters not statistically significant ($p >$ .05). These procedures identify the model that is most parsimonious in explaining the association of the social-background variables with each type of transition behavior. The resultant model includes the effects of all variables that, singly or in combination, affect transition behavior.

The results of the analysis are presented in Table 8.1. The models for age at school completion, age at first job, and the temporal ordering

Table 8.1
Models of the Net Effects of Social Background Variables on the Timing of Transition Events: American Males Born 1907–1952

Dependent Variable	Model[a]	X^2_{LR} [b]	df[c]	p[d]	Δ[e]
School interruption	(LSPE)(TLS)(TLP)(TLE)(TSP)	102.1	136	>.5	1.6
Age at school completion. . .	(LSPE)(TLS)(TLP)(TLE)	307.0	420	>.5	3.7
Age at first job.	(LSPE)(TLS)(TLP)(TLE)	311.3	420	>.5	3.7
Age at first marriage	(LSPE)(TLP)(TLE)(TSP)(TPE)	309.0	414	>.5	3.5
Temporal ordering of events .	(LSPE)(TLS)(TLP)(TLE)	187.1	280	>.5	2.7

[a]Each model shown was selected using reverse stepwise procedures to include all statistically significant ($p \leq .05$) parameters in the model and to exclude all parameters not statistically significant ($p > .05$) from the model.

T = Timing variable. School interruption (No/Yes); age at school completion; age at first job; age at first marriage (first quartile/second quartile/third quartile/fourth quartile); temporal ordering of events (normative/intermediate nonnormative/extreme nonnormative).

L = Level of education (0-11/12/13-15/16/17 or more).

S = Social class (white collar/blue collar/farm).

P = Size of place of residence (large city or suburb/small city/rural).

E = Paternal ethnic ancestry (Northern, Western, and Central European/Eastern European and Russian/Southern European/Hispanic and Black).

[b]X^2_{LR} is the likelihood ratio chi-square statistic.

[c]df are the degrees of freedom.

[d]p is the probability level that the chi-square statistic is due to chance.

[e]Δ is the index of dissimilarity between the observed sample frequencies and the expected sample frequencies obtained with that model.

of events each show statistically significant effects of the three background variables on transition behavior, effects that vary according to level of education. There are no interactions among the family-background variables in their effects on these transition behaviors. Social class, community size, and ethnic ancestry thus each exert a unique effect on age at school completion, age at first job, and the temporal ordering of events. Each of these variables index unique components of social background as it influences transition behavior. Social class, community size, and ethnicity also have unique effects on the probability of an interruption in schooling. In addition, there is an interaction between social class background and size of community in their effects on rates of school interruption. As observed earlier, there are no social class differentials in age at marriage that vary by level of education, but there are education-specific effects of ethnicity and community size on age at marriage. There is an interaction in the effects of social class and community size on age at marriage. Age at marriage also varies by the joint effects of community size and ethnicity.

Table 8.2 shows the net odds probability of an interruption in schooling lasting 6 months or more by social class background and size of community at age 16. The probability of an interruption in schooling varies relatively little by community size for men from blue-collar backgrounds. Men whose fathers were farmers, farm managers, or farm laborers but lived in small towns are less likely to interrupt their schooling than men who lived in rural areas. For men from white-collar origins, residence in a small city enhances the likelihood of school dropout, whereas residence in a large city or its suburb reduces the likelihood of school dropout. The combined effects of farm origin and rural residence or of white-collar origin and small town residence are higher than the additive effects of either social class or size of place of residence. The size of this interaction does not vary by level of schooling.

Community size and social class interact in their effects on age at marriage, although the size of the interaction is small (Table 8.1). The major difference is that rural origin men from blue-collar backgrounds tend to have a pattern of early marriage, whereas rural origin men whose fathers were engaged in farming avoid early marriage (Table 8.3). Community size also interacts with ethnic origin in its effects on age at

Table 8.2
The Net Odds Probability of an Interruption in Schooling by Social Class Background and Size of Community at Age 16: American Males Born 1907–1952

Community Size	Social Class		
	White Collar	Blue Collar	Farm
Large city or suburb.	0.917	1.054	1.034
Small city.	1.112	1.027	0.875
Rural	0.980	0.923	1.105

*Standardized value greater than 1.0.

**Standardized value greater than 2.0.

Table 8.3
The Net Odds Probability of Marrying Relatively Early or Late by Social Class Background and Size of Community at Age 16: American Males Born 1907–1952

Community Size	Social Class		
	White Collar	Blue Collar	Farm
	Net Odds Probability of Marrying Early		
Large city or suburb. . . .	1.007	0.948	1.047
Small city.	0.984	0.949	1.071
Rural	1.009	1.112	0.891
	Net Odds Probability of Marrying Late		
Large city or suburb. . . .	0.950	1.013	1.040
Small city.	1.054	1.005	0.945
Rural	0.999	0.983	1.018

marriage (Table 8.1). Men of Northern, Western, and Central European ancestry, as well as blacks and Hispanics, have low rates of early marriage if they grow up in large cities or suburbs and high rates of early marriage if they come from rural areas (Table 8.4). Southern European men have high rates of early marriage if they grow up in large cities and low rates of early marriage if they grow up in rural areas. This difference in behavior may have to do with the recency of the immigration of ethnic groups to the United States. Southern European immigrants to the United States come predominantly from rural areas of Europe and have settled in large American cities. Men of Southern European ancestry and from rural origins would be disproportionately composed of first generation immigrants. International migrants usually have later ages at first marriage (Hogan, 1978a).

In Chapter 7 I suggested that the greater frequency of interruptions in schooling, the later age at college completion, and the disorderly pattern of events characteristic of blacks and Hispanics may result from their deprived socioeconomic backgrounds, whereas the less frequent interruptions, the earlier age at college completion, and the normative order of events characteristic of men of Southern European, Eastern

Table 8.4
The Net Odds Probability of Marrying Relatively Early or Late by Size of Community at Age 16 and Paternal Ethnic Ancestry

Ethnic Ancestry	Community Size		
	Large City or Suburb	Small City	Rural
	Net Odds Probability of Marrying Early		
Northern, Western and Central European. . . .	0.721*	1.025	1.353*
Eastern European and Russian	1.144	0.802	1.090
Southern European	1.505*	1.344	0.495*
Hispanic and Black. . . .	0.806	0.905	1.372*
	Net Odds Probability of Marrying Late		
Northern, Western and Central European. . . .	1.129	1.011	0.876
Eastern European and Russian	0.898	1.029	1.083
Southern European	1.023	0.788	1.240
Hispanic and Black. . . .	0.965	1.220	0.849

*Standardized value greater than 1.0.

European, and Russian ancestry cannot be accounted for by their socioeconomic background. The effect parameters (gammas) estimated for the log-linear models shown in Table 8.1 provide a test of this hypothesis. Controlling for social class background and size of community of residence at age 16, men of black and Hispanic ancestry are more likely to experience an interrruption in schooling compared with other men, for those men with elementary school or 1 to 3 years of high school education (Table 8.5). The rate of school interruption is also higher than average among blacks and Hispanics with 4 years of high school. At more advanced levels of education, the blacks and Hispanics have lower net rates of school interruption than other men. This pattern is especially pronounced among men with 4 years of college. Men of Southern European ancestry experience lower than average rates of school interruptions at lower levels of education but higher than average rates of school

Table 8.5
The Net Odds Probability of an Interruption in Schooling by Paternal Ethnic Ancestry and Level of Schooling Completed, Controlling for Social Class Background and Size of Community at Age 16: American Males Born 1907–1952

Educational Attainment	Ethnic Group			
	Northern, Western, and Central European	Eastern European and Russian	Southern European	Black and Hispanic
Elementary 0-8, and High School, 1-3. . .	0.935	0.843	0.881	1.441**
High School, 4.	0.911	1.060	0.905	1.143
College, 1-3.	1.076	1.086	0.959	0.892
College, 4	1.108	1.158	1.112	0.701*
College, 5 or more . .	0.984	0.889	1.177	0.971

*Standardized value greater than 1.0.

**Standardized value greater than 2.0.

interruptions if they have 4 or more years of college. The men of Eastern European and Russian origin experience lower than average rates of school interruption when they have less than a high school or graduate school education, but higher than average rates of school interruption when they have 4 years of college.

Age at school completion also varies by ethnic ancestry and level of education, controlling for social class background and community size. Men of Northern, Western, and Central European origin are less likely than other men to finish graded school relatively early, but they are somewhat more likely to finish college relatively early (Table 8.6). Men of Eastern European and Russian ancestry show the opposite pattern, being more likely to finish graded schooling relatively early and more likely to finish 1 to 4 years of college relatively late. Men of Southern European ancestry avoid a late completion of graded schooling, but somewhat more commonly experience a relatively late college dropout. Black and Hispanic men show more variation in age at finish of 5 years or more of college, being more likely to complete such schooling either relatively early or relatively late. Blacks and Hispanics also tend to be relatively late at the completion of 4 years of college.

The previously observed pattern of ethnic differentials in the ordering of transition events reverses when controls are introduced for social class and size of community of origin (Table 8.7). Black and

Table 8.6
The Net Odds Probability of Completing Schooling Relatively Early or Late by Paternal Ethnic Ancestry and Level of Schooling Completed, Controlling for Social Class Background and Size of Community at Age 16: American Males Born 1907–1952

Educational Attainment	Ethnic Ancestry			
	Northern, Western, and Central European	Eastern European and Russian	Southern European	Black and Hispanic
	Net Odds of Completing School Early			
Elementary 0-8, and High School, 1-3 . .	0.749*	1.212*	1.013	1.087
High School, 4	0.801*	1.182*	1.043	1.012
College, 1-3	1.377*	0.970	0.859	0.871
College, 4	1.149	0.949	1.081	0.848
College, 5 or more . .	1.053	0.758	1.019	1.230
	Net Odds of Completing School Late			
Elementary 0-8, and High School, 1-3 . .	1.611*	0.834	0.767*	0.971
High School, 4	1.071	0.761*	1.145	1.071
College, 1-3	0.825	1.169	1.321	0.785
College, 4	0.665	1.469	0.900	1.138
College, 5 or more . .	1.057	0.917	0.958	1.076

*Standardized value greater than 1.0.

Hispanic men with grade school or some high school education are more likely to marry prior to completing school. They are less likely to do so if they have 4 or more years of college. The same pattern is observed among the men of Eastern European and Russian origin. This contrasts with the experience of men of Southern European origin who commonly have normative ordering patterns at the graded schooling level but, at the college level, are more likely to marry before college completion. Northern, Western, and Central European men who have 5 or more years of college are, on average, more likely to experience a normative or extreme nonnormative ordering pattern, and less likely to experience an intermediate ordering pattern, than other men.

Thus, at the college bachelor-degree level, blacks and Hispanics have lower levels of school interruption than other men but are more likely to complete school relatively late. Despite their late age at school

Table 8.7
The Net Odds Probability of Normative and Extreme Nonnormative Ordering of Life-Course Events by Paternal Ethnic Ancestry and Level of Schooling Completed, Controlling for Social Class Background and Size of Community at Age 16: American Males Born 1907–1952

Educational Attainment	Ethnic Ancestry			
	Northern, Western, and Central European	Eastern European and Russian	Southern European	Black and Hispanic
	Net Odds Probability of a Normative Ordering Pattern			
Elementary 0-8, and High School, 1-3 . .	1.011	0.786	1.570	0.802
High School, 4	0.895	1.019	1.297	0.845
College, 1-3	1.059	0.924	1.249	0.817
College, 4	0.843	1.149	0.732	1.411
College, 5 or more . .	1.238	1.176	0.537	1.278
	Net Odds Probability of Marriage before School Completion			
Elementary, 0-8, and High School, 1-3 . .	0.858	1.297	0.530	1.696
High School, 4	0.920	1.007	0.846	1.275
College, 1-3	0.883	0.938	1.434	0.842
College, 4	1.049	0.946	1.371	0.735
College, 5 or more . .	1.368	0.862	1.134	0.748

completion, the black and Hispanic college graduates tend to adhere to a normative ordering of events. Men of Eastern European and Russian origin with 4 years of college have average rates of school interruption but tend to complete school relatively late, delaying the beginning of first job and marriage until after the completion of their schooling. The introduction of controls for social class and community size thus reversed the transition behavior characteristic of blacks and Hispanics but left the behavior of men of Eastern European and Russian ancestry unchanged.

At the graduate and professional school level, men of Eastern European and Russian ancestry have lower rates of school interruption, whereas blacks and Hispanics have average rates of school interruption. The Eastern European and Russian men most commonly complete their graduate schooling in the middle quartiles of age at school completion, whereas the blacks and Hispanics tend to complete such training either relatively early or relatively late. Men from both groups tend to adhere to a normative ordering pattern.

It thus appears that differences in social class background and size of community of residence do account for the higher rates of school interruption and nonnormative ordering pattern characteristic of blacks and Hispanics. In fact, their patterns reverse when these family-background resource variables are included in the model.

Earlier I discussed the idea that men from poorer socioeconomic backgrounds who have late ages at school completion may marry prior to completing their schooling in order to capitalize on the financial assistance a working wife could contribute. It is interesting to observe that men of black, Hispanic, Eastern European, and Russian ancestry tend to adhere to normative ordering patterns despite their late ages at school completion, when family resources are taken into account. These results therefore indicate that the difference in financial resources of ethnic groups is an important factor in the determination of their ordering of events.

The models of Table 8.1 indicate that the gross effects of social class and community size persist when controls are introduced for all of the social background variables simultaneously. An inspection of the gamma parameters of the models indicate that there are no major differences between the previously described gross effects of social class and community size on transition behavior and the net effects estimated by these models (tabulations not shown).

CONCLUSIONS

The analyses presented in Part III of this book have empirically tested the hpothesis that social background characteristics differentiate the transition process through which American adolescents become adults. These analyses have confirmed that social class of family of origin, size of community of residence at age 16, and paternal ethnic ancestry each uniquely affect the timing and ordering of school completion, first job, and first marriage. Social background differences in educational attainment are an important cause of these differentials in transition behavior. Lower educational attainments are one reason why men from blue-collar and farm origins, rural communities, and blacks and Hispanics in general have earlier ages at school completion, the beginning of work, and first marriage.

Men who complete post-high-school levels of education remain in school longer and finish school at a later age than men with an elementary or secondary school education. Men tend to delay the start of their first jobs and their first marriages until after their schooling is completed. But the prolongation of school enrollment associated with a college education requires the postponement of first job and first marriage until relatively advanced ages, if men adhere to the usual ordering pattern of transition events. The longer men remain in school, the more likely they are to begin working at their first job and/or to marry prior to completing school.

Among men with a college education, men from blue-collar and farm origins, from rural communities, and of black and Hispanic ancestry more frequently experience one or more interruptions in schooling, and they have later ages at the completion of schooling. Associated with these delays in completing schooling are slight delays in the beginning of first job and first marriage. These slight delays are insufficient, however, to prevent a large proportion of these men from beginning work and first marrying prior to finishing their schooling. In contrast, there are remarkably few social background differentials in the transition behavior of men who complete less than a college education.

Among persons with less than a college education, school completion, full-time entry into the labor force, and the formation of family of procreation are temporally separate transitions, with relatively little overlap. Among men with a college education, these transitions are compacted into a shorter time interval. There is a greater degree of simultaneity in the transitions of college educated men, and such men are more likely to marry prior to completing their schooling and beginning their first, full-time jobs. This compacting of transition events is most pronounced among the college-educated men from blue-collar or farm origins, from rural communities, and of black and Hispanic ancestry.

These effects of social background characteristics on the transition behavior of college-educated males do not vary systematically among birth cohorts. However, there have been intercohort increases in college attendance, and a growing proportion of college-educated men in each cohort have come from lower status social backgrounds. This change in the social background and educational composition of the cohorts has meant that an increased proportion of men have been subject to the transition pattern characteristic of the college-educated, lower status men. As a result, the transition behavior of birth cohorts of American males has shifted to a pattern resembling that of college-educated men from blue-collar and farm origins, and from rural communities.

Intercohort increases in the age at school completion and in the probability of beginning work and/or first marrying prior to completing schooling thus are not simply a function of increased levels of education associated with modernity. Rather, the social background characteristics of males brought into the school system as a result of social welfare expenditures have been productive of intercohort changes in transition behavior. Intercohort increases in social welfare expenditures on education attracted increased percentages of men from all social backgrounds into the schools, but the expenditures were insufficient to permit men from poorer social backgrounds to complete their schooling as quickly, and with as few interruptions, as men from richer social backgrounds. Many of the men from poorer social backgrounds chose to attend college despite the greater likelihood that financial pressures might force interruptions in their schooling or delays in its completion. Men from social backgrounds that provided greater resources could choose to attend college with the prospect of fewer interruptions in schooling, and a relatively early age at school completion. These different circumstances surrounding the school-completion transition had unique effects on the timing of first job and first marriage, with resulting ramifications for the entire transition to adulthood. Thus, the ways in which men from different social class, community size, and ethnic backgrounds have responded to historical changes in the opportunities for a college education have been productive of intercohort changes in the timing and ordering of events making the transition from adolescence to adulthood.

IV

The Consequences of Early Life-Course Transition Behavior

The life course consequences of the timing and ordering of school completion, beginning of first job, and first marriage for occupational and earnings attainments and for marital stability are identified in Part IV of this book. The life-course perspective that guides this study suggests that the timing and ordering of early life transitions are contingencies that affect the later life history (Elder, 1974a). The nature and size of the consequences of early-life transition behavior for career and family histories may vary over the life course. For example, some timing patterns may have important consequences for career achievements, immediately after the transition to adulthood, consequences that are altered by the passage of time and the intervention of mitigating factors or compensatory action. Other timing patterns may have career consequences that persist over the life course.

Previous studies have provided evidence that the timing of early life-course transitions affects the occupational and earnings attainments of American men. Interruptions in schooling may reduce the earnings attainment of men, and an early age at first job seems to depress occupational attainments (Featherman and Carter, 1976; Ducan *et al.*, 1972; Ornstein, 1976). An early age at marriage, an early age at first childbirth, and a premarital conception or birth depress career attainments (Duncan *et al.*, 1972; Coombs and Freedman, 1970; Freedman and Coombs, 1966). But these studies also indicate that a substantial number of the associations are explained by the poorer social origins of men who are "off-time'' in their transitions or who have disorderly sequences of transition events.

Most previous studies have used absolute age at the time of a transition. The analysis presented in Part III demonstrated the importance of distinguishing whether a man is relatively early or late in a transition, or on time in a transition with reference to men at the same level of educational attainment. Part IV of this book therefore emphasizes the life-course consequences of the *relative timing* of each transition, rather than examine the effects of absolute age at each transition. This decision, although based on substantive considerations, facilitates the statistical separation of the effects of age at school completion and years of schooling completed. The consequences of the *temporal ordering* of school completion, beginning of first job, and first marriage for careeer achievement and marital stability also are traced in Part IV.

The relative timing of each transition, and the temporal ordering pattern of the transitions, are defined as in Part III. Since the consequences of transition behavior for career achievements and family stability may vary over the life course, the analysis is conducted for groups of men at different points in the life course. The occupational and earnings attainments of men are examined at three career stages: (*a*) men at the start of their careers (operationally defined as those beginning their first job in the five-year period prior to the 1973 survey); (*b*) men who are at a point in their careers of consolidation and building (operationalized as men who began working at their first full-time jobs 10 to 14 years prior to the survey); and (*c*) men who are in the prime of their careers (having begun their first job 25 to 29 years prior to the survey). The consequences of the timing of transition events on marital instability are examined for successive 5-year marriage cohorts.

In general, I anticipated that the consequences of the timing of transition events would be largest in the early adult years and would diminish as a person ages. Such a pattern would be reflected in the analysis by a finding that the occupational and earnings attainments consequences of transition behavior are greatest among the youngest job-tenure cohort, of somewhat diminished importance among men who have been working 10 to 14 years, and least among those men who are in the prime of their careers. Similarly, differentials in the prevalence of marital instability will be greatest among the most recent marriage cohort, if the consequences of transition behavior diminish over the life course. On the other hand, differentials in career attainments or marital instability that are most pronounced among the middle or later cohorts but do not occur among the youngest cohort are probably best interpreted as the result of intercohort changes in the consequences of transition behavior. An exact test of the hypothesis that the consequences of transition behavior diminish over the life course requires life-history data on the occupational and earnings attainments and the marital stability of men from a number of different cohorts. Intercohort analysis of the consequences of transition behavior over the life course would provide a test of the hypothesis. Unfortunately, the OCG-II survey did not collect this type of life-history data. Instead, the consequences of transition behavior at different points in the life course must be inferred from intercohort comparisons of the experiences of men in 1973. Such an approach is problematic, since any intercohort differences would be interpreted as resulting from life course stage (Baltes *et al.*, 1979). This shortcoming must be kept in mind in interpreting the results described in Part IV.

A variety of social background characteristics that are known to affect occupational and earnings attainments also differentiate the transition behavior of men. Controls for these background variables are introduced in the occupational and earnings attainment models in order to isolate the true effects of transition behavior on attainments. This analysis is restricted to ever-married white males who are currently in the experienced civilian labor force with 1972 earnings of at least $1000. This restriction limits the analysis to men who have completed school, are in the labor force, have some earnings, and have married; it eliminates the potentially confounding effects of race. Where possible, controls are included for the father's occupational status (Duncan Socioeconomic Status Scale), the father's years of completed education, and whether a man is from a farm background. Years of graded schooling and years of college are included in the models to control for differing levels of educational attainment. Since military service is an important factor influencing the transition to adulthood and may also affect occupational and earnings attainments (Mason, 1970), it is included as a variable in the models. Variables for occupational status and number of weeks worked during the year are included in the 1972 earnings attainment equations. The inclusion of these independent variables in the models permits the identification of the ways in which family background resources and education are converted into occupational and earnings attainments for men with each type of transition behavior.

The consequences of transition behavior for marital stability are examined among men who have been married at least once, and who therefore have been exposed to the risk of separation or divorce. (Men whose first marriage ended because of the deaths of their wives are excluded from the analysis.) In addition to marriage cohort, controls are included for level of education and race, two variables known to have a strong association with marital instability (Carter and Glick, 1970; Bumpass and Sweet, 1972).

The occupational consequences of the timing and ordering of the early life transition events are the subject of Chapter 9. The analysis of occupational attainments includes an examination of transition behavior differences in intergenerational (father to son) and career (first job to 1973 occupation) occupational mobility, classifying respondents according to ordered major occupation groups. Transition group differences in the process of converting family background resources and education into occupational status also are examined. The consequences of transition behavior for earnings attainments are reported in Chapter 10, for marital stability in Chapter 11. In Chapter 12, the major findings of this study are reviewed. There, theoretical conclusions are drawn about differentials and changes in the causes and consequences of early life course transitions.

9

The Transition to Adulthood and Career Occupational Attainments

In this chapter, the consequences of the timing and ordering of early life transitions for the occupational attainments of American men are identified. In the first part of this chapter, the processes by which men with different transition behaviors are assigned to specific occupational groups are described. In the second part of the chapter, the occupational status attainments of men with different transition behaviors are examined.

OCCUPATIONAL MOBILITY

Social scientists have a continuing interest in understanding the ways in which the social class structure persists over time. Attention has been directed toward the persistence of social class standing across the generations and over the lifetimes of individuals. Higher education is a mechanism by which parents can increase the chances of a favorable social class position for their children (Blau and Duncan, 1967; Svalastoga, 1965; Boudon, 1973). The timing and ordering of school completion, first job, and marriage are influenced by characteristics of social background. These transition behaviors may affect the entry-level occupation of men, thus determining their social class position in early adulthood. Off-time or disorderly transitions may depress social-class entry levels and/or may burden upward-mobility career chances.

These two hypotheses are tested by examining the intergenerational and intragenerational occupational mobility matrices of men with each type of timing and ordering pattern for differences in the structure of mobility. In order to provide a relatively refined test for differences in mobility chances, an eight-category occupational classification is used: self-employed professionals; salaried professionals; managers; proprietors, sales and clerical personnel; craftsmen; servicemen; operatives, and laborers; and farmers and farm laborers. These occupational groups are ranked according to status levels; the highest status position is occupied by self-employed professionals and the lowest by farmers and farm laborers (Featherman and Hauser, 1978).

Persons from higher social class backgrounds more frequently have on-time transitions and a normative order of events (Chapter 5). The occupational origins of men with various transition behaviors consequently are different. These differences in occupational origins produce differentials in occupational mobility that are not associated with actual mobility chances (Hauser and Featherman, 1977). Appropriate statistical tests for differences in occupational mobility among the transition groups must control for variation in occupational margins. This is done by carrying out log-linear tests of transition-group differences in occupational mobility. The baseline model assumes associations between transition-group distributions and occupational-origin and destination distributions. The baseline model also assumes a constant association of occupational origins and destinations among all groups. A statistical test is performed to measure the improvement in fit obtained when a parameter indicating transition-group differences in occupational mobility (upward–downward–mobile) is added to the model. The results of these tests for transition-group differences in intergenerational occupational mobility for each transition are shown in Table 9.1.

There are few differences in intergenerational occupational mobility associated with the timing of transition events for any of the job cohorts. Timing of school completion has a statistically significant ($p = .01$) effect on intergenerational occupational mobility among men who have been working fewer than 5 years. Timing of first job has significant effects ($p < .01$) among those men who first began work 10 to 14 years prior to the survey date and is of marginal significance ($p = .068$) among men who began work in the 5 years prior to the survey. Timing of first marriage and the temporal ordering of events do not affect intergenerational occupational mobility, regardless of year of labor-force entry.

Descriptive statistics for the intergenerational occupational mobility differences observed in the log-linear analysis are presented in Table 9.2. As with the log-linear models, the effects of differing origin and destination marginals on mobility rates have been removed to permit the identification of true differences in intergenerational mobility. This was done by applying iterative procedures for proportional adjustment that

Table 9.1
Log-Linear Models of Difference in Mobility from Father's Occupation to First Job by Timing of Transition Events for Job Tenure Cohorts: Ever-Married White Males Born 1907–1952 in the Experienced Civilian Labor Force

Tenure Cohort and Transition Event	χ^2_{LR} [a]	Degrees of Freedom	p
0-4 Years			
Timing of education	16.9	6	.010
Timing of first job	11.9	6	.068
Timing of marriage.	6.6	6	.378
Temporal ordering of events	1.1	4	.893
10-14 Years			
Timing of education	8.5	6	.216
Timing of first job	21.0	6	.003
Timing of marriage.	5.3	6	.509
Temporal ordering of events	5.9	4	.220
25-29 Years			
Timing of education	6.5	6	.389
Timing of first job	9.7	6	.149
Timing of marriage.	3.1	6	.796
Temporal ordering of events	5.9	4	.220

[a]Likelihood ratio chi-square statistic measuring the change in χ^2_{LR} due to the addition of a timing of events by mobility (upward/downward/stable) parameter to the fitted model.

assigned the origin and destination distributions for the total population to the mobility matrix for each group. The iterative procedures preserve the underlying structure of the mobility matrix (see Hauser and Featherman, 1977).

The net, or minimum, mobility figure indicates the minimum percentage of the respondents who must have first jobs different from the occupations of their fathers. (Since the origin and destination distributions were statistically adjusted to be identical for every group, the minimum mobility index of 28.1% is the same for every transition group.) The observed mobility index describes the actual percentage of men who had first jobs different from those of their fathers. The expected mobility index indicates the percentage of men who would be expected to be mobile if father's occupation and son's first job were statistically independent. The circulation mobility index shows the percentage of men who were occupationally mobile in excess of the percentage of men who

Table 9.2
Occupational Mobility Statistics from Father's Occupation to First Job for Selected Transition Events and Job Tenure Cohorts: Ever-Married White Males Born 1907–1952 in the Experienced Civilian Labor Force

	Changing Major Occupation Group (%)[a]				
	Mobility[b]	Observed[c]	Expected[d]	Circulation Mobility[e]	Mobility Index[f]
0-4 Years					
Timing of Education					
First quartile . .	28.1	69.1	81.9	41.0	76.2
Second quartile. .	28.1	69.5	81.9	41.4	77.0
Third quartile . .	28.1	67.7	81.9	39.6	73.6
Fourth quartile. .	28.1	72.7	81.9	44.6	82.9
Timing of First Job					
First quartile . .	28.1	65.6	81.9	37.5	69.7
Second quartile. .	28.1	68.5	81.9	40.4	75.1
Third quartile . .	28.1	69.0	81.9	40.9	76.0
Fourth quartile. .	28.1	70.7	81.9	42.6	79.2
10-14 Years					
Timing of First Job					
First quartile . .	28.1	62.3	81.9	34.2	63.6
Second quartile. .	28.1	71.1	81.9	43.0	79.9
Third quartile . .	28.1	67.9	81.9	39.8	74.0
Fourth quartile. .	28.1	73.1	81.9	45.0	83.6

[a]Mobility statistics shown are for occupational mobility matrices adjusted to the origin and destination distribution of the total ever-married white male population.

[b]Net mobility; index of dissimilarity comparing row and column marginals.

[c]Percentage off main diagonal.

[d]Percentage off the main diagonal under model of independence of rows and columns.

[e]Circulation mobility = (observed - minimum).

[f]Mobility index = $\left(\frac{\text{observed} - \text{minimum}}{\text{expected} - \text{minimum}}\right) \times 100$.

were necessarily mobile (given the differences between both origin and destination occupational distribution). The mobility index measures the degree to which the actual circulation mobility in the group approached the circulation mobility expected if the origin and destination statuses were independent. The mobility index ranges from 0 to 100. A mobility index of 0 would indicate the maximum degree of inheritance of fathers' occupation by sons. A mobility index of 100 would signify the maximum degree of occupational mobility between fathers and sons.

Men who have worked fewer than 5 years and were relatively late in the completion of their education display greater occupational mobility than men who completed their schooling relatively early or on time (Table 9.2). The mobility index of 82.9 for men in the fourth quartile is 5.9 to 9.3 percentage points greater than for men with an early or on-time education transition. For both the tenure cohort working 0 to 4 years and the cohort beginning work 10 to 14 years before the survey, those men beginning their first jobs relatively early display the least occupational mobility whereas those men beginning work relatively late show the greatest mobility from their father's occupation.

Men who completed their schooling and/or began their first jobs relatively late may display greater occupational mobility because such delays provide time for the development of increased numbers of non-familial personal and professional contacts by the men, contacts who may be able to provide job search assistance. Men beginning to work relatively early, on the other hand, may have developed fewer acquaintances who can be used for job search behavior, and are forced to rely on familial assistance in locating an appropriate first job. Such assistance may involve the father getting his son a job as an apprentice in the same occupation or in the same firm. Men who are proprietors or farmers may bring their sons directly into the family business at a relatively early age.

The beginning of first job occurs at roughly comparable ages for each of the three job-tenure cohorts. This means that differences in intergenerational occupational-mobility chances reflect intercohort shifts in the effects of the timing of transition events. Men who have been working 25 to 29 years by the survey date began work between 1944 and 1948, in the immediate post-war period. Men who have been working 10 to 14 years began their first jobs from 1959 to 1963, a time of peace and a prosperous, if sluggish, economy. Men beginning work immediately prior to the survey began working between 1969 and 1973, during the Vietnam War era of prosperity with inflation. The oldest job-tenure cohort is disproportionately composed of relatively old veterans (see Chapter 3).

Career occupational mobility from first job to 1973 occupation does not vary by timing of education for any of the job-tenure cohorts (Table 9.3). The timing of first job is of marginal importance ($p = .065$) for career occupational mobility among men working 10 to 14 years but is unimportant among the other job-tenure cohorts. The timing of first marriage may have an impact on career occupational mobility among the

Table 9.3
Log-Linear Models of Differences in Mobility from First Job to 1973 Occupation by Timing of Transition Events for Job Tenure Cohorts: Ever-Married White Males Born 1907–1952 in the Experienced Civilian Labor Force

Tenure Cohort and Transition Event	χ^{2a}_{LR}	Degrees of Freedom	P
0-4 Years			
Timing of education	3.4	6	.762
Timing of first job	3.6	6	.733
Timing of marriage.	11.0	6	.092
Temporal ordering of events	9.4	4	.054
10-14 Years			
Timing of education	7.0	6	.333
Timing of first job	12.0	6	.065
Timing of marriage.	8.4	6	.219
Temporal ordering of events	7.1	4	.140
25-29 Years			
Timing of education	4.9	6	.560
Timing of first job	2.4	6	.877
Timing of marriage.	8.9	6	.191
Temporal ordering of events	7.1	4	.140

[a] Likelihood ratio chi-square statistic measuring the change in χ^2_{LR} due to the addition of a timing of events by mobility (upward/downward/stable) parameter to the fitted model.

youngest cohort (p = .092) but has no effect among the other cohorts. The temporal ordering of events is important for career mobility only among men working less than 5 years.

Men who have been working since 10 to 14 years prior to the survey and who began their first job relatively late display less occupational mobility from first job to occupation in 1973 than do men with an early or on-time first job beginning (Table 9.4). Among men who have worked fewer than 5 years, those married in the first or second quartile of age at marriage display less occupational mobility than men marrying relatively late. This may indicate that it is easier to change jobs when one is free of familial responsibilities. This is confirmed by the tendency for men who marry prior to completing schooling to show much less job mobility in their early careers. Men who choose to marry relatively early, before the completion of other life-course transitions, thus are more likely to find themselves locked into a first job in the early years of their career. These restricted mobility rates in the early career seem to dissipate within 10 years of the career beginning, however.

Table 9.4
Occupational Mobility Statistics from First Job to 1973 Occupation for Selected Transition Events and Job Tenure Cohorts: Ever-Married White Males Born 1907–1952 in the Experienced Civilian Labor Force

Tenure Cohort and Transition Event	Changing Major Occupation Group (%)[a]				
	Minimum[b]	Observed[c]	Expected[d]	Circulation Mobility[e]	Mobility Index[f]
0-4 Years					
Timing of Marriage					
First quartile . .	25.7	49.2	82.2	23.5	41.6
Second quartile. .	25.7	49.8	82.2	24.1	42.7
Third quartile . .	25.7	51.8	82.2	26.1	46.2
Fourth quartile. .	25.7	53.7	82.2	28.0	49.6
Temporal Ordering Pattern					
Normative.	25.7	51.5	82.2	25.8	45.7
Intermediate Non-normative. . . .	25.7	52.4	82.2	26.7	47.3
Extreme nonnormative	25.7	45.5	82.2	19.8	35.0
10-14 Years					
Timing of First Job					
First quartile . .	25.7	58.4	82.2	32.7	57.9
Second quartile. .	25.7	60.5	82.2	34.8	61.6
Third quartile . .	25.7	56.7	82.2	31.0	54.9
Fourth quartile. .	25.7	54.1	82.2	28.4	50.3

[a]Mobility statistics shown are for occupational mobility matrices adjusted to the origin and destination distribution of the total ever-married white male population.

[b]Net mobility; index of dissimilarity comparing row and column marginals.

[c]Percentage off main diagonal.

[d]Percentage off the main diagonal under model of independence of rows and columns.

[e]Circulation mobility = (observed - minimum).

[f]Mobility index = $\left(\frac{\text{observed - minimum}}{\text{expected - minimum}}\right) \times 100$.

OCCUPATIONAL STATUS

While the timing of transition events display rather limited influence on occupational mobility, it may have effects on occupational status levels attained by 1973. To test this hypothesis, the mean occupational status levels of men with different timing patterns on the transition events were calculated (Table 9.5). Among men working 0 to 4 years, an earlier timing of the education transition is associated with higher occupational status in 1973. The pattern reverses, however, when the means are standardized for level of schooling completed, with a later age at school completion being associated with higher occupational status. The same direct association between age at school completion and occupational status is observed for the tenure cohorts working 10 to 14 years and 25 to 29 years. The differences are small, though consistent. Comparing the standardized fourth quartile age at school completion to the standardized first quartile, the occupational status advantage amounts to 3.4 points among those working 0 to 4 years, 5.3 points among those working 10 to 14 years, and 2.7 points among those working 25 to 29 years. An early age at school completion thus has negative effects on occupational attainments, effects that persist throughout the life course.

The pattern is not as clear-cut for age at first job. Mean occupational status is higher among those men beginning first job relatively early or relatively late among each of the job-tenure cohorts. When the figures are standardized for level of education, the curvilinear pattern persists in reduced form among those men working 0 to 4 years. Among men working 10 to 14 and 25 to 29 years the pattern appears to be direct, a later timing of first job resulting in higher occupational status in 1973, with the difference between the fourth and first quartile amounting to 6.52 and 2.99 status points, respectively. It is not possible to assess the extent to which these different patterns result from life-course developments rather than intercohort change. One possibility that seems plausible is that an early or a late timing of first job results in initially favorable occupational positions at the time of labor-force entry. The reduced career mobility of men entering their first job relatively early, noted above, may hinder attempts to enhance occupational achievements, whereas the men who begin their first jobs relatively late are more occupationally mobile and can capitalize on their higher entry levels. Within a decade after labor-force entry these processes would result in depressed occupational attainments among those men who begin working relatively early and in relatively good occupational attainments for those who entered the labor force relatively late.

An early age at first marriage is associated with depressed occupational attainment among each of the job-tenure cohorts. When controls are introduced for level of education, the pattern of effects varies among the cohorts. For men who entered the labor force in the five-year period prior to the survey, a later age at first marriage is associated with higher occupational status levels. There are no differences in occupational status by the timing of first marriage among men entering the labor force 10 to 14 years before the survey. Among those men who have been working

Table 9.5
Mean 1973 Occupational Status by Timing of Transition Events for Job Tenure Cohorts: Ever-Married White Males Born 1907–1952 in the Experienced Civilian Labor Force

Transition Event	Tenure Cohort					
	0–4 Years		10–14 Years		25–29 Years	
	Mean	Standardized Mean[a]	Mean	Standardized Mean	Mean	Standardized Mean
Timing of Education						
First quartile	55.48	38.71	47.77	41.18	43.56	47.59
Second quartile	46.68	38.27	43.33	45.27	41.84	48.76
Third quartile	47.75	41.01	44.27	45.18	43.82	49.50
Fourth quartile	41.87	42.10	45.54	46.51	44.35	50.30
Timing of First Job						
First quartile	54.84	41.80	46.34	42.18	41.58	46.49
Second quartile	47.82	36.85	42.14	44.37	40.26	48.54
Third quartile	43.90	38.70	42.85	45.08	46.35	51.60
Fourth quartile	46.17	42.79	49.68	48.70	44.40	49.48
Timing of Marriage						
First quartile	42.88	39.06	42.42	44.54	42.00	49.05
Second quartile	49.28	40.20	45.39	45.71	43.27	50.04
Third quartile	52.72	41.96	46.30	45.29	44.50	49.74
Fourth quartile	49.95	42.94	48.16	45.01	43.54	46.74
Temporal Order of Events						
Normative	36.92	37.91	38.98	44.29	39.98	49.25
Intermediate nonnormative	40.27	40.03	42.15	45.54	44.55	48.50
Extreme nonnormative	57.63	43.79	60.99	47.99	57.35	51.41

[a] Directly standardized for education using the education distribution of the total job cohort.

25 to 29 years, men who married late have somewhat depressed occupational attainments. There thus seem to be no clear patterns in the effect of age at marriage on occupational status attainments.

In all job-tenure cohorts, men who marry prior to finishing school have much higher occupational attainments than men who complete the transition to adulthood in a normative fashion. Most of this differential is accounted for by the greater educations of men who marry before completing school. Even with controls for education, however, men with an extreme nonnormative ordering pattern achieve somewhat higher occupational status positions than other men. This advantage amounts to nearly six points among men at the start of their career, but declines over the life course to about two points by 25 to 29 years after labor force entry.

THE OCCUPATIONAL ATTAINMENT PROCESS

These differences in occupational status attainment reflect controls for the educational compositions of the transition groups but may not exist net of differences in family background and military service histories. Furthermore, the analysis of mean occupational status levels does not reveal whether the *process* of occupational attainment (i.e., the way in which background resources and education are converted into occupational attainments) differs among men according to their timing of transition events. In order to test for differences in the occupational attainment process, separate structural equations models of the occupational attainment process were estimated for each of the timing groups for each transition. A statistical test for significant differences among the regression coefficients of the structural equation models was then carried out for each transition event and for the ordering of events. The results of these tests are shown in Table 9.6.

The timing of school completion affects the process of occupational attainment only among those men who have been working 10 to 14 years. Although the occupational mobility analysis indicated that men who have just begun working are more occupationally mobile if they finished school relatively late, men working less than 5 years are equally successful at converting their schooling and armed forces experience into occupational status, regardless of their timing of school completion. Conversely, although the timing of school completion does not affect the occupational mobility of men working 10 to 14 years, it does influence the conversion of personal measures into occupational attainments.

Among men working 10 to 14 years, those completing their schooling relatively late have a more favorable process of occupational attainment than men who complete their schooling relatively early (Table 9.7). In

Table 9.6

Linear Regression Tests of Differences in the Process of Occupational Status Attainment by Timing of Transition Events for Job Tenure Cohorts: Ever-Married White Males Born 1907–1952 in the Experienced Civilian Labor Force with Earnings of at Least $1000

Attainment and Transition Event	Tenure Cohort								
	0–4 Years			10–14 Years			25–29 Years		
	F[a]	df[b]	p[c]	F	df	p	F	df	p
1973 Occupational Status									
Timing of education	1.03	18, 1287	NS	2.43	18, 1682	<.01	1.36	18, 1369	NS
Timing of first job	2.45	18, 1287	<.01	1.63	18, 1682	<.05	1.04	18, 1369	NS
Timing of marriage.	0.88	18, 1287	NS	1.78	18, 1682	<.025	0.99	18, 1369	NS
Temporal order of events. . .	2.43	12, 1293	<.01	2.44	12, 1688	<.01	1.99	12, 1375	<.025

[a] F statistic for test of differences in the parameters of structural equation models of the attainment process among timing groups.

[b] Degrees of freedom.

[c] P is the probability level that the observed F statistic is a result of chance. NS indicates not significant.

Table 9.7

Structural Equation Models of the Occupational Attainment Process for Selected Transition Events and Job Tenure Cohorts: Ever-Married White Males Born 1907–1952 in the Experienced Civilian Labor Force with Earnings of at Least $1000

Transition Event and Tenure Cohort	Independent Variables[a]					
	Graded Schooling	College	Military Service	Intercept	R^2	Differences in occupational attainment due to process[b]
TIMING OF EDUCATION						
10-14 Years						
First quartile	0.99	7.77**	3.69	16.56	.486	-1.87
Second quartile.	3.78**	7.18**	1.86	-6.97	.411	--
Third quartile	4.04**	7.57**	0.63	-13.35	.495	-0.79
Fourth quartile.	2.35**	7.24**	4.88**	2.20	.454	1.59
TIMING OF FIRST JOB						
0-4 Years						
First quartile	0.00	9.68**	10.22*	17.50	.456	0.37
Second quartile.	3.49	9.13**	3.57	-16.21	.546	--
Third quartile	0.68	8.59**	1.63	7.62	.519	1.71
Fourth quartile.	2.63**	7.46**	-2.04	-1.26	.433	3.77
10-14 Years						
First quartile	3.38**	7.28**	0.16	-5.91	.479	-2.07
Second quartile.	2.70**	6.96**	1.30	1.06	.375	--
Third quartile	3.48**	7.95**	1.67	-7.81	.510	-0.39
Fourth quartile.	2.46**	7.02**	1.00	8.18	.441	3.94

TIMING OF MARRIAGE						
10-14 Years						
First quartile	3.32**	7.07**	1.22	-4.05	.454	0.42
Second quartile.	3.18**	7.00**	2.45	-5.30	.447	--
Third quartile	1.94**	7.55**	5.46**	9.35	.448	0.72
Fourth quartile.	2.51*	8.53**	0.55	2.54	.503	0.04
TEMPORAL ORDER OF EVENTS						
0-4 Years						
Normative	0.60	8.73**	4.91**	11.92	.452	--
Intermediate nonnormative . .	2.18	7.59**	-0.36	-0.28	.411	2.46
Extreme nonnormative.	1.93	7.09**	3.51*	4.24	.376	3.85
10-14 Years						
Normative	3.03**	7.98**	0.94	-3.42	.402	--
Intermediate nonnormative . .	3.16**	5.95**	2.75	-1.78	.296	1.08
Extreme nonnormative.	0.41	6.46**	4.34*	34.35	.372	0.75
25-29 Years						
Normative	3.24*	6.56**	0.82	-1.44	.336	--
Intermediate nonnormative . .	1.96*	4.65**	10.02*	0.59	.309	-1.27
Extreme nonnormative.	1.12	4.57**	3.85	26.55	.315	-0.49

[a] Metric regression coefficients shown are net of the effects of father's occupation and education and of farm background.

[b] Intergroup differences in mean occupational attainment due to process are determined by finding the residual difference in occupational attainment levels between a comparison population and the standard population using the means of the independent variables of the comparison population and the structural equation model of the standard population. The standard population for each transition event and birth cohort is indicated by a dash.

*$p < .05$

** $p < .01$

large part, this is a result of the higher rate of conversion of military service experience into job status among men who finished their schooling relatively late. These men entered the labor force between 1958 and 1962. Men who served in the military and finished their schooling relatively late are disproportionately representative of men who used G.I. Bill benefits to attend college. For these men, the combination of military service experience during the cold war and a college education completed after military service proved advantageous in the process of career attainments. This initial advantage in occupational status attainment probably disappears over the course of the career, so that its effects are not evident among men who have been working since the period immediately following World War II.

If military service in combination with a post-military college education has proven historically advantageous, with the initial advantage dissipating over the life cycle, what explains the lack of differentials among timing of education groups for men working only 0 to 4 years? These men began work from April 1968 to March 1973 during the peak of the Vietnam War years. The veterans of the Vietnam War who completed their educations under G.I. Bill benefits appear not to have benefited from this pattern of career entry, relative to men with more common patterns of career entry. This represents an intercohort shift in the treatment of veterans coincident with the trauma of the Vietnam War years. However, even though Vietnam War veterans with a college education appear not to have garnered the advantages historically associated with college-educated veteran status, they have not suffered disadvantages relative to other men entering the labor force in the same years.

The process of occupational attainment varies by the timing of first job for men at the beginning of their careers, and for men who have been working 10 to 14 years. By 25 to 29 years after career entry, the timing of first job is not a significant influence on occupational status attainments. There are no clear patterns in the regression coefficients of the groups of men working fewer than 15 years, but for both recent job-tenure cohorts, the process of converting background and educational resources into occupational attainments is more favorable for men who began their first jobs relatively late (Table 9.7). It is noteworthy that these are the same men who experience higher intergenerational occupational mobility. As discussed earlier, it appears that men who began their first jobs relatively late are more successful at converting their personal resources into relatively high-status entry occupations. Men who began their first jobs relatively early were probably more dependent on their families of origin for assistance in job placement. Although such men are more occupationally mobile over their early careers, their initial failure to convert their personal resources into high entry-level occupations has effects that persist through the first 14 years of the career. By 25 to 29 years after career entry, the timing of first job no longer affects relative occupational standing.

The timing of first marriage influences the conversion of personal resources into occupational status only among those men who have been working 10 to 14 years (Table 9.6). This contrasts with the occupational mobility analysis, which indicated that the timing of first marriage was important early in the career but not among men working 10 years or longer. However, the differentials in the occupational attainment process among men working 10 to 14 years are small and unsystematic. Overall, differences in the process of occupational achievement produce less than a difference of one status point among the age-at-marriage group.

The temporal order of events by which a man completed the transition to adulthood produces differences in the process of occupational attainment for men in all job-tenure cohorts (Table 9.6). Men with a normative ordering pattern tend to receive a higher rate of occupational return to each year of schooling, particularly at the college level, compared with other men in the same job-tenure cohort (Table 9.7). Among the two older job-tenure cohorts, the occupational status returns to service in the military are higher among men with nonnormative ordering patterns. Among men working fewer than 5 years, the occupational status returns to military service are about equal for men with normative and extreme nonnormative ordering patterns.

This pattern of results supports the idea that there have been intercohort shifts in the process of occupational status attainment among veterans. Men who serve in the military and complete their college education after their military service are especially likely to marry before completing school. Among pre–Vietnam War era veterans this pattern was not particularly disadvantageous despite the lower occupational returns to education, because of the superior benefits accruing to military service experience. Among the Vietnam War era veterans, the pattern of a higher rate of return to military service did not characterize men who married prior to completing their schooling.

Although the process of occupational attainment varies among the ordering groups, these differences represent no particular net advantage or disadvantage in terms of mean occupational attainments among the two more recent cohorts. Among men at the beginning of their careers, a nonnormative ordering pattern may even represent a slight advantage in the achievement of entry-level occupational status. Among all three job-tenure cohorts, the levels of explained variance in occupational attainments are highest among men with normative orders. The occupational attainments of men with nonnormative orders are more heavily dependent on chance.

CONCLUSIONS

The timing and ordering of early life-course transition events do constitute contingencies for occupational attainments over the later life course. It appears that men who make the transition to adulthood relatively early rely more on familial connections for placement in their first jobs. These initial jobs depend relatively little on educational attainment and provide a poor basis for career advancements. Men who marry relatively early, or before the completion of their educations, are especially likely to have depressed career occupational mobility. They experience difficulties in converting their educational attainments into occupational achievements. Conversely, men who begin their first job relatively late, after the completion of schooling and before marriage, are able to capitalize on their educations to attain entry level occupations of higher status than their fathers. These entry-level occupations provide a good basis for upward occupational mobility over the course of their careers. These patterns vary according to job-tenure cohort and military service history. It appears that the contingent effects of transition behavior on occupational attainments are relatively pronounced in the early phases of the career, but dissipate over the life course.

10

The Transition to Adulthood and Career Earnings Attainments

In this chapter, the consequence of the timing and ordering of school completion, first job, and first marriage for earnings in the later life course are identified. As in Chapter 9, this analysis is restricted to ever-married white men in the experienced civilian labor force. The experiences of three job-tenure cohorts—men working 0 to 4 years, 10 to 14 years, and 25 to 29 years—are examined. The analysis begins with an examination of mean 1972 earnings differences among these men classified according to transition behavior, with and without controls for educational attainment. Structural equation models of the earnings attainment process then are estimated for men in each job-tenure cohort and with each type of transition behavior. A comparison of the parameters of the earnings equation models indicates differences among the groups in the process by which personal resources are converted into earnings attainments.

EARNINGS

Among men working 0 to 4 years, a relatively late age at school completion, first job, and first marriage are associated with above average earnings (Table 10.1). This pattern persists with controls for education, with the earnings advantage of being late on any of the three transitions amounting to $1000 or more. Men who marry before completing their schooling also report higher than average earnings attainments, but all except about $500 of the difference is accounted for by their above-

Table 10.1
Mean Earnings in 1972 by Timing of Transition Events for Job Tenure Cohorts: Ever-Married White Males Born 1907–1952 in the Experienced Civilian Labor Force

Transition Event	Tenure Cohort					
	0–4 Years		10–14 Years		25–29 Years	
	Mean	Standardized Mean[a]	Mean	Standardized Mean	Mean	Standardized Mean
Timing of Education						
First quartile	8971	7574	12929	11591	12990	14037
Second quartile	8261	7647	12336	12819	12531	13900
Third quartile	8330	7769	11890	11896	12916	13931
Fourth quartile	8710	8725	11397	11501	12418	13506
Timing of First Job						
First quartile	8330	7392	12075	11223	12696	13712
Second quartile	7679	6815	11616	12092	11651	13460
Third quartile	7855	7454	12162	12573	13698	14992
Fourth quartile	9516	9085	12535	12273	12563	13637
Timing of Marriage						
First quartile	7747	7463	11342	11688	12967	14954
Second quartile	8666	8080	12590	12619	12159	13501
Third quartile	9759	8694	12521	12283	13488	14924
Fourth quartile	10826	9932	12234	11553	11910	12471
Temporal Order of Events						
Normative	7506	7623	11108	12414	12067	14306
Intermediate nonnormative	8267	8287	10985	11743	12640	13697
Extreme nonnormative	9356	8110	15248	12755	15735	14030

[a]Directly standardized for education using the education distribution of the total job cohort.

average educational attainments. For men at later points in their careers, the timing of transition events is not systematically related to earnings attainments.

THE EARNINGS ATTAINMENT PROCESS

The process of earnings attainment varies by the timing of education among men who began working between 1959 and 1963, but does not differ among the older or younger job-tenure cohorts (Table 10.2). Among the men working 10 to 14 years the rate of earnings return to a year of college is higher among the men who finished school relatively early, but the return to military service experience is higher among men who finished school at approximately average ages (Table 10.3). Men who finished school in the second age quartile enjoy the greatest net advantage accruing to differences in the process of earnings attainments. Other men suffer earnings deficits of $960 or higher as a result of differences in process. In Chapter 9 it was noted that men from this cohort who served in the military and then finished college under G.I. Bill benefits did not suffer disadvantages in the process of occupational attainments. This statement is not true of the earnings attainment process. Men who complete school relatively late bacause of service in the military are treated no differently than other men who completed their schooling relatively late.

The timing of first job affects the earnings attainment process of men during the first five years of their careers, but it is not an important contingency for earnings of men during their later career (Table 10.2). Among men in the first years of their career, the earnings return to a year of graded schooling is more than $300 for men who began working at a median age at first job, or later, compared to $10 returns to an additional year of graded schooling for men beginning their first job relatively early (Table 10.3). The net advantage of differences in the earnings attainment process is $395 for men in the third quartile of age at first job, and $1484 for men with a fourth quartile age at first job. Although a later age at first job is associated with above-average earnings, the levels of explained variance in earnings are higher among those men who began working relatively early. Service in the military and the number of weeks employed during the previous year are factors of greater importance in the earnings attainment process of men who began working relatively early compared to men who began working relatively late.

Timing of first marriage does not significantly affect the process by which men convert their human capital resources into earnings. The temporal ordering of school completion, beginning of first job, and first

Table 10.2
Linear Regression Tests of Differences in the Process of Earnings Attainment by Timing of Transition Events for Job Tenure Cohorts: Ever-Married White Males Born 1907–1952 in the Experienced Civilian Labor Force with Earnings of at Least $1000

Attainment and Transition Event	Tenure Cohort								
	0–4 Years			10–14 Years			25–29 Years		
	F[a]	df[b]	p[c]	F	df	p	F	df	p
Earnings									
Timing of education	1.40	24, 1279	NS	1.80	24, 1674	< .01	0.74	24, 1361	NS
Timing of first job	2.39	24, 1279	< .01	1.23	24, 1674	NS	0.81	24, 1361	NS
Timing of marriage.	1.30	24, 1279	NS	1.11	24, 1674	NS	1.40	24, 1361	NS
Temporal order of events. . .	2.47	16, 1287	< .01	3.23	16, 1682	< .01	0.67	16, 1369	NS

[a] F statistic for test of differences in the parameters of structural equation models of the attainment process among timing groups.

[b] Degrees of freedom.

[c] p is the probability level that the observed F statistic is a result of change. NS indicates not significant.

marriage influence the earnings attainment process of men during the first fifteen years of their careers (Table 10.2). The nature of this influence is different for men who have been working 0 to 4 years compared to men working 10 to 14 years (Table 10.3). Among men beginning their careers, a normative order of events is associated with a higher rate of earnings returns to graded schooling, but a lower rate of return to a college education. The earnings return to an additional point of occupational status also is higher among men with a nonnormative order of events. Men with an intermediate ordering pattern have much higher earnings if they served in the military, but military service history makes no difference among men with other ordering patterns. Overall, differences in the process of earnings attainment at the beginning of the career favor men with nonnormative orders, with the annual earnings advantage amounting to $800 or more.

The pattern is reversed among men who have been working 10 to 14 years. Among these men, the earnings return to an additional year of schooling, at both the graded and college levels, is higher among men with a normative ordering of transition events. The earnings returns to an additional week worked are especially low among men who marry before completing school, and are higher among men with intermediate ordering patterns. Men who have a nonnormative ordering pattern due to military service have earnings that are much higher than men who have similar transition schedules but did not serve in the military. Among men with a normative ordering of events, service in the military has no effect on earnings. Overall, differences in the process of earnings attainment produce more than a $700 advantage for men with a normative sequence of transitions.

Why is a normative ordering pattern unfavorable to earnings attainments in the early career, favorable for men observed at mid-career, and irrelevant for men who have been working for 25 to 29 years? These differences among the job cohorts may reflect maturation effects or may represent true intercohort differences. The explanation I find most probable is that men who are married at the time they begin to seek their first full-time civilian jobs have an initial advantage in the labor market because employers regard married men as more stable workers than single men. (This is true, insofar as married men display less occupational mobility in their early careers than do men who marry after beginning work.) Men who are single in the early years of their career tend to experience quicker career advancement. Within a decade of beginning work, the occupational status disadvantage associated with a normative order of events has diminished greatly, and the earnings deficit has become an earnings advantage. By the time the men have reached a mature

Table 10.3

Structural Equation Models of the Earnings Attainment Process for Selected Transition Events and Job Tenure Cohorts: Ever-Married White Males Born 1907–1952 in the Experienced Civilian Labor Force with Earnings of at Least $1000

Transition Event and Tenure Cohort	Independent Variable[a]							
	Graded Schooling	College	Military Service	Occupational Status	Weeks Worked	Intercept	R^2	Differences in Earnings Attainment Due to Process[b]
TIMING OF EDUCATION								
10–14 Years								
First quartile	-70	1364**	474	57**	146*	-1637	.415	-1301
Second quartile.	110	1702**	1411*	59**	140**	-1417	.251	--
Third quartile	259	996**	1249*	43**	176**	-4852	.354	-960
Fourth quartile.	-221	758**	479	70**	191**	-1677	.290	-1545
TIMING OF FIRST JOB								
0–4 Years								
First quartile	0	497*	841	12	179**	-2899	.374	-59
Second quartile.	-28	467**	1006**	24*	155**	-1674	.318	--
Third quartile	382	628**	567	-6	153**	-5439	.146	395
Fourth quartile.	329	411*	651	62**	145**	-3279	.228	1484

TEMPORAL ORDER OF EVENTS								
0-4 Years								
Normative.	263	230	507	13	138**	-3780	.136	--
Intermediate nonnormative. .	108	708**	2392**	42*	118**	-2170	.209	818
Extreme nonnormative	-35	366*	681	40**	200**	-1857	.253	1225
10-14 Years								
Normative.	286*	1514**	109	49**	157**	-3040	.277	--
Intermediate nonnormative. .	160	918**	1475*	29	212**	-6054	.248	-731
Extreme nonnormative	-1040*	948**	2419**	94**	137	6207	.278	-986

[a]Metric regression coefficients shown are net of the effects of father's occupation and education and of farm background.

[b]Intergroup difference in earnings attainment processes are determined by finding the residual difference in earnings between a comparison population and the standard population using the means of the independent variables of the comparison population and the structural equation model of the standard population. The standard population for each transition event and birth cohort is indicated by a dash.

*$p < .05$.

**$p < .01$.

stage in their careers, the timing and ordering of events marking the transition to adulthood no longer have any impact on attainment.[1]

CONCLUSIONS

The results of this analysis demonstrate that the timing and ordering of early life transistions constitute important contingencies for earnings attainments in the later life course.[2] The nature of these contingent effects vary among the three job-tenure cohorts. These intercohort variations may reflect the effects of maturation of labor-force entrants over the course of their careers or may result from different age-constant intercohort differences in the process of achievement. In the absence of life-history data, it was not possible to choose formally between these two alternative explanations for the findings. The analysis does suggest a number of tentative conclusions which may serve as a basis for future research.

In general, men who complete school and enter the labor force relatively early appear to rely more on familial connections for placement in their first jobs. The types of jobs they enter provide a relatively poor basis for career advancement. For these men, the occupational and earnings returns to an additional year of schooling are depressed. In contrast, men who first complete school, next enter the labor force, and finally marry, are able to capitalize on their educations to attain entry-level occupations that provide a good basis for occupational mobility over the course of their careers. These men frequently achieve high status jobs which produce higher earnings returns to their educations.

Initially, married men who seek employment tend to find better paying and somewhat higher status jobs than single men. This may be associated with the employer's perception that the married man will make a more stable worker than the single man. This is undoubtedly true. Married men display less occupational mobility in their early careers than do men who marry after beginning work. But the man who is single has greater freedom to seek a better job. Unrestricted by familial responsibilities, single men tend to enjoy quicker career advancement.

[1]A complete test of this hypothesis about the relationship between the ordering of events and earnings achievements would require data on earnings at different points in the careers of several job-tenure cohorts. These data are not available in the Occupational Changes in a Generation II survey. Their collection and analysis could prove a fruitful avenue of future research.

[2]The structural equation models reported in this chapter also were estimated for relative earnings attainments, using a logged earnings variable. The substantive results did not differ from those reported for real earnings in this chapter.

Within a decade of beginning work the occupational status disadvantages attached to being single when first seeking employment in a first job are greatly reduced, and the earnings difference has become an actual advantage.

An apparent exception to these generalizations involves veterans of World War II, Korean War, and cold war military service. These men more frequently suffered interruptions in their schooling and delays in their career entry because of military service obligations. After their military service many of these men continued their educations, completing college under G.I. Bill benefits. Because of their relatively advanced ages they often married prior to completing school and beginning work. These men do not seem to suffer the occupational attainment disadvantages ususally associated with a disorderly transition to adulthood. The earnings deficits in mid-career associated with such transition behavior is ameliorated to a large extent. Vietnam War veterans who completed their educations under the G.I. Bill appear not to have benefited from this pattern of career entry, relative to nonveterans with the same patterns of career entry. Thus, although these Vietnam War veterans did not enjoy the career returns to veteran status to which other men were accustomed, they suffered no particular disadvantages as a result of their veteran status, compared to other men with the same transition patterns. The occupational and earnings consequences of the timing and order of the transition to adulthood thus have shown historical intercohort change, as well as variation by military service experience and by career stage in the life course.

11

The Transition to Adulthood and Marital Stability

The analysis presented in Chapters 9 and 10 provided evidence in support of the hypothesis that the timing and sequencing of early life transitions are contingencies for occupational and earnings achievements in the later life course. This chapter directs attention to another domain of achievement—marriage. The results of Chapters 9 and 10 indicate that an early marriage, or marriage prior to the completion of schooling, creates structural incompatibilities between a man's career and family commitments, lowering life course career achievements. This chapter tests the hypothesis that an early marriage, or a marriage prior to the completion of schooling and beginning of the first full-time job, is more likely to be terminated through separation and/or divorce.

The analysis described in this chapter is restricted to the population of ever-married men who have been subject to the risk of termination of first marriage. Men whose first marriage ended through the death of the wife and who were widowers at the time of the OCG-II survey are excluded from the analysis, because the survival chances of a spouse are not expected to vary systematically by early life transition behavior. The remaining men are classified into those who are still in an intact first marriage and those men whose first marriage is no longer intact.[1]

[1]If an OCG-II respondent has remarried after the termination of his first marriage, it is not possible to determine whether his first marriage ended through divorce or widowhood. Other research indicates, however, that for most remarried men, the first marriage was terminated by divorce (Sweet, 1973). Information is not available on the timing of the termination of the first marriage, the background characteristics of the first wife for men no longer in their first marriage, or the fertility of the couple in the man's first marriage.

Previous research has demonstrated that rates of marital instability vary according to husband's education and race (Hogan, 1977). Since the timing of transition events varies according to race and educational attainment, these variables are included as controls in this analysis of marital instability. Marriage cohort is incorporated into this analysis as a control for differing lengths of exposure time to the risk of dissolution of first marriage, as well as to permit a test for intercohort change in the effects of the timing of transition events on marital stability. As in Chapters 9 and 10, attention is directed toward the effects of the relative timing of transition events compared to other men with a comparable level of education. Because marriage prior to school completion and beginning of first job is associated with an early absolute age of marriage which is, in turn, associated with a higher probability of martial dissolution, a control variable for age at marriage is incorporated into the model estimating the effects of temporal order of transition events on marital stability.

Since the dependent variable is dichotomous, log-linear modified multiple regression models were estimated for each of the transition events. The models allow for the joint effects of the control variables (education, race, and marriage cohort) on marital stability and for the association of these control variables with the independent transition variable. The direct effects of each transition variable on marital instability, controlling for these other associations, then were estimated (see Table 11.1). Tests were also performed for the existence of differences in the effects of transition behavior on marital instability among education, race, and marriage cohort groups (Table 11.1).

ANALYSIS

The relative timing of school completion and of first marriage have statistically significant effects on the probability of a dissolution of first marriage for American men born in this century. The relative timing of first job has no effect on marital instability. The temporal order of events significantly affects marital instability.

Men who complete school relatively early or relatively late have higher rates of marital instability than men who complete school on time (Table 11.2). Men who marry at a relatively early age, compared with other men at the same level of education, have rates of marital instability more than 50% higher than men marrying on time or relatively late. Since chronological age at first marriage affects rates of marital insta-

Table 11.1
Log-Linear Models of the Net Effects of Timing of Transition Events on Marital Instability: Ever-Married Males Born 1907–1952

Transition Event	χ^2_{LR} [a]	df [b]	p [c]
Timing of Education			
Direct effect	19.6	3	<.01
Interaction effect with			
Education	14.2	12	NS
Race.	0.2	3	NS
Marriage cohort	5.9	6	NS
Timing of First Job			
Direct effect	5.9	3	NS
Interaction effect with			
Education	14.3	12	NS
Race.	0.7	3	NS
Marriage cohort	5.5	6	NS
Timing of First Marriage			
Direct effect	14.1	3	<.01
Interaction effect with			
Education	9.4	12	NS
Race.	7.5	3	NS
Marriage cohort	32.5	6	<.01
Temporal Order of Events			
Direct effect	8.6	2	<.025
Interaction effect with			
Education	1.4	8	NS
Race.	1.5	2	NS
Marriage cohort	5.4	4	NS
Age at first marriage	1.9	4	NS

[a] χ_{LR} is the likelihood ratio chi-square statistic. The statistic shown for the effect of each transition event is net of the effects of education, marriage cohort, and race on marital instability. A control for age at first marriage also is included in the model for the effect of temporal ordering of events on marital instability.

[b] df are the degrees of freedom.

[c] p is the probability level that the chi-square statistic is due to chance. NS indicates $p > .05$.

bility, it is not surprising that relative age at first marriage is of importance. It seems likely that men who marry early are relatively immature

Table 11.2
The Net Odds Probability of First Marriage Ending in a Separation or Divorce by the Timing of Transition Events: Ever-Married Males Born 1907–1952

Transition Event	Odds Probability		
	Direct Effects		
Timing of Education			
First quartile	1.155**		
Second quartile.	0.905		
Third quartile	0.916*		
Fourth quartile.	1.044		
Timing of Marriage			
First quartile	1.449**		
Second quartile.	0.940		
Third quartile	0.772**		
Fourth quartile.	0.951		
Temporal Order of Events			
Normative.	0.903		
Intermediate Nonnormative. . . .	1.020		
Extreme nonnormative	1.086		
	Interaction Effects		
	Marriage Cohort		
	1920-47	1948-61	1962-73
Timing of Marriage			
First quartile	1.108*	1.061*	0.850**
Second quartile.	1.091*	1.097*	0.835**
Third quartile	1.010	0.984	1.006
Fourth quartile.	0.819**	0.873**	1.400**

*Standardized value greater than 1.0.

**Standardized value greater than 2.0.

at the time of marriage. Their selection of a marriage partner might be ill-considered because of this immaturity, or problems associated with the sudden entry of an immature man into a marital union may produce strains that result in marital discord. The result in both cases would be the same—a higher rate of marital dissolution. It is probably the association of an early age at first marriage with an early age at school completion that results in the higher rate of marital instability reported by men who complete school relatively early.

The negative effects of an early age at first marriage are most pronounced among men who were married prior to 1962. Men married after this date display a lesser effect of age at marriage on rates of marital instability. In fact, the direct effects of age at marriage on marital instability, in combination with the interaction effects of marriage cohort with the timing of marriage, produce a pattern in which, among men married from 1962 on, both relatively early and relatively late marriages have a higher probability of dissolution than other marriages. This represents a sharp reversal from earlier times. It may be that the greater availability of contraceptive methods and of abortion during the 1960s and 1970s reduced the number of couples who were forced into a marriage as a result of premaritally conceived pregnancies. A greater proportion of early marriages during the recent period, therefore, would have been freely chosen unions, perhaps resulting in the breakup of fewer early marriages. It is unclear what factors have changed the advantage historically associated with a late age at marriage into a disadvantage.

A normative order of events is associated with the lowest rate of marital instability, whereas men who marry before the completion of schooling have rates of marital instability 20% higher. The negative effect of a nonnormative ordering pattern has remained constant over time; there have been no intercohort decreases in the effect of temporal ordering patterns on marital instability. A disorderly sequence of transition events raises marital instability regardless of whether the marriage is at an early or late age and regardless of the level of educational attainment. These differentials are exactly the sort expected under the hypothesis that a disorderly sequence of life-course events in the transition from school boy to adult male increases the likelihood of a marital disruption.

CONCLUSIONS

This analysis has demonstrated that a relatively early marriage, as well as marriage prior to the completion of schooling and the beginning of a first, full-time job, increase the probability that this first marriage will terminate through separation or divorce. Off-time and out of sequence transitions in the early life course thus are deleterious for familial achievements, as well as for career achievements. Marriage prior to the completion of the other transitions associated with the passage from youth to adulthood places an American male in a structurally incompatible nexus of roles. This structural incompatibility lessens the chances of career achievements and marital stability in the later life course.

12

Social Change and the Transition to Adulthood

The timing and sequencing of the early life transitions of twentieth-century American males have varied among birth cohorts. These inter-cohort changes in transition behavior have resulted from differences in social structural conditions at the time the cohorts were undergoing the transition to adulthood, and from the unique historical experiences of the cohorts. Transition behavior also has varied among men according to their social class, size of community of origin, and paternal ethnic ancestry. Although the effects of these social group memberships on transition behavior have remained largely invariant among the birth cohorts, the differing social-class, community-size, and ethnic-ancestry compositions of the cohorts account for some of the intercohort changes in transition behavior. Thus, it is necessary to consider men's historical and social structural milieu, as well as their social group memberships, in order to understand the timing and sequencing of their early life transitions. The life-course perspective utilized in the study described in this book has focused attention on each of these factors.

Over the course of the twentieth century, cohort succession has provided the mechnanism by which the American population was transformed from a rural–agrarian into an urban–industrial society. New cohorts were trained in the skills, and inculcated with the beliefs and attitudes, necessary for life in the modern world. Mass, public education had the function of accomplishing this training and socialization of the new cohorts. Thus, over the course of the twentieth century, the age-specific rates of school enrollment have increased on an intercohort basis, initially at the primary school level, and subsequently at the secondary school level. These changes in school enrollment have produced intercohort increases in the age at which birth cohorts began their transition out of school. The post–World War II expansion of college enrollment has caused intercohort delays in the age at which birth cohorts complete the education transition.

Government decisions about the level of public support for school enrollment have produced intracohort differentials in school ènrollment. Education at the primary and secondary school levels has been financed almost entirely by government expenditures. Most men were able to complete such graded schooling regardless of their social class, community, and ethnic origins. The small differentials in rates of high school attendance and completion among these groups probably result more from subgroup variations in educational aspirations and encouragement than from differences in financial resources. Consequently, there have been few socioeconomic differentials in the first, second, and third quartiles of age at the school-leaving transition among males completing equivalent levels of graded schooling.

In contrast, government expenditures on college education have not fully covered the cost of enrollment. Rates of college attendance have been lower among poorer socioeconomic groups because of a shortage of economic resources, as well as because of lower educational aspirations. Programs of educational scholarships, grants, and loans have enabled men from a variety of socioeconomic backgrounds to enroll in school, but this assistance often was insufficient to permit continuous, full-time enrollment in college. G.I. Bill benefits have been another important mechanism permitting some men from poor socioeconomic backgrounds to attend college, but the requisite military duty led to an interruption in schooling lasting 2 years or longer. Thus, blue-collar and farm origin men, men from rural communities, and blacks and Hispanics have had lower rates of college attendance; those who have managed to complete college have experienced one or more interruptions in their schooling more often than other men. Because of their disadvantaged position in the American opportunity structure, the relatively few college graduates from these groups were considerably later in their age at school completion, and they experienced more variability in their age at school completion.

Intercohort changes and socioeconomic differences in age at the beginning of the first, full-time civilian job have paralleled those of the school-completion transition. Men tended to delay the start of their first job until after their schooling was fully completed but began working shortly thereafter. Among men with a college education, those from better socioeconomic origins conformed more closely to this pattern than did other men. The blue-collar and farm origin men, men from rural and small town communities, and blacks and Hispanics more frequently began working at a full-time job prior to the completion of college. This pattern apparently resulted from the greater financial needs of these men. Because some of these men began work relatively early, while still in school, and others began their first job only after a relatively late completion of schooling, the variability of age at first job was greater among men from deprived socioeconomic origins.

Men born in the early part of the twentieth century experienced rapid intercohort declines in the median age at first marriage. Variability in age at marriage decreased as a result of the near disappearance of bachelorhood among men 30 and older. This decline in age at marriage probably was related to intercohort changes in educational attainment and entry-level first jobs. The data suggest that most men preferred to marry relatively early—as soon as they located a satisfactory mate and financial circumstances were auspicious. The school system probably serves as a better mechanism for bringing together potential marriage partners than does adolescent work in a factory or on the family farm. Furthermore, college attendance frequently has necessitated residential migration away from the parental household into a private apartment or dormitory. The reduction in interpersonal contacts between young persons and their parents has probably reduced parental ability to influence the choice of a marriage partner. Thus, the prolongation of school enrollment has increased contacts with potential mates, while reducing parental control over the timing of marriage.

The rapid intercohort increases in educational attainment have meant that young persons entering the labor market offered better manpower skills to potential employers than their less educated elders. Higher educational attainments produced intercohort improvements in the competitive positions of men as they entered the labor force. The socioeconomic status of first job was higher among the better educated cohorts, perhaps producing intercohort declines in the age at which men achieved the economic sufficiency targets that would allow them to marry. Thus, the historical expansion of the educational system has improved the efficiency of the marriage market, as well as the economic positions of men in the marriage market.

Intercohort changes in marriage behavior resemble differentials of social class, ethnic ancestry, and community size. This is not coincidental. The intercohort changes in transition behavior, in part, have been produced by changes in the compositions of cohorts attending college. The decision of the body politic to democratize admissions to American's colleges and universities through limited financial aids programs, without supporting the entire cost of that education, produced patterns of post-secondary school enrollment, labor-force entry, and marriage that were reflected in intercohort changes in transition behavior. For example, the intercohort increases in college attendance by men from poorer socio-economic origins have, to some degree, caused the higher rates of marriage before school completion observed among the more recent birth cohorts. There were no social class differences in age at marriage, controlling for level of schooling completed. Men from poorer socioeconomic backgrounds have a later age at school completion than other men, but they have not foregone marriage beyond the normatively preferred age (as would be necessary to delay marriage until after school completion). For men with delays in the completion of schooling, marriage while enrolled in school may provide economic support (from a working wife) that would be unavailable from the family of origin. The higher rates of college enrollment among men from poorer socioeconomic origins, and the delays in school completion characteristic of these men, thus have jointly produced some of intercohort tendencies toward a higher probability of marriage prior to school completion.

The post–World War II decision to delay the labor-force entrance of many mobilized soldiers by offering G.I. Bill support for college enrollment accelerated this pattern of change. It created a group of military-experienced birth cohorts among whom schooling was completed relatively late, at widely varying ages, and many persons married and/or began their first, full-time jobs while enrolled in school. To the extent that the veterans attending college under G.I. Bill benefits were from poor socioeconomic backgrounds, intercohort changes in transition behavior were assured.

Twentieth-century improvements in the expectation of life have increased the probability that both parents will be alive when men undergo the transition to adulthood. The twentieth-century decrease in average age at childbirth means that more parents were of prime working age at the time their sons carried out these early life transitions. Decreases in completed family size have reduced the numer of siblings with whom parental support was shared. These changes have enhanced the ability of families to support their sons over a prolonged period of school enrollment. This support may even extend to assisting a son who wishes to marry prior to achieving economic self-sufficiency. These demographic changes thus have been associated with intercohort delays in the age at school completion and beginning of first job, with reductions in age at first marriage, and with increases in the probability of marriage prior to the completion of schooling and beginning of work.

The transition behavior of the twentieth-century birth cohorts has been influenced by societal economic conditions as well. Men making the transition to adulthood during prosperous times were able to prolong their school enrollment in order to achieve the maximum amount of education possible. This sort of human capital investment resulted in placing these men in relatively favorable positions for labor-market entry. During prosperous times, men not only remained in school longer, they also spent more time after the completion of their schooling in search of a suitable first job. Economic prosperity permitted these men to be more flexible in marriage decisions; they tended to marry at an earlier age than men from birth cohorts making the transition to adulthood during less prosperous years, and more frequently chose to marry before completing their schooling.

Men undergoing the transition to adulthood during times of slow economic growth and high unemployment were forced to adopt a much different strategy in their transition to adulthood. Their initial reaction was to remain in school and to postpone searching for a job. This was only a short run expedient, however. Few of these men remained in school until a relatively late age. Most began to work at an earlier age than would otherwise have been the case. Because of poor economic conditions, these men delayed marriage until school was completed and they had begun to work. They did not postpone marriage indefinitely, however. Most of these men chose to marry before becoming unusually late in the marriage transition, despite the unfavorable economic circumstances of the time.

Thus, men undergoing the transition to adulthood during auspicious times were able to maximize their educations and early career achievements without postponement of marriage. Men undertaking the passage to adulthood during inauspicious years were forced to engage in minimally satisfying behavior. They stayed in school as long as possible and, when forced to leave school, began work at once. They postponed marriage somewhat, but married before the postponement made them unattractive in the marriage market.

The greatest disruptive situation faced by men undergoing the transition to adulthood was a wartime mobilization of young men into the armed forces. Military obiligations were most burdensome when they occurred suddenly, and unexpectedly. Men faced with the prospect of immediate induction into the armed forces were forced to make quick decisions about school enrollment and marriage. Some men chose to marry at once, before entry into the military. Others delayed marriage until after their return to civilian life. This produced considerable variability in the average age at marriage. After military service, some men chose to return to school under G.I. Bill benefits, whereas others let their schooling end at the point at which it had been disrupted. The men who returned to college after military service faced the prospect of a very late age at school completion and beginning of first, full-time civilian job. Many of these men married on time even if that meant they had to marry before completing their schooling and beginning work. For most men, therefore, military service represented an obstacle to the smooth completion of the transition from adolescence to adulthood.

Nonetheless, for some men from lower status socioeconomic backgrounds, the interruption in the usual life course produced by service in the military may actually have proven advantageous. After serving in the military, such men qualified for veterans' benefits that helped to pay for a college education. Although those benefits were limited, their availability provided an incentive to these men to consider a college education. The decision to attend college was crucial in breaking the socioeconomic tie to family of origin, and facilitated upward intergenerational socioeconomic mobility. In addition to benefiting the individual, it contributed to the democratization of college attendance that produced the modern pattern of transition behavior.

Taken together, the intercohort increases in median age at school completion, the increased variability in age at school completion, the decreased median age at marriage, and the decreased variability in age at marriage produced a greater degree of overlap between the school completion, first job, and marriage transitions. This overlap caused departures from the usual ordering pattern of events so that fewer men first completed school, then began work, and finally married. The duration of time necessary to complete the entire transition to adulthood (measured as the number of years between the age at which one-quarter of the men completed school and three-quarters of the men married) displayed marked intercohort declines. Men with higher levels of education experienced a shorter transition period. This pattern was particularly pronounced among men from poor socioeconomic origins who attended college.

The timing and sequencing of school completion, beginning of first job, and marriage constituted important life-course contingencies for career socioeconomic attainments. Men who completed the transition to adulthood relatively early relied more on familial connections for placement in their first job, rather than on educational credentials. Because such employment frequently began prior to the completion of schooling, the occupational and earnings returns to schooling were depressed. The entry level position of these men provided a poor basis for career advancement.

Conversely, men who completed their schooling before beginning work were able to capitalize on their educational credentials to attain an entry occupation of higher status than their fathers' occupation. A good entry-level occupation provided a sound basis for upward occupational mobility and higher earnings over the course of the career. The advantages associated with a relatively late education and first-job transition persisted throughout the consolidation phase of the career. By the time a man had been working 25 years or longer, however, the occupational and earnings advantages associated with these patterns of transition behavior had disappeared.

Initially, married men tended to find better paying and somewhat higher-status jobs than single men. But married men were less mobile in their early careers than men who married after beginning work. Unrestricted by familial responsibilities, the single men achieved quicker career advancement. Within a decade of beginning work, the occupational status disadvantage associated with being single at the beginning of first job was reduced greatly, and the earnings disadvantage had become an earnings advantage.

Veterans of World War II, Korean War, and cold war military service were apparent exceptions to these generalizations. These men did not experience the occupational attainment disadvantages usually associated with a disorderly transition to adulthood. Among these military-service veterans, the mid-career earnings deficits associated with marriage before school completion were ameliorated to a large extent. Men who served in the armed forces during the Vietman War and completed college after marriage, on the other hand, experienced the socioeconomic attainment deficits usually associated with such a disorderly sequence of events. There apparently was an intercohort change in the occupational and earnings attainment returns to being a veteran. Veteran status was a positive personal attribute among men seeking work before the Vietnam War. Although veteran status did not actually become a liability during the Vietnam War years, it did not produce the career advantages with which it had been associated historically.

The timing and sequencing of transition events also influenced marital stability. Men who married relatively early had higher rates of marital instability than men who married on time or late. The association between an early marriage and marital instability decreased in recent years, perhaps because a smaller proportion of such marriages occurred as a consequence of premarital pregnancy. The recent improvement in the availability of reliable contraceptives and safe abortions was an important historical factor in this change.

Men who married before completing their schooling experienced higher rates of marital instability, controlling for age at marriage. This was true of both veterans and nonveterans and of men from every marriage cohort. Thus, an inter-mixture of the marriage transition with the school-completion and first-job transitions was doubly disadvantageous—it lowered career socioeconomic attainments and increased the likelihood of a separation or divorce. The successful completion of schooling required long hours of study. Upward career mobility depended upon the availability of time to search for a suitable entry-level occupation, geographic mobility, and the flexibility to work long hours, for what was often a relatively low starting salary. Marital stability probably was enhanced by residential stability, long hours spent together by the couple, and a freedom from financial worry. Thus, it was stressful to be married while enrolled in school or in the early years of the career. The intercohort increase in the probability of marriage prior to the completion of school and beginning of work undoubtedly was one of the factors producing intercohort increases in marital instability.

PROSPECTS FOR FUTURE CHANGE

Although this study of the interrelations of social change, social group differentiation, and the transition to adulthood was based on cohorts of American men born from 1907 to 1952, it provides a sound basis for predictions about the transition behavior of birth cohorts born after 1952. The intercohort expansion of the average level of education has proceeded as far as possible through the universalization of graded schooling. Future intercohort improvements in average level of education must come through increases in the proportion of the birth cohort completing college. The members of the lower socioeconomic groups provide a ready pool of recruits for college enrollment. But unless government or private aid programs for college enrollment are expanded substantially, these men will not attend college. The recent modification of college benefits for military service veterans have closed another important avenue for increases in college enrollment among the lower classes. Thus, it appears that the democratization of college enrollment characteristic of the post–World War II period may not continue.

As greater proportions of successive birth cohorts have completed high school and attended college, ceiling effects that prevent large intercohort increases in educational attainments have appeared. Unless enrollments in graduate and professional education enlarge drastically, future intercohort increases in educationl attainment will be small and will be a product of the expansion of college attendance among lower socioeconomic groups. A diminution of intercohort upgradings in educational attainment will eliminate the educational advantages of new cohorts of young men as they enter the labor market. It will be more difficult for young men to attain entry-level occupations that provide a good basis for upward career mobility. The current national economic malaise probably has created financial obstacles to extended college enrollment and forced more men to hold part-time or full-time jobs while still enrolled in school. It has become imperative for young men to find employment quickly after finishing school. Current structural circumstances thus produce difficult school and work transitions for cohorts of young men undergoing the transition to adulthood.

These structural circumstances, and the attendant difficulties in the school completion and first job tansitions, probably will cause these young men to delay their marriages. Recent changes in contraceptive technology and sexual mores will enable many of these men to postpone marriage without foregoing the sexual and companionate pleasures historically associated with marriage. A later age at first marriage, in combination with a somewhat earlier age at school completion, will mean fewer marriages occurring prior to the completion of schooling and beginning of work and a lengthening of the years required to complete the transition to adulthood.

These expected patterns of transition behavior may help to improve the career achievements of these men, to some extent counteracting the unfavorable effects of current structural circumstances. Thus, by adapting the timing and sequencing of their early life transitions to current social structural circumstances, cohorts of men now undergoing the transition to adulthood may ameliorate the unfavorable effects of these circumstances on their later life course. Innovative behavior of this sort would be consistent with the coping behavior with which previous cohorts of men have responded to inauspicous circumstances during their transition to adulthood.

ISSUES FOR FUTURE RESEARCH

The actual behavior of men during their passage to adulthood is certainly more complex than the simple model of behavior that was the basis of this analysis. There are transitions besides school completion, job entry, and marriage that mark the passage to adulthood. These include establishing a place of residence that is independent of the family of origin, becoming economically self-supporting (through either earned or unearned income), and having one's first child. Although data limitations prevented consideration of these other transitions in this study, their timing and sequencing should be a focus of future research.

Furthermore, the variables used in this analysis were simplified representations of a complex reality. The number and duration of interruptions in schooling vary among men. Actual educational histories often are quite complex. Men "complete" their schooling only in the sense that schooling is interrupted at some point (perhaps with the awarding of a diploma or degree) and is not resumed after that date. By reentering school, men can, at any time, change the age at which they are defined as completing school. The financial resources potentially available for college expenditures, as well as the sources of economic support actually received while in school, must be known in order to fully understand the educational histories of men. This study, lacking these data, drew conclusions on the basis of inferences from limited educational histories.

Men repeatedly enter into and exit from the labor force before finally beginning their first, relatively permanent, full-time job. These early labor force experiences presumably are influential in determining the "first job" as defined in this book. Periods of employment during interruptions in schooling also merit attention. A fully developed model of transition behavior must consider these complexities in school exit and labor-force entry.

Future research should examine the normative structures governing the timing and sequencing of early life transitions. There is almost no empirical evidence about the existence of transition norms, nor about supporting societal sanctions. It is not known how these norms have changed over the course of the century, nor how they differ among social class, residential, or ethnic subgroups in the population. It is too late to collect data on normative expectations about transitions from men who have already undergone the transition to adulthood. A major research priority should be the collection and analysis of such data for persons preparing to undergo the passage from youth to adulthood.

Males and females occupy different positions in the social structure. Females are subject to different normative expectations about educational, career, and familial achievements, and their attainment processes vary. Therefore, the transition to adulthood is different for males and females. The remarkable changes in female labor-force participation and fertility that have characterized the twentieth century undoubtedly have had a tremendous impact on the early life transitions of American females. It is essential that future research on the life-course behavior of females examine these issues.

This demographic analysis has been enriched by the utilization of a life-course perspective. The interplay of historical events, social structural organization, and position in the social structure define the social milieux within which individuals act out their lives. Interindividual differences in human behavior must be studied with reference to the social and historical milieux. Whatever success this study has had in enhancing our understanding of the early life transitions of twentieth century American men is due to its adherence to this key principle of the life-course perspective.

References

Baltes, P. B., S. W. Cornelius, and J. R. Nesselroade
1979 "Cohort effects in developmental psychology." Pp. 61–87 in R. Nesselroade and P. B. Baltes, (eds.), *Longitudinal Research in the Study of Behavior and Development*. New York: Academic Press.

Bayer, A. E.
1969 "Life plans and marriage age: An application of path analysis." *Journal of Marriage and the Family* 31: 551–558.

Blau, P. M., and O. D. Duncan
1967 *The American Occupational Structure*. New York: John Wiley and Sons.

Bogue, D. J.
1969 *Principles of Demography*. New York: John Wiley and Sons.

Boudon, R.
1973 *Education, Opportunity, and Social Inequality*. New York: John Wiley and Sons.

Bowles, S.
1972 "Schooling and inequality from generation to generation." *Journal of Political Economy* 80: S219–S251.

Bowles, S. and H. Gintis
1976 *Schooling in Capitalist America*. New York: Basic Books.

Bumpass, L. L., and J. A. Sweet
1972 "Differentials in marital instability: 1970." *American Sociological Review* 37: 754–766.

Carter, H., and P. C. Glick
1970 *Marriage and Divorce: A Social and Economic Study*. Cambridge, Mass: Harvard University Press.

Coleman, J. S.
1961 *The Adolescent Society*. New York: Free Press.

Coombs, L. C., and R. Freedman
1970 "Pre-marital pregnancy, childspacing, and later economic achievement." *Population Studies* 24: 389–412.

Duncan, B.
1965 "Dropouts and the unemployed." *The Journal of Political Economy* 53: 121–134.
1968 "Trends in output and distribution of schooling." Pp. 601–674 in E. B. Sheldon and W. E. Moore, (eds.), *Indicators of Social Change: Concepts and Measurements*. New York: Russell Sage Foundation.

Duncan, O. D., D. L. Featherman, and B. Duncan
1972 *Socioeconomic Background and Achievement*. New York: Seminar Press.

Easterlin, R. A.
1978 "What will 1984 be like? Socioeconomic implications of recent twists in age structure." *Demography* 15: 397–432.

Elder, G. H., Jr.
1974a "Age differentiation and the life course." Pp. 165–190 in A. Inkeles, J. Coleman, and N. Smelser (eds.), *Annual Review of Sociology, 1975*, Vol. 1. Palo Alto, California: Annual Reviews.
1974b *Children of the Great Depression*. Chicago: University of Chicago Press.
1978a "Approaches to social change and the family." *American Journal of Sociology* 84(Supplement): S1–S38.
1978b "Family history and the life course." Pp. 17–64 in T. K. Hareven (ed.), *Transitions: The Family and the Life Course in Historical Perspective*. New York: Academic Press.
1980 "Adolescence in historical perspective." Pp. 3–46 in J. Adelson (ed.), *Handbook of Adolescent Psychology*. New York: John Wiley and Sons.

Featherman, D. L.
1971 "The socioeconomic achievement of white religio-ethnic subgroups: Social and psychological explanations." *American Sociological Review* 36: 207–222.

Featherman, D. L., and T. M. Carter
1976 "Discontinuities in schooling and the socioeconomic life cycle." Pp. 133–160 in W. H. Sewell, R. M. Hauser, and D. L. Featherman (eds.), *Schooling and Achievement in American Society*. New York: Academic Press.

Featherman, D. L., and R. M. Hauser
1975 "Design for a replicate study of social mobility in the United States." Pp. 219–251 in K. C. Land and S. Spilerman (eds.), *Social Indicator Models*. New York: Russell Sage Foundation.
1978 *Opportunity and Change*. New York: Academic Press.

Freedman, R., and L. C. Coombs
1966 "Childspacing and family economic position." *American Sociological Review* 31: 631–648.

Freeman, R. B.
1976 *The Overeducated American*. New York: Academic Press.

Friedenberg, E. Z.
1963 *Coming of Age in Amcrica*. New York: Vintage Books.

Goodman, L. A.
1971 "The analysis of multidimensional contingency tables: Stepwise procedures and direct estimation methods for building models for multiple classifications." *Technometrics* 13: 36–61.
1972 "A modified multiple regression approach to the analysis of dichotomous variables." *American Sociological Review* 37: 28–46.

Gross, A. J., and V. A. Clark
1975 *Survival Distributions: Reliability Applications in the Biomedical Sciences*. New York: John Wiley and Sons.

Haraven, T. K.
1978 "The dynamics of kin in an industrial community." *American Journal of Sociology* 84(Supplement): S151–S182.
Hauser, R. M., and D. L. Featherman
1977 *The Process of Stratification: Trends and Analyses.* New York: Academic Press.
Hirschman, C. and J. Matras
1971 "A new look at the marriage market and nuptiality rates, 1915–1958." *Demography* 8: 549–569.
Hogan D. P.
1976 "The passage of American men from family of orientation to family of procreation: Patterns, timing, and determinants." Doctoral dissertation, University of Wisconsin.
1977 "Ethnic differences in marital instability." *Proceedings of the Social Statistics Section of the American Statistical Association*, Part II, Pp. 598–602.
1978a "The effects of demographic factors, family background, and early job achievement on age at marriage." *Demography* 15: 161–175.
1978b "The variable order of events in the life course." *American Sociological Review* 43: 573–586.
1980 "The transition to adulthood as a career contingency." *American Sociological Review* 45: 261–276.
Hollingshead, A. B.
1949 *Elmtown's Youth.* New York: John Wiley and Sons.
Kaestle, C. F., and M. A. Vinovskis
1978 "From fireside to factory: School entry and school leaving in nineteenth-century Massachusetts." Pp. 135–185 in T. K. Haraven (ed.), *Transitions: The Family and the Life Course in Historical Perspective.* New York: Academic Press.
Katz, M. B., and I. E. Davey
1978 "Youth and early industrialization in a Canadian city." *American Journal of Sociology* 84(Supplement): S81–S119.
Kett, J. F.
1977 *Rites of Passage: Adolescence in America 1790 to Present.* New York: Basic Books.
Kitagawa, E. M., and P. M. Hauser
1973 *Differential Mortality in the United States: A Study in Socioeconomic Epidemiology.* Cambridge, Mass.: Harvard University Press.
Kobrin, F. E., and C. Goldscheider
1978 *The Ethnic Factor in Family Structure and Mobility.* Cambridge Mass.: Ballinger Press.
Mare, R. D.
1979 "Social background composition and educational growth." *Demography* 16: 55–71.
Mason, W. M.
1970 "On the socioeconomic effects of military service." Doctoral dissertation, University of Chicago.
Matras, J.
1973 *Populations and Societies.* Englewood Cliffs, New Jersey: Prentice-Hall, Inc.
Mills, C. W.
1959 *The Sociological Imagination.* New York: Oxford University Press.
Modell, J.
1978 "Patterns of consumption, acculturation, and family income strategies in late

nineteenth-century America." Pp. 206–240 in T. K. Haravan and M. A. Vinovskis (eds.), *Family and Population in Nineteenth-Century America.*

1980 "Normative aspects of American marriage timing since World War II." *Journal of Family History* 5: 210–234.

Modell, J., F. F. Furstenberg, Jr., and T. Herschberg

1976 "Social change and transitions to adulthood in historical perspective." *Journal of Family History* 1: 7–32.

Modell, J., F. F. Furstenberg, Jr., and D. Strong

1978 "The timing of marriage in the transition to adulthood: Continuity and change, 1860–1975." *American Journal of Sociology* 84: S120–S150.

Modell, J., and T. K. Hareven

1978 "Transitions: Patterns of timing." Pp. 245–269 in T. K. Haraven (ed.), *Transitions: The Family and the Life Course in Historical Perspective.* New York: Academic Press.

Neugarten, B. L., and G. O. Hagestad

1976 "Age and the life course." Pp. 35–55 in R. H. Binstock and E. Shanas (eds.), *Handbook of Aging and the Social Sciences.* New York: Van Nostrand Reinhold.

Neugarten, B. L., and J. W. Moore

1968 "The changing age status system." Pp. 5–21 in B. L. Neugarten (ed.), *Middle Age and Aging.* Chicago: University of Chicago Press.

Neugarten, B. L., J. W. Moore, and J. C. Lowe

1965 "Age norms, age constraints, and adult socialization." *American Journal of Sociology* 70: 710–717.

Ornstein, M. D.

1976 *Entry Into the American Labor Force.* New York: Academic Press.

Panel on Youth

1974 *Youth: Transition to Adulthood.* Report of the Panel on Youth of the President's Science Advisory Committee (1972). Chicago: University of Chicago Press.

Riley, M. W.

1976 "Age strata in social systems." Pp. 189–217 in R. H. Binstock and E. Shanas (eds.), *Handbook of Aging and the Social Sciences.* New York: Van Nostrand Reinhold.

1979 "Aging, social change and social policy." Pp. 109–120 in M. W. Riley (ed.), *Aging From Birth to Death: Interdisciplinary Perspectives* Boulder: Westview Press.

Ryder, N. B.

1965 "The cohort as a concept in the study of social change." *American Sociological Review* 30: 843–861.

1969 "The emergence of a modern fertility pattern: United States, 1917–66." Pp. 99–123 in S. J. Behrman, L. Corsa, and R. Freedman (eds.), *Fertility and Family Planning: A World View.* Ann Arbor: University of Michigan Press.

Sewell, W. H.

1964 "Community of residence and college plans." *American Sociological Review* 29: 24–38.

1971 "Inequality of opportunity for higher education." *American Sociological Review* 36: 793–809.

Sewell, W. H., and R. M. Hauser

1975 *Education, Opportunity and Earnings: Achievement in the Early Career.* New York: Academic Press.

Sewell, W. H., and V. P. Shah
1968 "Social class, parental encouragement, and educational aspirations." *American Journal of Sociology* 73: 559–572.

Svalastoga, K.
1965 *Social Differentiation*. New York: David McKay Company.

Sweet, J. A.
1973 "Differentials in remarriage probabilities." University of Wisconsin, Center for Demography and Ecology Working Paper 73–29.
1979 "Changes in the allocation of time of young women among schooling, marriage, work, and childbearing: 1960–1976." Paper presented at the annual meeting of the Population Association of America, Philadelphia, Pennsylvania.

Uhlenberg, P.
1978 "Changing configurations of the life course." Pp. 65–97 in T. K. Hareven (ed.), *Transitions: The Family and the Life Course in Historical Perspective*. New York: Academic Press.

U.S. Department of Health, Education, and Welfare, National Center for Health Statistics.
1964 "United States Life Tables: 1959–61." Public Health Service Publication No. 1252, Volume 1, Number 1. Washington, D.C.: U.S. Government Printing Office.

U.S. Bureau of the Census
1965 "Estimates of the population of the United States, by single years of age, color, and sex: 1900 to 1959." *Current Population Reports*, Series P-25, Number 311. Washington, D.C.: U.S. Government Printing Office.
1973 *Statistical Abstract of the United States: 1973*. Washington, D.C.: U.S. Government Printing Office.
1974a "Estimates of the population of the United States, by age, sex, and race: April 1, 1960 to July 1, 1973." *Current Population Reports*, Series P-25, Number 519. Washington, D.C.: U.S. Government Printing Office.
1974b *Statistical Abstract of the United States, 1974*. Washington, D.C.: U.S. Government Printing Office.
1975a *Historical Statistics of the United States, Colonial Times to 1970*, Bicentennial Edition, Parts 1 and 2. Washington, D.C.: U.S. Government Printing Office.
1975b *Statistical Abstract of the United States: 1975*. Washington, D.C.: U.S. Government Printing Office.
1977 "Estimates of the population of the United States, by age, sex, and race: July 1, 1974 to 1976." *Current Population Reports*, Series P-25, Number 643. Washington, D.C.: U.S. Government Printing Office.
1978 *Statistical Abstract of the United States: 1978*. Washington, D.C.: U.S. Government Printing Office.

Waring, J. M.
1975 "Social replenishment and social change." Pp. 237–256 in *American Behavioral Scientist* 19:2. Edited by Anne Foner.

Winsborough, H. H.
1978 "Statistical histories of the life cycle of birth cohorts: the transition from schoolboy to adult male." Pp. 231–259 in K. E. Taeuber, L. L. Bumpass, and J. A. Sweet (eds.), *Social Demography*. New York: Academic Press.
1979 "Changes in the transition to adulthood." Pp. 137–152 in M. W. Riley (ed.), *Aging from Birth to Death: Interdisciplinary Perspectives*. Boulder: Westview Press.

Subject Index

N

O

R

S

STUDIES IN POPULATION

Under the Editorship of: H. H. WINSBOROUGH

Department of Sociology
University of Wisconsin
Madison, Wisconsin

Samuel H. Preston, Nathan Keyfitz, and Robert Schoen. **Causes of Death: *Life Tables for National Populations.***

Otis Dudley Duncan, David L. Featherman, and Beverly Duncan. **Socioeconomic Background and Achievement.**

James A. Sweet. **Women in the Labor Force.**

Tertius Chandler and Gerald Fox. **3000 Years of Urban Growth.**

William H. Sewell and Robert M. Hauser. **Education, Occupation, and Earnings:** *Achievement in the Early Career.*

Otis Dudley Duncan. **Introduction to Structural Equation Models.**

William H. Sewell, Robert M. Hauser, and David L. Featherman (Eds.). **Schooling and Achievement in American Society.**

Henry Shryock, Jacob S. Siegel, and Associates. **The Methods and Materials of Demography.** *Condensed Edition by Edward Stockwell.*

Samuel H. Preston. **Mortality Patterns in National Populations: *With Special Reference to Recorded Causes of Death.***

Robert M. Hauser and David L. Featherman. **The Process of Stratification:** *Trends and Analyses.*

Ronald R. Rindfuss and James A. Sweet. **Postwar Fertility Trends and Differentials in the United States.**

David L. Featherman and Robert M. Hauser. **Opportunity and Change.**

Karl E. Taeuber, Larry L. Bumpass, and James A. Sweet (Eds.). **Social Demography.**

Thomas J. Espenshade and William J. Serow (Eds.). **The Economic Consequences of Slowing Population Growth.**

Frank D. Bean and W. Parker Frisbie (Eds.). **The Demography of Racial and Ethnic Groups.**

Joseph A. McFalls, Jr. **Psychopathology and Subfecundity.**

Franklin D. Wilson. **Residential Consumption, Economic Opportunity, and Race.**

Maris A. Vinovskis (Ed.). **Studies in American Historical Demography.**

Clifford C. Clogg. **Measuring Underemployment: Demographic Indicators for the United States.**

David L. Brown and John M. Wardwell (Eds.). **New Directions in Urban–Rural Migration: *The Population Turnaround in Rural America.***

A. J. Jaffe, Ruth M. Cullen, and Thomas D. Boswell. **The Changing Demography of Spanish Americans.**

Robert Alan Johnson. **Religious Assortative Marriage in the United States.**

Hilany J. Page and Ron Lesthaeghe. **Child Spacing in Tropical Africa.**

Dennis P. Hogan. **Transitions and Social Change: *The Early Lives of American Men.***

In preparation

F. Thomas Juster and Kenneth C. Land (Eds.) **Social Accounting Systems: *Essays on the State of the Art.***